Geronticide

of related interest

The Psychology of Ageing
An Introduction 3rd Edition
Ian Stuart-Hamilton
ISBN 1 85302 771 5

Spirituality and Ageing
Edited by Albert Jewell
ISBN 1 85302 631 X

Understanding Dementia
The Man with the Worried Eyes
Richard Cheston and Michael Bender
ISBN 1 85302 479 1

Drug Treatments and Dementia
Stephen Hopker
ISBN 1 85302 760 X

Including the Person with Dementia
in Designing and Delivering Care
'I Need to Be Me'
Elizabeth Barnett
ISBN 1 85302 740 5

Care Services for Later Life
Transformations and Critiques
Edited by Tony Warnes, Lorna Warren and Mike Nolan
ISBN 1 85302 852 5

Geronticide
Killing the Elderly

Mike Brogden

Jessica Kingsley Publishers
London and Philadelphia

The right of Mike Brogden to be identified as author of this work has been asserted by him in accordance with the Copyright, Designs and Patents Act 1988.

First published in the United Kingdom in 2001 by
Jessica Kingsley Publishers Ltd
116 Pentonville Road, London
N1 9JB, England
and
325 Chestnut Street
Philadelphia
PA 19106, USA.

www.jkp.com

© Copyright 2001 Mike Brogden

Library of Congress Cataloging in Publication Data
A CIP catalog record for this book is available from the Library of Congress

British Library Cataloguing in Publication Data
A CIP catalogue record for this book is available from the British Library

ISBN 1 85302 709 X

Printed and Bound in Great Britain by
Athenaeum Press, Gateshead, Tyne and Wear

Contents

Acknowledgements

Given a text that draws on so many diverse sources and academic traditions, recognition of the contribution of the many different writers and scholars, past, present and futuristic, cannot be adequate. But of those to whom this book owes most, two stand out. The fine collection of folk stories by D.L. Ashliman, is an invaluable source containing timeless wisdom, and grim humour. From a different tradition, Michael Kearl's continuing work, on the sociology of death, enlivens a potentially banal subject with insights, scholarship, as well as empirical detail.

Most of this work was conducted in Northern Ireland. Concern, as in this text, with the fundamental and neglected ideology of ageism, was frequently perceived as an irrelevance, a distraction from the local sectarian obsession. In Belfast, there were mixed contributions, both negative and positive. On the bleaker side, one should recognise that the divisions in that benighted society are not confined to bleak, low rent, housing executive estates. Family and community, concealing the major schisms of child, partner, and elder abuse, remain publicly elevated and privately disturbed. The elderly, like other victims of private space crime (and the victimisation of ethnic minorities), are perceived to be of little significance as compared with the rewards accruing from a piece of the peace-making pie in the major Northern Ireland industry of 'mediation' consultants and human rights' Commissioners.

But any conflict also elevates those whose humour and intelligence raises them above grappling for the financial and status spoils of the 'Peace' Process. Only a few can be mentioned. Much was alleviated by the Truman Street 'geriatric walkers'.

Given the kaleidoscope of materials used in this text, friends, colleagues, and students were pumped dry for sources and literary gleanings. Ray Geary, in particular, had most patience and most to offer. Colleagues such as Chris Greer revived their own literary pasts. Keith Bryett's e-mails like the arrival of Graham Ellison, were a welcome relief from indigenous scholarly incest and ambition. The original ideas for the text were sparked by an adviser from one of the local ageing enterprises, for whose work and quality of research my admiration grows daily. In my writing life, I have never encountered a publishing office as thorough and so painstakingly meticulous as in the work of Amy Lankester-Owen, her colleagues, and the remarkable anonymous copyeditor. Together, they prevent me saying in the time-honoured, if inverted tradition, that 'any mistakes are theirs, any virtues mine'.

To Preeti

CHAPTER 1

Living Too Long?

Introduction

In *The Time Machine*, H. G. Wells' narrator remarks on the absence of an older generation in the new world. In the land of everlasting youth, the problem of ageing – if it is a problem – has been apparently resolved. A genre of utopian and dystopian writers raise often unanswered questions about the place of the elderly in future society. In the past, as in the present, that experience has often been grim.

This book is about, bluntly, the killing of old people. We will argue that all societies – so-called 'primitive', early modern, medieval, colonial, Victorian, pre-industrial, industrial and others – have regularly condoned the killing of older people. Procedures have varied. The elderly Inuit may have been cast aside on an ice floe after a ritual chant, but his experience was not that different from the pauper forced into the Victorian workhouse on a less-than-subsistence diet or the older female resident of a modern nursing home starved of life-maintaining medicine because of a rationing process that discriminates against the elderly.

The simple fact is that old age in itself has been one *criterion for selecting people to die*. As the philosopher Battin (1992) says:

> Not all family life is harmonious, and underlying pathology can often be exacerbated by the stresses of a family member's terminal illness. ... 'All right, Granny, it's time to go' is a message that we can imagine being conveyed in a variety of ways, exhibiting an entire range from the faintest suggestion to outright coercion. (p.136)

However, as we shall show, the picture is slightly more complicated in two ways. The elderly are not a homogeneous group. Typically, it has been the very old (the liminal) who have been subject to inveterate disposal. That is especially true if they were of marginal caste or social class – at the bottom of the socio-economic ladder. Occasionally, that decision-making (often sins of omission rather than of commission – though both can be intentional) is further qualified by factors of gender (elderly women have often been a particular target), of ethnicity (minority groups and stranger elderly have regularly suffered geronticide), and of disability.

In this book, we explore not the 'voluntary' act itself – for example, through the euthanasia 'technology' pioneered by such agencies as the Hemlock Society and its affiliates.[1] Instead, our focus is on those occasions when other parties determine that older people should lose their fundamental right to life. Societies which otherwise preach tolerance, civility, and human rights prompt elders – marked out by the social prejudices attached to ageing and by other negative stereotyping – to accept a premature death. There is nothing new in such homicides. Only the techniques have changed over time. Death happens to the elderly in various ways:

- *by rationing health resources* in favour of other age cohorts, under the impact of changing demography. Older people die earlier – and perhaps more painfully – than would have happened if younger people were not given health-sustaining priority.

- *by ceremonial slaughter* where a social group – tribe, or so-called 'primitive society' – decreed that the individual elder was a hindrance to the collective.

- *by attrition* under the impact of a modernisation process that abandoned impoverished elderly in the living charnel house of the Victorian workhouse.

- *by degrees,* as the elderly are processed as waste commodities on the conveyor belt of the modern nursing or care home.

This chapter outlines the key problems in understanding the selective termination of the lives of elderly people in societies past and present.

- Killing the elderly has little to do with biological ageing – it is a function of differentials in power and of inequality.

- Scientific studies show that the limits of the human lifespan have not yet been reached – we may only have seen the beginning of the attempt to create a population weighted towards the elderly.

- The social consequences of biological ageing have frequently been the focus of literary discourse, rather than that of planners and policy makers.

- Historical solutions have frequently been to kill the elderly – more frequently by death-hastening devices rather than by direct geronticide.

- The concept of *the elderly* is a euphemism. It conceals differences of gender, of social class, of ethnicity, of disability, and between the 'young-old' and the 'old-old'.

The social context of ageing and geronticide

The study of geronticide, killing elderly people, relies on an analysis of the social context in which old age is perceived and experienced. The violent death of the elderly – geronticide, senecide, and often patricide and matricide, whether at the hands of oneself or of others, willingly or unwillingly – is a social phenomenon, an outcome of social evaluations of the older person's worth. Ageing itself – an inevitable process – is not a problem. Nor is it equivalent to illness. A crude demographic determinism which sees the elderly as a problem is misconceived. It confuses a biological process – growing old – with the social and political factors that determine the treatment of the elderly. The problem is one of societal reaction not one of biology.

The wider debate about the role of older people in society derives from the traditions of European social science – how old age and the physiological process of ageing may be understood socially – placing attitudes to the inevitable demise of the elderly within a context of social relationships and structural forces. Ageing as a process can be addressed from biological or psychological perspectives, but the definition of old age as a life stage is a social construction. The impact of biological and psychological ideas about the termination of the lives of the elderly is integrated into more general social attitudes.

Ageing populations are a global phenomenon. All industrial and most non-industrial countries show the same trends: a growth in the proportion of people aged over 65 years; an increase in the absolute numbers of older people; and improvement of life expectancy at birth. Such changes have appeared gradually in some countries and more rapidly in others. However, the broad phenomenon of an ageing population is to be found all across the developed and developing world (Ehrlich and Ehrlich 1996).

Is longer life possible?

Infinite life has long been a desire. The Epic of Gilgamesh tells the story of an ancient Middle Eastern king who struggled to find the secret of eternal life. In a Faustian bargain, Gilgamesh was given the secret ingredient which would allow him to live for ever. Despite his powers, he was unable to fulfil his part of the pact and eventually died. In *Götterdämmerung*, Wagner's epic based on the Norse saga, even the gods die. Life is finite. The problem occurs when that term is extended beyond traditional assumptions.

Today the cryonics movement, in which wealthy individuals are frozen on death with the prospect of reawakening when medical science so permits, evidences the desire of some people to live longer. The dream of increasing the allotted span remains. George Bernard Shaw contemplated the scientific possibility in *Back to Methuselah* (1921). In his inimitable style, Shaw pondered the variations in life spans between such species as parrots and dogs, turtles and wasps, questioning the traditional assumption that man's years would always be numbered as three score and ten. Barring accidents, could science not some day vastly increase human longevity?

While the Gilgamesh Utopia is fantasy, some scientists suggest that a 50 per cent increase in the age span to some 120 years is feasible in theory. The lifespan can potentially be increased.

Biblical sources offer one horizon for traditional Christians. Psalm 90 verse 10 gives the human lifespan as threescore years and ten. However, there is a more obscure biblical reference ('for that man is also flesh; yet his days shall be an hundred and twenty years' – Genesis 6:3) that indicates that 120 years may be nearer the potential of the human body. Recent physiological evidence combined with a recalculation of historical mortality data, suggests that that latter figure may be nearer to human potential.

Francis Bacon (1561–1626) was the first to speak about the prolongation of life as a new task for physicians, dividing medicine into three offices: 'First, the preservation of health, second, the cure of disease, and third, the prolongation of life,' and extolled the 'third part of medicine, regarding the prolongation of life: this is a new part, and deficient, although the most noble of all.' However, the medical profession did not even consider facing this task until a rich clientele appeared in the late eighteenth century. The 'new rich' refused to die in retirement and insisted on being carried away through death from natural exhaustion while still at work. 'He refused to accept death unless he was in good health in an active old age' (Illich 1991, p.190).

Stratification determined Victorian lifespan. While for most people the new medicine of the industrial revolution was unavailable, it made it possible for the wealthy elderly to extend their working lives. For the bourgeoisie, living and working conditions had eased in the nineteenth century. But increased employment opportunities for the weak, sickly and old hardly favoured the majority's life chances. As Illich (1991) pointed out, sedentary work, hitherto rare, had come into its own: 'A general affected by gout could now command a battle from his wagon, and decrepit diplomats could travel from London to Vienna or Moscow' (p.191). A new class of clerical workers appeared, freed from the life-threatening physical stresses of employment. The old male elite had a greater chance of survival because their lives had become physically less demanding. Ageing was a way of capitalising life. As Illich describes it, years at the desk, either at the counter or the school bench, began to bear interest on the market. The youthful middle class, whether gifted or not, were now for the first time sent to school, thus allowing the old to stay on the job. The bourgeoisie could afford to eliminate 'social death' by avoiding retirement. But nevertheless, for lesser beings in Victorian society, premature elderly deaths could be regarded as socially beneficial by the early eugenicists. They should be persuaded of their debt to society and go quietly (see Smyth 1888, pp.173–174; Weisman 1899/1982).

Central to this notion of extending the lifespan through medicine was a view that old age and death were a disease. In James Gunn's 'New Blood' (in *The Immortals* (1958)) the main character comments that death is a disease caught at birth, a disease of ageing from which no one can be inoculated. Identifying old age as a disease suggests that old age can be treated, even cured.[2] If the cause of ageing can be determined, a way may be found to slow it down or even to reverse it. A different genre of authors, notably Simone de Beauvoir, have argued the contrary, that disease is contingent, whereas ageing is the law of life itself.

Science and increasing the lifespan

As early as 1558 Luigi Cornaro, a Venetian nobleman, wrote a treatise (at the age of 83) entitled *The Sure Certain Method of Attaining a Long and Healthful Life*. But not until the nineteenth century do records show biological attempts to calculate potential longevity – as in the work of the British actuary, Benjamin Gompertz. In his Law of Mortality, Gompertz, in 1825, showed that the mortality rate increases in a geometric progression. Hence when death rates are plotted on a logarithm scale, a straight line known as the Gompertz function is obtained. The Gompertz model (as more fully developed a century later) aimed to predict maximum life expectancies for various species. It assumes that the risk of dying accelerates at a constant rate over time for all organisms, from insects to mammals. The model allows scientists to express life expectancy as a product of two factors – environment (from stressful to benign) and genetics – a kind of built-in species clock, '... a burden of ageing that keeps accumulating, like interest compounding on a debt' (Kearl 1999).

These two factors can be combined to calculate a maximum age that any member of a given population could reach. According to that model, the Genesis figure of one hundred and twenty years might, in fact, represent the average human life expectancy if medical science could duplicate life-extending experimental mechanisms effective in laboratory rodents.[3]

Drawing on Gompertz, Finch and Pike[4] use ethological data to extrapolate human lifespan potential. The chances of dying, they argue, increase by approximately 9 per cent each year after puberty – meaning the risk of dying in any given year doubles with every eight years lived. This relation appears to be true for humans under an extreme variety of environmental conditions. Kearl quotes the example of Australian soldiers in Japanese prisoner-of-war camps during World War II who suffered death rates approximately 30 times higher than Australian men of the same age living at home. The rate of increase in deaths between age groups remained the same for prison and home populations: 24-year-olds died in the same ratio to 48-year-olds, regardless of whether they lived in jungle death camps or in Australia. Similar correlations have been observed in other mammals.

Finch and Pike's study examines the mortality data from a variety of species to see what useful conclusions about lifespan could be drawn from the Gompertz model, in order to develop estimates for potential human lifespan. Ethological data, especially from those species most closely related to humans, fits the Gompertz curves closely, with no sign of a levelling off in extreme old age. The model appears to account successfully for much of the ageing process. However, anomalies were reported in some species, especially at the extreme-old-age end of the lifespan spectrum. Many invertebrates and some reptiles exhibit an old-age plateau. After approximately 90 per cent of the population have died, the mortality rate seems to become constant rather than continuing.

The researchers also analysed factors causing early death from disease and from wider environmental hazards such as accidents and natural disasters. People in Western societies are much less susceptible (up to 10 times lower) to death from those exigencies, compared to people living in non-industrial countries. There has been a qualitative increase in primary health care through prevention: better diets, clean water, hygiene, and effective sewage treatment systems. Medical services have been much improved, from preventive screening to reactive medical care and treatment once diagnosed. Finch and Pike calculated what it would take for humans to live to the age of 120 – the kinds of medical advances (preventive, and reactive welfare and medicine) that would make it possible for half the population to reach the maximum.

First, if disease and environmental risks of death were reduced to roughly one-fiftieth of the level currently found in the most medically advanced areas of the world, half of 50-year-olds might expect to reach 120. However, this would require extreme medical advances. (Reliable cures for the three leading causes of death after 50 years of age – cancer, heart and vascular diseases, and diabetes – would only raise average life expectancy at 50 to approximately 95 years.)

Second, if the ageing clock could be manipulated, slowing it by 45 per cent would increase life expectancy to the 120-year threshold. There is evidence that that clock can in fact be altered. Some species live longer than others; the questions are why, and how such evidence can be applied to the human population. Species which are capable of asexual propagation are the longest living. Modest rates of asexual reproduction can produce quite dramatic effects on the age distribution of the resulting population. While the age-frequency distribution of an asexually reproducing organism eventually attenuates, this will occur at a considerably greater age than in an otherwise similar sexual population. Asexually reproducing individuals are not immune from the effects of ageing, but are potentially less susceptible to early ageing than sexual organisms. Humans, as organisms whose ancestors long since abandoned asexuality, are destined to die at a relatively early age. In rodents, long-term maintenance on low-calorie diets retards ageing by nearly 50 per cent (although it is questionable whether such findings can be generalised to a human population).

Theoretically, given changes in the environment and potential future manipulation of the ageing clock, it is possible that the lifespan has not yet reached its potential. We are only at the beginning of the process of thinking through what to do with an increasingly elderly, non-working, but consuming, population.

Some people will still die early for genetic reasons. Natural selection cannot eliminate this genetic propensity from the population. Since older individuals have already passed on their genes to their offspring before they decline, early deaths have little impact on the frequency of deleterious genes in subsequent populations. The cumulative effect of genetic susceptibility for some to early death will inevitably be a gradual decline and dysfunction with increasing age. A long-living population will necessarily evolve to senescence. The signs are that some time in this millennium this social problem may have to be confronted. The alternative biblical source of 120 years may yet be a reality.

Ageing and decline: Consequences of extending the lifespan

Science has suggested that *the disposal time may be postponed but the liminal status – the period between fully active life and death – may be extended.* (See Chapter 2 for a fuller discussion of this.) But there are major literary divides in the perceptions of that near-immortal state. At one end of the spectrum is Tolkien's character Treebeard in *The Lord of the Rings.* (1954–55). Treebeard is quite literally as old as the hills. As in much Chinese folklore, Treebeard's age is something to be in awe of, it commands the respect of legend. As he has grown older, he has grown wiser and more powerful. Similarly Tom Bombadil, another of Tolkien's creations, is hundreds of years old. He is purposeful, thoughtful and considerate. Despite his age, or perhaps because of it, he is full of song, rhyme, and good humour.

But at the other end of the spectrum Maurice Jastrow interprets a biblical characterisation of ageing (Ecclesiastes 12:1–6). Ageing inevitably means decay and senescence.

> Remember now thy Creator in the days of thy youth… While the sun, or the light, or the moon be not darkened, nor the clouds return after the rain [diminution of sight, extinction of intellectual powers]: in the day when the keepers of the house [the arms] shall tremble, and the strong men [the legs] shall bow themselves, and the grinders [the teeth] cease because they are few, and those that look out of the windows [the eyes] be darkened, and the doors shall be shut in the streets [digestive and urinary difficulties], when the sound of the grinding is low [deafness], and he shall rise up at the voice of the bird [poor sleep, early wakening], and all the daughters of music shall be brought low [difficulties in speech]; also when they shall be afraid of that which is high [breathlessness in

going up or down stairs] and fears shall be in the way, and the almond tree shall flourish [white hairs], and the grasshopper shall be a burden [fading of sexual power] ... or ever the silver cord be loosed [bending of the spinal column], or the golden bowl be broken, or the pitcher be broken at the fountain, or the wheel be broken at the cistern [malfunction of the liver and kidneys] (quoted in De Beauvoir 1973, p.107).

Fear of growing old features frequently in literature. For example, Lewis Carroll's *Alice's Adventures in Wonderland* (1865) and *Through the Looking Glass* (1871) contain a constant refrain about the fear of growing old, the precursor of death. Humpty Dumpty grimly suggests that an early death by murder or suicide would be one way to keep him from 'growing older'. In Alan Absire's novel *Lazarus* (1985) the main character explores the period of the liminal, and the horrors of immortality. Jesus has raised Lazarus from the grave in the New Testament miracle. But an extended lifespan is not the same as enjoying a full lifestyle, as Lazarus learns through decades of his pre-grave experience. Once an energetic carpenter with a vibrant young wife, Lazarus now stinks of the grave. His skin is corpse-like grey. He cannot indulge in sexual relations, sleep or even saw and hammer wood. He sees his young wife grow old and die. The novel ends bleakly as this animated corpse finds that his 'resurrection' brought neither joy nor significance.

A similar theme projected into the future rather than back to Biblical times appears in the play *Fortitude* by Kurt Vonnegut (1965). Science's ambition to prolong human life meets a comic corrective in the fantasy of Dr Frankenstein and his wealthy, 1000-year-old patient. Sybil is now a mere head, piped and wired to a laboratory of mechanical organs, which fulfil all her bodily functions. Despite Sibyl's artificial sweetness (as stimulated by a computer), she knows that life is really for death because, as her friend tells the ingenious doctor who has created immortality: she knows that hell exists and calls the doctor its inventor. Frankenstein himself ends as another product of his own ingenuity – as Sibyl's immortal companion on his infernal machine.

Shakespeare recognised that the later years of life were a problem if prolonged indefinitely:

> The sixth age shifts
> Into the lean and slipper'd pantaloon,
> With spectacles on nose and pouch on side,
> His youthful hose, well saved, a world too wide
> For his shrunk shank; and his big manly voice,
> Turning again toward childish treble, pipes
> And whistles in his sound. Last scene of all,
> That ends this strange eventful history,

> Is second childishness and mere oblivion,
> Sans teeth, sans eyes, sans taste, sans everything.
> (*As You Like It*, Act 2, Scene 7).

Tennyson furnishes a similar moral tale about the problem of extending the lifespan. Tithonus was a handsome young man who so delighted in being alive that he asked Aurora, goddess of the morning, to make him immortal. She did, but as it had not occurred to him to request perpetual youthfulness as well, he simply became an old man who could not die. Eventually taking pity on him, after listening to his repeated prayer that he should be freed from his never-ending dissolution, the goddess turned him into a grasshopper. As Blythe (1979) notes, in Tennyson's poem we hear the voice of all those people who have long passed the 'goal of ordinance' and who are yet cursed to open their drugged gaze on morning after new morning. The poem is an eloquent case for those whose last fate is to be toyed with by time, to be mutilated and mocked by it.

Jonathan Swift confronted the same problem in *Gulliver's Travels* (1726) with his account of the *struldbruggs* in the Land of Laputa. Swift's satire, according to Landa (1960), depicts the vanity and penalties of undue ageing. The *struldbruggs* were elevated amongst their kin by the gift of immortality, a status which the traveller initially assumes to be the most advantageous that man can acquire, allowing him to accumulate wealth and wisdom indefinitely. It assumed perpetuity of youth health, and vigour.[5] But he is soon disabused. In practice, the *struldbruggs* commonly acted like mortals until about 30 years of age,

> after which by degrees they grew melancholy and dejected ... When they came to fourscore years, ... they had not only all the follies and infirmities of other old men, but many more which arose from the dreadful prospects of never dying. They were not only opinionative, peevish, covetous, morose, vain, talkative, but uncapable of friendship, and dead to all natural affection ... Envy and impotent desires are their prevailing passions. ... whenever they see a funeral, they lament and repine that others are gone to an harbour of rest, to which they themselves can never hope to arrive ... The least miserable among them appear to be those who turn to dotage and entirely lose their memories; these meet with more pity and assistance, because they want many bad qualities which abound in others....

> As soon as they have completed their term of eighty years, they are looked on as dead in law ... After that period they are held incapable of any employment of trust or profit...

> At ninety they lose their teeth and hair, they have at that age no distinction of taste, but eat and drink whatever they can get, without relish or appetite. The diseases they were subject to still continue ... In talking they forget ... the names of persons, even of those who are their nearest friends and relations. For the same

reason, they never can amuse themselves with reading, because their memory will not serve to carry them from the beginning of a sentence to the end ...

They are despised and hated by all sorts of people... (Swift 1726/1960, pp.171–172)

A more recent criticism of undue ageing appears in Richard Cowper's *The Tithonian Factor* (1983), in which the over-hasty use of life-extending technology produces a *struldbrugg*-like longevity. (The beneficiaries of that technology are later discomfited by finding that humans do indeed have a joyous afterlife!) Sterling's *Holy Fire* (1997) explores a different problem with the extended age span – boredom. Mia Ziemann is 93 years old and has infinite life owing to a medical life extension programme. Sound in mind and limb, she just finds life to have lost all its pleasures.

The dystopian consequences of undue ageing are explored in several Gothic fantasies and science fiction accounts. Some see it as an infinitely tedious punishment as meted out to Ixion, Tantalus, Sisyphus, and the Wandering Jew.[6] Early science fiction writers initiated this theme – Walter Besant in *The Inner House* (1888) proposes that immortality would lead to social sterility, an opinion shared by many later writers.[7] Karel Capek in *The Makropolous Secret* (1925) regards it as an unmitigated curse. Immortality is regarded as the ultimate stagnation and the end of innovation in David H. Keller's (1934) story 'Life Everlasting'.[8] Boredom and sterility must eventually set in.

Chiron, the Thessalian God of healing, classically confronted one of the problems of immortality by abdicating that power. He had been tutor of Asclepius, Nestor and Achilles. When he was accidentally shot by a poisoned arrow, Chiron relinquished his immortality to escape the pain through death. Long-living with pain was a curse, not a blessing.

This fate of elderly long-living is a common theme of ballads and short stories. In medieval days, popular concern often revolved around what to do if the elderly lived too long. Thus in the Grimms' story *The Three Old Men* the characters are bemused by the prospect of those living beyond the accustomed lifespan and their subsequent problems.

Montaigne ridiculed those who wished to extend their life

'Tis the last and extreme form of dying ... what an idle conceit is it to expect to die of a decay of strength which is the effect of the extremest age, and to propose to ourselves no shorter lease on life ... as if it were contrary to nature to see a man break his neck with a fall, be drowned by shipwreck, be snatched away with pleurisy or the plague ... we ought to call natural death that which is general, common and universal. (Quoted in Illich 1991, p.190)

In Illich's rhetorical denunciation of the development of modern medicine, there appears an account of elderly status in the Middle Ages. In the sixteenth century 'the young wife is death to an old man', and in the seventeenth 'old men who play with young maids dance with death'. At the court of Louis XIV 'the old lecher was a laughing stock'. Ashliman (1999) cites a variety of aphorisms to exemplify the same theme – such as 'there is no fool like an old fool', 'an old man who takes a young wife invites death to the wedding' and 'when the old cow dances, her claws rattle'.

Being elderly is often regarded as symptomatic of being ill. That juxtaposition may furnish a disavowal of the elderly – it removes their human self and denies them personhood, and makes them fit for disposal as detritus.

Although the meaning and the value attached to old age vary in different societies, old age nevertheless remains a fact that runs throughout history, arousing identical reactions. Physically, it is without any question a decline, and for that reason most people have dreaded it. The early Egyptians cherished the hope that they might defeat it. There is a papyrus that reads: 'The beginning of the book on the way of changing an old man into a young one.' It advises the eating of fresh glands taken from young animals (De Beauvoir 1973).

Outline of the book

But irrespective of personal experiences, history demonstrates that larger societal forces have decided that those final years should be terminated early. Two general processes have been apparent. *Direct killing* of the elderly and, much more frequently, *death-hastening* devices, through various techniques of social and physical deprivation, have been a consistent feature of societies past and present.

Despite many official disavowals, there are few societies in which the elderly are all treated in a benevolent way until final natural death. Geronticide is a social construct. Decisions to kill the elderly, humanely or otherwise, are made by people. They are not inevitable, decreed by some anonymous fate.

Four overlapping approaches to the practice of geronticide can be identified

- demographic explanations (popularly known as the *demographic time-bomb thesis*)

- the *political economy perspective* (economic scarcity leads to early death for the elderly and their discard as non-productive junk)

- the *modernisation thesis* (that social and economic changes under industrialisation deleteriously affected attitudes towards older people, often leaving them as marginal or isolated, and often welcoming the release of death)

- *bureaucratisation and geronticide* (the thesis that the elderly are disposed of by pragmatic, unconscious decision-making processes in industrial society that resolve problems not through evil machinations but by anonymous clinical procedures and impartial officials).

The four approaches are addressed separately in Chapters 2 to 5 as they furnish contrasting explanations of public attitudes, and private and public practices, in relation to geronticide. Moving from the realm of social theory to the historical evidence from popular discourse, Chapter 6 demonstrates that different data sources may furnish a novel account of the continuity of the practice – poets may exaggerate but academics may not see the wood for the trees. Geronticide representations in popular discourse (normally in death-hastening form) have been a continuing feature of human society, as evidenced by a variety of literary and scientific sources, from biblical days to science fiction.

Chapter 7 represents a slight diversion. It deals with the topic of elderly voluntary euthanasia. Focusing on physician-assisted suicide, it argues that legislation in favour of that practice may offer too much unchecked discretion to medical practitioners. Euthanasia legislation is often justified in relation to the relief of incurable illness and severe pain. In practice, it may be used most frequently for older people suffering from a range of psychosocial problems, which could to some extent be relieved by social and psychological measures without resort to euthanasia practices.

Finally, Chapter 8 – initially through the vehicle of the case of Dr Harold Shipman – develops the social policy implications of our theoretical, historical, and empirical excursion into death-hastening processes for the elderly. Prevention at the procedural level has basic flaws. Older people are not passive in their experience of the death-hastening process. The problem is one of finding an adequate platform from which they can defend themselves. The chapter concludes by advocating a proactive and progressive adaptation of universal human rights principles.

Geronticide and the elderly: Definitions

Geronticide, if it is taken to mean the deliberate and systematic killing of the elderly solely because they are elderly, either by others or through social pressure to commit suicide, is a modern term (see e.g. Posner 1995; Post 1991) to describe a common refrain in literature and anthropological studies that stretches back to antiquity. Writing of the island of Ceos, Strabo (cited in Jones 1938) asserts that 'It is reputed that there was once a law among these people, which appears to have ordered those who were over sixty years of age to drink hemlock, in order that the good might be sufficient for the rest' (p.169). Diodorus (cited in Oldfather 1838) offers another example:

And the inhabitants, they tell us, are extremely long-lived, living even to the age of one hundred and fifty years, and experiencing for the most part no illness.

Anyone also among them who has become crippled or suffers, in general, from any physical infirmity is forced by them, in accordance with an inexorable law, to remove himself from life. And there is also a law among them that they should live only for a stipulated number of years, and that at the completion of this period they should make away with themselves of their own accord, by a strange manner of death; for there grows among them a plant of a peculiar nature, and whenever a man lies down upon it, imperceptibly and gently he falls asleep and dies. (p.13)

That theme, represented in utopian and dystopian writings, has been a recurrent motif in literature from Sir Thomas More's *Utopia* (1516) through to Anthony Trollope's *The Fixed Period* (1882) and to modern science fiction writers. It forms a counterpoint to discussions of suicide and euthanasia, invoking the coerced rather than the autonomous suicide, and incremental arguments of the transition from voluntary to involuntary euthanasia with any relaxation of legal controls.

However, portraying the elderly as a group especially subject to homicidal social pressure is a moveable feast. For the most part, the boundary between 'middle age' and 'old age' is one which varies in different situations. In earlier societies 'old' designated people between 35 and 60 years of age, and these indeed were often granted special status and privilege. However, once a person became senile and could no longer contribute to family and society, he or she might be pushed from a position of honour, and even executed or abandoned (as in Chapter 3). In Western society, De Jouvenal (1966) summarises the prevailing view in assigning to 'old age' the normal demographic classification of people aged 65 years and over, 'whatever may be their actual situation in terms of profes-sional activity or state of health' (p.6). That figure is a relatively artificial but stand-ardised measure which may be applied to everyone.

Yet the age of 65 as the demarcation of old age is not entirely arbitrary (Hugman 1998). It reflects the most widely used age criterion in Western societies for the receipt of retirement pensions. It is probable in such societies that a person aged over 65 years will have retired from full-time paid employment, and most people in this age group will be eligible for some type of pension on the grounds of age alone.

Alternatively, it might be possible to fix a comparative measure, from the known incidence of the relationship between increasing age and levels of disability and illness in Western society. In that case, the figure of 75 years would appear to be most appropriate as it is within the over-75 age group that disability and ill-health become identifiably correlated with chronological age. Such an approach has actually led to the demarcation of the 'old-old' as a more coherent focus for the study of geronticide practices.

Both these boundary markers demonstrate the social nature of the definition of old age. People may not stop working at the age when they could receive retirement pension. In that sense, the average age of retirement as a definition of old age is *socially normative* rather than *neutrally descriptive*. It describes what exists, reflecting a generalised view that older people should not work. Similarly, where levels of disability or ill health are the criteria for defining the old-old, there will also be reservations. While it may be that amongst the over-75s, the incidence of health, social and economic needs rises dramatically, such a focus means ignoring deprivations below that chronological age. Further divisions could be made, such as that between people under and over 80 years or 90 years of age, in which other age-related factors may be identified – disability, social isolation, the predominance of women and differentially gendered death ratios.

Consequently, demarcating 'old age' in strictly chronological terms is bound to be imprecise in including some and excluding others. It would be especially arbitrary when applied to the non-industrialised world. However, the age groupings do have a degree of common currency. The categories 'over 65 years' (often referring to the young-old) and 'over 75 years' (the old-old) are utilised throughout gerontological study as a means of ensuring comparability.

But we need to distinguish between ageing and senescence. Ageing is the mere passing of years, without any implication of degradation. Everybody ages – a natural process; but some decline into senescence because of factors often external to the ageing process. In routine life styles, some people inevitably (unequally) die from exposure to the pitfalls of everyday life, but now over a longer period of time. The number of older people will necessarily decline, not because of a diminution in faculties (hearing, vision, manual and physical dexterity, and so on), but simply because they are differentially exposed to physical perils. Stratification affects longer living.

But the key distinctions in considering the elderly as a problem of dependency are the relationships

- between the young-old and the old-old
- between ageing and senescence
- between those with power and those without.

An astronomical increase in lifespan may be of little value if the latter years still tail into frail decay, with the more powerful members of society ensuring an inequitable distribution of supportive resources. Ageing is the mere passing of years, without any implication of degradation. Senescence is ageing plus degradation, and exposes one to inequalities of power.

An extreme version of this division between the young-old and the old-old is coupled with the notion of rights. Killing an elderly person in Western society means *inter alia* extinguishing his or her rights to be a person. But if life is to be subjected to a rights test, a person in an irreversible coma, young or old, does not enjoy such rights. Being in a coma is in effect being dead as defined by the absence of rights. An extreme view of the old-old would therefore simply encompass those who by virtue of senility or some other terminal phase have abdicated willingly, or unwillingly, the rights of being a person and hence of life. To 'die at the right time' – that is when one is wasted by life, and meaningful rights have been surrendered – was not a value invented by Nietzsche's Zarathustra in *Also Sprach Zarathustra* (1883–85).

A less extreme construction of the old-old accommodates those who are dependent as well as being conscious that their dependency is a handicap to others with whom they have an affinity. In exceptional situations, that second group may not be distinguished from other vulnerable populations. The brutal decision by the Nazi creators of the Holocaust that some elderly people could be included within the general termination of disabled people and the 'mentally unfit' was not diminished by re-labelling the state killing agency the 'Charitable Foundation for Institutional Care'. (The rationale offered by Hitler was simple – it would furnish 'a certain saving in hospitals, physicians, and nursing personnel'. (quoted in Friedlander, 1995, p.63)) Almost by accident, the elderly – or rather those elderly designated as disabled – were included in the wider Holocaust cull. Old age homes, amongst others, had to be registered with the Reich Ministry of the Interior, in readiness for involuntary euthanasia of the elderly as part of the larger population deemed to be a drain on the state's resources.

The old-old may be demarcated by poverty as well as by physical and mental dependence. As noted in Chapter 2, the old-old population will grow the fastest, perhaps by as much as 60 per cent in the next 30 years in most developed countries. About 80 per cent of the elderly population in Western societies have no problems and require no special assistance. Approximately another 5 per cent are institutionalised, and a further 15 per cent have frequent or constant problems living independently (Heumann and Boldy 1993). It is this 20 per cent who constitute the old-old and the group most susceptible to geronticide practices in the present day and whose position can be regarded as senescent.

All indications are that this group will also have the greatest need for supportive housing and services to cope with their advanced frailties. However, for the past decade or more most governments in developed countries have been committed to lower taxes and to withdrawing subsidised support service programmes. The pressure has been to lessen state support rather than to expand it, or at least to subject elderly needs to the inequalities of provision by the market. The changes in technology, in health and in wealth can have only a marginal effect on the burden on others of longer lives. But intervention on the scale necessary to construct both a fair and equal condition of age, as well as to minimise the dependence of the elderly in a range of ways on their juniors, is highly unlikely by governments committed to *laissez faire* market economy capitalism. It certainly is impossible in the non-industrial countries.

Such limitations are a social construction, the subject of social and economic inequalities. The caveat of differential experiences of disadvantage is crucial. Utilising that terminology does not ignore the critical influence of other forms of inequality and of social stratification. However, investigating the social dimensions of geronticide involves inquiring into the way social needs and responses are perceived in age-related terms, while risking reinforcing the equation of old age and dependency by the forces of social reaction.

Notes

1   Bizarrely summed up by Derek Humphry (1994): 'The plastic bag is getting the same sort of public relations reputation as the wire coat hanger did in the abortion debate, except that the bag is 100 per cent effective' (p.1017).

2   Supposedly effective elixirs at solving the 'disease' problem of ageing are common. Most recently, a French doctor published research – in front of a credulous ageing audience – which sought to demonstrate that dehydroepiandrosterone might just work – 'France enjoys love affair with "elixir of life."' *The Times,* 14 April, 2000

3   Barash (1983) draws an arguable parallel between long-living rats and isolated groups of peoples – the long-living Abkasians, Vilcambans, and the Hunzas. These groups have poverty (for example the consumption of very little meat) and a high child mortality rate in common. The key to longevity, he argues, may lie in a stringent but adequate diet that contains all the necessary nutrients, but in minimum supply. After the childhood deaths, the survivors can expect a long life.

4   Quoted in Kearl (1999).

5   Alan Harrington in *Paradise 1* (1977) introduces the intriguing idea that immortality can be achieved by immunity from ageing but not from injury. Accidents - 'acts of God' - kill randomly but biological processes can potentially be controlled.

6   In William Godwin's *St Leon* (1799), Charles Maturin's *Melmoth the Wanderer* (1820), Eugene Sue's *The Wandering Jew* (1844/5), W. Harrison Ainsworth's *Auriel* (1850), and W. Clark Russell's *The Death Ship* (1888).

7   Including Harold Scarborough in *The Immortals* (1924), and Aldous Huxley in *After Many a Summer* (1939).

8   In *Life Everlasting and Other Tales.*

CHAPTER 2

Death by Demography and Longevity

When God created the world he gave the ass, the dog, the monkey, and man each a lifespan of 30 years. The ass, knowing that his was to be a hard existence, asked for a shorter life. God had mercy and took away 18 years. The dog and the monkey similarly thought their prescribed lives too long, and God reduced them respectively by 12 and 10 years. Man, however, considered the 30 years assigned to him to be too brief, and he petitioned for a longer life. Accordingly, God gave him the years not wanted by the ass, the dog, and the monkey. Thus man lives 70 years. The first 30 are his human years, and they quickly disappear. Here he is healthy and happy; he works with pleasure, and enjoys his existence. The ass's 18 years follow. Here one burden after the other is laid on him; he carries the grain that feeds others, and his faithful service is rewarded with kicks and blows. Then come the dog's 12 years, and he lies in the corner growling, no longer having teeth with which to bite. When this time is past, the monkey's 10 years conclude. Now man is weak headed and foolish; he does silly things and becomes a laughing stock for children. (Quoted in Ashliman 1997)

In his novel *All Moonshine* (1907), Richard Whiteing brought the whole world population to the Isle of Wight to ridicule the idea of an overburdened earth. Right now, you may still be able to stand the whole world population on that island – but it will be becoming a little crowded. In particular, the weak and the lame – the number using wheelchairs and Zimmer frames – may seem disproportionately higher.

This chapter considers the effect of the demographic character of the growth of the elderly population – the extent to which that expansion affects attitudes towards their survival and the pressure on them to 'move over'. In the first place, we consider the relative growth of the older population both in the West and in non-industrial countries. The overall figure, however, does not allow for the inequalities in power and in access to resources by the elderly, as determined by factors such as gender, socio-economic class, and ethnicity as well as by the relative faster growth of the elderly in the so-called Third World countries. The increased dependent population is affected by the 'normal' problems of elderly living, for instance a higher propensity to violent deaths in traffic accidents and to suicide-promoting illnesses such as depression. It also necessarily involves both higher economic costs as well as increased demands on a labour force of (mainly) female carers. One typical result of societal reaction to that demographic expansion has been in the development of death-hastening processes through rationed discrimination in relation to health resources for the elderly. However, a crude deterministic view of the demographic time bomb ignores the differentiation amongst the elderly and the inequalities dividing them.

The Problem of Longevity

If men were certain that the present over-population would eventually engulf them, would they be right in withdrawing such things as insecticide, fertiliser, and anti-malarial and anti-tuberculosis drugs. If men breed like rabbits, should they not die like rabbits? (Inaugural address by the President of the American Sociological Association, September 1952)

An ageing world population raises questions about the experiences of older people, and about the appropriate ways in which their needs – from health to housing to economic security – can be met. It problematises social attitudes to the functions and roles, if any, of the elderly.

Gregory King (1648–1712), who pioneered long-range global population projections, wrote that 'if the World should continue to 2000 AD, it might then have 6,500 million [people]'. The world's population will reach the size projected by King early this century. A combination of fewer early deaths and increased longevity for older people has become popularised as the problem of the demographic time bomb. The French mathematician, the Marquis Jean-Antoine-Nicolas Carriar de Condorcet (1743–1794), had pondered the problem:

This average span of life which we suppose will increase indefinitely as time passes, may grow in conformity either with a law such that it gradually approaches a limitless length but without ever reaching it, or with a law such that through the centuries it reaches a length greater than any determinate quantity that we may assign to it … we are bound to believe that the average length of life will for ever increase unless this is prevented by physical revolutions. (Cited by Carey 1999) [1]

Thomas Malthus (1798) published his *Essay on the Principle of Population as it Affects the Future Improvement of Society*, arguing that because of the tendency of the population in the absence of war, famine and the plague,[2] to increase exponentially society would be in danger of continually outgrowing resources. In his later (1803) edition, Malthus called for check by 'voluntary restraint'. But he had little belief in the effectiveness of that moral process. As he pointed out, the situation may be self-correcting – when there are more people than the earth can accommodate, the surplus will eventually die, one way or another.

An ageing population has been a key feature of Britain's post-war social history. The percentage of the population of 65 and over in England and Wales has increased from 10.9 per cent in 1951 to over 16 per cent in the new millennium (some 2 per cent will be at least 85 years old). There are also noticeable changes in terms of the increasing proportion of those of 75 and over. In 1991, 44 per cent of the elderly population were at least 75 years old, compared to 33 per cent in 1951. Over the last 30 years, the numbers of people aged 60 and over increased by 13 per cent.

The ageing of the population reflects the convergence of two main factors: first, the downward trend in the birth rate, so that the proportion of older people is increasing faster than the proportion of children in the population; and second, improvements in life expectancy (an increase of 20 years over the course of the twentieth century, in the case of Britain).

However, the rate of increase is noticeably slowing. There has been a relative decrease in the number of 'young elderly', especially those in their sixties. But this has been more than compensated by a rapid growth in those aged 85 and over. The 'old elderly' (what we refer to in this text as the old-old group) are the survivors of the larger cohort born in Britain in the first decade of the twentieth century.

The elderly represent an increasing dilemma for policy makers and resource providers. That problem is indicated by the increased discussion of euthanasia, by public debates over disproportionate dependency costs, and by concerns with elderly care and shelter. The elderly are already pictured as frequent victims in violent crime in the media – stereotypes abound of older people as prey to homicide and other violence either in the extended household or in the nursing home (Brogden and Nijhar 2000).

Most of these problems are perceived to stem from the demographic time bomb – the increased number of non-working older people in the population. Kearl (1999) expresses the dilemma in imagining the problems that would occur if a researcher ever found the cure for cancer. He or she would be met not by praise but by a government frenetic about higher health and social security costs. Greater tax revenue would be required to provide for the old, given increased illness and welfare benefits. Longer lifespan costs money. The United Kingdom, like other parts of the Western world, is about to pay the price for advances since the Second World War in improving public health and encouraging expectations about the quality of life.

Population ageing in Western society

The demographic approach to geronticide is centred on the implications of the growth of the numbers of older people, globally as well as in European society, and the relationship this has to other sections of the population (De Jouvenal

1966). Governments around the world are only starting to come to grips with the challenges posed by a dramatic demographic shift. In industrial nations, there is a lower percentage of children than at any time in world history, while there is a larger proportion of older people. The problem is one of how to ensure that the increasing health needs and other necessary resources (and costs) of an ageing population are met while, simultaneously, the tax base shrinks as the percentage of employed people declines.

Until the Industrial Revolution, few lived beyond the age of 65 years – only 2–3 per cent of the population was over 65 at any one time – compared with a projected rise to 20 per cent by 2030. In Britain, according to the US Office of National Statistics, the number of people aged 90 and over will quadruple within the next 70 years. Currently 67,000 men and 273,000 women are in their nineties. By 2066, this will increase to 390,000 men and 800,000 women. Currently just over nine million people – 15 per cent of the population – are 65 and over. By 2066, this will have risen by more than 50 per cent to 14.5 million (24 per cent of the total).

The United Nations estimates that by the year 2025 there will be 822 million people in the world aged 65 and over, a number greater than the present combined populations of Europe and North America. In 30 years, a quarter of the population in Western Europe, for example, will be over 60, compared to only one-fifth in 1994. The numbers of old-old are increasing sharply internationally – a rise from 400 million now to 1.3 billion in 2050 in the number of 65–85 year olds, and from 26 million to 175 million in the over 85s. One out of every ten persons is now 60 years or over. By 2050, one out of five will be 60 years or over, and by 2150, one out of three persons.

In other words, the oldest segment of the population is not just growing larger; it is also getting older. The old-old are increasing at a faster rate than the total elderly population. In 1990, fewer than one in ten elderly persons was aged 85 and over. By 2045, the oldest old will be one in five. In the UK in 1950, there were 300 centenarians. By 2021 it is estimated that 22,493 women and 4386 men will be over the age of 100. The oldest old will be three times as numerous in 2050 as they are now (Royal Commission on Long-Term Care 1999). Internationally, the number of very old people of 80 plus is projected to grow by a factor of eight to ten from 1950 to 2050.

The demographic time bomb can be expressed longitudinally. In 1900, only 3.1 million of the population of the United States (4 per cent of the total population) was aged 65 and over. The life expectancy of a newborn white child was only about 50 years and was less than 35 years for a black child. In 30 years, the average life expectancy for whites shot up to 60 years, and blacks to 50 years, and the number of elderly people more than doubled to 6.7 million (about 5 per cent of the total population). In 1960, the elderly population had doubled again with some 16.7 million people aged 65 and older (about 9 per cent of the total population). Life expectancies for whites were 70 years, and 60 years for minority groups.

A further doubling had occurred by 1994 – some 31 million people (12 per cent of the total population) were aged 65 years and over. In another 35 years, it could double again. Some 62 million American citizens (almost one in five of the population) will be aged 65 and over by the year 2025. By 2045, the elderly population will reach some 77 million, more than the total population of the United States in the 1900s. Today, 50 per cent of Americans will survive beyond the age of 74. In 1946, half could expect to live to age 67 and in 1900, half of the American population died before reaching 50 years of age (US Department of Commerce, Economics and Statistics, 2000).

In Britain, the number of people of pensionable age is projected to increase from 10.7 million in 1996 to 11.8 million in the year 2010. This will rise to 14 million by 2021 and will peak at just over 17 million. Allowing for changes in women's retirement age (from 60 to 65), the population of pensionable age will rise to 12 million by 2021 and reach nearly 15.5 million around the year 2038. While the maximum lifespan for a human being has not changed (the upper limit is between 110 and 120 – see Chapter 1), average life expectancy has increased (Age Concern 1999a).

The outcome for Western societies is that the proportion of people aged over 65 years appears to have doubled in the latter half of the twentieth century, while the percentage of people aged over 75 may have increased by a little under three times (United Nations 1998). Between 1950 and 1996, the average number of births per woman worldwide declined from five to three. During the same period, average life expectancy at birth increased by 21 years in non-industrial countries and by 8 years in industrial ones.

Non-industrial societies and the demographic time bomb

Projections show that population ageing is likely to impact more harshly on non-industrial countries because of a more rapid decline in fertility. The speed of ageing increase is faster than in developed countries. There will be less time to adapt to the consequences of an ageing population.

The number of people aged 60 and older increased by 125 per cent in industrial countries to 214 million in 1995; and by 200 per cent in countries such as China, India, and Brazil to reach 330 million. UN projections show this trend accelerating. Between 1995 and 2025, the population aged 60 and older may increase to 54 per cent in industrial countries. But by 2050, non-industrial countries could have more than four times as many elderly people as industrial countries (United Nations 1998).

Currently, only 9.2 per cent of the population of non-industrial countries are above the age of sixty. But more than a quarter of people aged 75 and over live in just two countries – China and India. A steep increase in this proportion is already pre-programmed in the age structure of China. Over the next 15 years, a moderate increase in the age structure occurs followed by a steep increase. Within less than four decades, China's old-age dependency burden will be higher than North America's and about the same as that in Western Europe today.

But while Western Europe's old-age dependency burden has been built up over more than a century, and has had a relatively long period for the gestation of social security schemes for the elderly, China has little time.[3] Strict population policies lowered its fertility rate from 4.8 children per woman in the 1970s to 1.8 in 1996, while life expectancy has increased by 28 years since 1950. In the next 30 years, China's population aged 60 and older may grow seven times as fast as its total population. In the West, it took 115 years for the elder population to increase from 7 per cent to 17 per cent but a comparable change will occur in China in just 27 years.[4]

There is also an urban versus rural dimension to the ageing programme internationally – rural dwellers may have fewer resources than those in urban areas. In the West, some 77 per cent of the elderly are living in urban areas in the year 2000. But the majority in developing regions still live in rural locations. The problems for the elderly inhabitants of the non-industrial world may make those of the Western elderly pale into insignificance.

The dependency ratio and the social crisis

Control over fertility is one side of the population control mechanism to deal with the demographic explosion. Age of death is the other. These considerations anticipate a point in the near future where, if present trends continue, an 'imbalance' of older people to younger people will be reached where the changed proportions will have profound effects on every aspect of social organisation. The 'crisis' or 'time bomb' ideas are based on an assumed link between the absolute numbers and proportions of older people and the ratio of dependence. This ratio is the number of people economically 'active' compared to those who are in some way economically 'dependent' such as school or college students (Hugman 1998). In the UK, there are currently 3.7 people of working age (20–64 years) to each person aged 65 and over. By 2020, this ratio will have fallen to 3.1 and by 2040 to 2.1. This will be offset, but only partly, by a fall in the numbers of people below working age (Age Concern 1997). In the United States in 1990 there were 20 elderly persons for every 100 of working age. But by the year 2025, there will be 32 elderly persons for every 100 of working age (US Department of Commerce, Economics and Statistics 2000). The dramatic change is not just in the overall ratio but in the balance between the so-called dependent groups within it.

The idea of crisis arises from presumptions about the dependence (economic and otherwise) of older people, which are derived not only from predicted numbers and proportions but also at the same time from particular perceptions of old age as a part of human experience. The crisis notion is based on social prejudices about ageing, such as adaptability to change, capacity to develop new skills, or to make an active contribution to society. The cornerstones of these social assumptions are fertility rates, mortality rates and the extent of international migration (De Jouvenal 1966). The conflation of these factors in advanced industrial societies has meant that four related phenomena have emerged:

- an increase in the proportion of older people in the population

- an increase in the actual number of older people

- an increase in the average age of populations

- a corresponding negative constellation of values about the elderly has been reinforced.

The reason why fertility rates are an important aspect of the demographic approach is that the increase in the proportions of older people in European societies does not arise solely from the growth in actual numbers of those aged over 65 years and a decline in mortality rates but also from the decline in the numbers of people aged less than 20 years. In this sense, the concept of an 'ageing' population relates to the age structure of society as a whole, not to one cohort in isolation. Proportionately fewer people are being born as well as more people living longer. The result is a social crisis – an interpretation of demographic change.

Gender and the demography of ageing

In the UK in 1996, out of a population of 59 million, two-thirds (6,900,000) were women aged 60 and over (of whom 5,482,000 were aged 65 and over); nearly four million were men aged 65 and over. Almost three-quarters of those aged 85 and over were women, 794,000 compared to 273,000 men (including 5670 female centenarians and 655 male centenarians).[5]

By the year 2000, the figures of gendered life expectancy in the UK have changed. Men are now catching up with women, with men likely to live five years longer than was predicted a decade ago. A man aged 35 years can now expect to live to the age of 85 years and one month compared with 80 years and one month.[6] The life expectancy of women has climbed from 84 years and 7 months to 88 years and 1 month. A man aged 40 can expect to live until he is 84 years and 10 months, as compared to 80 years and 1 month. For a woman aged 40, life expectancy is 87 years and 10 months compared with 84 years and 7 months. A 50-year-old man is forecast to die at 84 years and 2 months – an extra 4 years' life expectancy. A woman at the same age is expected to live to 87 years and 2 months, up from 84 years and 8 months. For women, the biggest improvement is among 60- to 70-year-olds, whose likelihood of dying in that period has fallen by 20 per cent. For men the major change is among the 50- to 60-year-olds, whose death rate has fallen by up to 35 per cent (Institute of Actuaries 1999).

Universally, ageing populations will give the planet a more feminine aspect. The age pyramid is biased towards the more traditionally socio-economically disadvantaged gender. The greater life expectancy of women compared to men is a global phenomenon. In many countries, there are twice as many women aged 60 or older as men. Women may live, on average, between five and nine and a half years longer than their male co-nationals. International figures do not demonstrate much geographical difference in life expectancy, with a variation for women of 3.7 years and for men of 4.8. What is most apparent is that women in all countries, on average, are longer-lived than their male counterparts.

More than two-thirds of Western Europeans who die at age 85 or older are women. Because of the age difference, women are more likely than men to die of the lingering conditions that afflict the old. In Britain, before the age of 65, men are three times more likely to suffer heart disease than women and twice as likely to die from lung cancer (Age Concern 1999a). Men (reportedly) leave serious medical conditions too late by not visiting the doctor – women visit the doctor around twice as often as men and form the majority of the patients treated in hospital. Men also seem more accident-prone, constituting the majority of accident and emergency cases. However, health differences largely disappear with age. Among men and women aged 65 and older, the top ten death causes are almost identical – headed by heart disease and cancer (Age Concern 1999a). As a result, increases in life expectancy for men will mean that fewer Westerners will die suddenly, and more will die in ways that consume costly healthcare services.

Women are less likely than men to die in a hospital and more likely to die in a nursing home. Only 56 per cent of women died in hospitals in 1992, compared with 62 per cent of men. Yet 23 per cent of all deaths for women were in nursing homes, compared with just 12 per cent for men. The 'normal' occupant of a care home is female (Age Concern 1999a).

In Britain, 3.1 million women do not qualify for a full basic pension. Two-thirds of men over 65 years have a private pension but only one-third of women. As many as three-quarters of pensioners on income support are female, and many more women than men live on income just above the poverty level. Three out of five older women are single, the majority of the former living on a basic pension. Women's private pensions are less than 10 per cent of men's when they retire (Age Concern 1999b).

Social class and demography

> But the complication of medicine had another effect. It restricted treatment to those who could afford it. ... Everything was sacrificed to the Great God of Medicine – all so that a few people could live a few years longer. (James Gunn, *The Immortals*, 1958, pp.138–139)

Compassion for the poor and disabled will not necessarily be the primary consideration in doling out such a precious commodity as medicine. A major factor in ageing is its relationship to poverty and to social class. In the words of the Royal Commission on Long-Term Care (1999):

> ...until the twentieth century in western industrial societies, life for most people could, with justification, have been described as nasty, brutish, and short. It could be particularly brutish for people who were unfortunate enough to grow old and be poor. (p.1)

The population is subject to major social change in composition. The proportionate size of the population that is the most deprived is expanding rapidly. It is also becoming less self-sufficient. In Britain, lower social class males can expect to live to just over 70 years, whereas for males in the upper social classes the average life span is nearly 80 years. Poverty is usually associated with gender and with increasing age (Laczko 1990). Economic hardship characterises much of the older population. In 1995/96, 48 per cent of pensioner households depended on state benefits for at least three-quarters of their incomes – one in eight receiving all income from state benefits. (Glennerster 1999) Where the head of the household is aged 65 and over, a higher proportion of income is spent each week on the basics of housing, fuel and food, than in other households. In England in 1996, 18.7 per cent of single older people lived in poor housing conditions rising to 19.9 per cent for those over the age of 75 years. Nearly two-thirds of those over 70 years are among the poorest 40 per cent of the population, and people over 70 are only half as likely as those in other age groups to be among the richest 40 per cent of the population. Excluding the value of their home, 57 per cent of those aged 55–69 have savings and investments worth less than £3000, with only 8 per cent having savings and investments over £30,000 (Royal Commission on Long-Term Care 1999).

Despite the major advances in support for the elderly in industrial societies since the Second World War, 10–15 per cent of them in some of these countries live below the poverty line. They own no home; they have no cash savings. If they are lucky, they have a meagre pension and are eligible for government-subsidised medical and social services. The luckiest of the poor elderly are able to obtain subsidised housing, but the demand far exceeds the supply. Longer lives create problems when inequality of provision is supported by the more powerful. Unless costs are spread across society in a fair and progressive way, the chances are that poverty and a lack of dignity and choice will be the reality for many (Royal Commission on Long-Term Care 1999).

Pensioners living alone who are mainly dependent on state pensions experience the most severe deprivation. Over half their expenditure is on basic necessities. In 1996/97 one-adult retired households mainly dependent on benefits spent 10.8 per cent of their average weekly expenditure on fuel, light and power, compared with 4.7 per cent for single non-retired households; and 18.7 per cent of old people lived in unfit housing. In 1996, in the 65–74 age group, 21 per cent of men and 39 per cent of women lived alone, and 31 per cent of men and 58 per cent of women aged 75 and over lived alone and were less likely to possess conventional assets such as central heating, washing machines and telephones, and much less likely to have personal transport. The old are not merely liable to other forms of dependence but they are also economically the weakest section of the population, drawing disproportionately upon state benefits. Old Mother Hubbard inevitably had an empty cupboard.

Ethnicity and the ageing population

Not only do gender, nationality and social class divide older people, but there are also racial and ethnic distinctions which must be recognised. The bias is a black and white phenomenon. In 1985, there were approximately 7.3 million people resident in European Economic Community (EEC) countries who were born elsewhere. Like those minority ethnic people born in the EEC, elders from such backgrounds may be divided from the mainstream of European society through racism as well as by age (De Jouvenal 1966). Ethnic minorities are more likely than their white counterparts to have experienced other forms of discrimination, of gender and of social class. For these people, old age may represent only one dimension of multiple marginalisation. Minorities constitute some 6 per cent of the population of the UK. Eight per cent of the black Caribbean population was aged 65 and over, 5 per cent of Indians, 3 per cent of Bangladeshis, 2 per cent of Pakistanis and 2 per cent of black Africans (Age Concern 1999b).

Ethnic health discrimination has been documented. In the United States for example, Afro-Americans with symptoms of heart trouble are only about half as likely to be referred for the best testing and treatment. Members of that ethnic group suffering from cancer in nursing homes are severely under-treated for pain – many not even receiving aspirin. Black and other minority patients are more likely to be discharged from hospital in unsuitable conditions. Despite equal Medicare coverage, affluent white elderly patients often receive better medical care than African Americans or poor people of all races. African American academics express concern that new limits on healthcare present new opportunities to victimise minorities: [7] 'People know they don't get the health care they need while they're living. So what makes them think it's going to be more sensitive when they're dying?'.[8]

Other divisions of social structure may also be identified. In the UK, disability is a major issue for some older people. By the year 2029, projected numbers of disabled older people will increase from the present 2 million to 6.5 million (General Household Survey 1998). There are religious and sectarian diversities, psychological differences and biological variations, which in older age may exacerbate the wider social distinctions which can be seen in every age group. Older people, as with younger people, represent a considerable diversity. At the same time, there is a common range of ageist social factors and perceptions through which old age as a phenomenon is constructed.

Demography and a finite food supply

A key demographic argument is that the increase in the elderly, non-working population will contribute to future food shortages, especially in non-industrial countries. Can we any longer feed such an increasing non-working population? Since the time when Malthus launched the debate, some 200 years ago, research has mushroomed on the subject. But there is no clear conclusion. The literature on estimating the earth's population-carrying capacity reveals diverse results (Heilig 1994). How many people can be fed on earth if we take into account technical, ecological, political and social constraints? Can an increasing elderly population be sustained? H.G. Wells (1901) had foreseen the current debate when he forecast a world in which the expansion of animal species and of green conservation habitats would constrain the world population to some two billion people.

Most experts would accept that the current six billion world population could be supported. Beyond that figure, practical problems arise – the intervening variables of policy failures, post-colonial exploitation, corruption, ethnic conflicts, communications, access to and application of technical expertise, and inequalities in the control of resources such as land and water.

Pearson and Harper (1945) calculated that between 902 million and 2.8 billion people could be supported by the earth's agriculture. Clark (1967) estimated the sustainable population maximum of the earth to range between 40 and 157 billion! However, in the 1970s Buringh, Van Hearnst and Starling (1975) considered the world food production potential equivalent to just 5.3 billion people. In the early 1980s, a large Food and Agriculture Organization (FAO) study concluded that between 3.9 and 32.4 billion people could be fed (depending on the level of agricultural inputs) (FAO 1988)

It may be that we have already passed the limits of sustainability and are on the way to ecological disaster. In 1992, the World Resources Institute published a wealth of data suggesting early finite ecological limits in many sectors of the economies, including agriculture. Most recently Ehrlich and Ehrlich (1996) analysed the subject – it is 'doubtful – whether food security could be achieved indefinitely for a global population of 10 or 12 billion people'. They thought it 'rather likely that a sustainable population, one comfortably below Earth's nutritional capacity, will number far fewer than the present population.'

Heilig (1994) illustrates the problem with the metaphor of a pipe through which the earth's food resources have to pass before they can be used for feeding people. The diameter of the pipe is large on the 'input' side but narrow at the 'output' end. The decreasing diameter symbolises different kinds of restrictions to the earth's carrying capacity – technological, economic, ecological and socio-cultural. Even in its extreme version, the measure ignores economic, social, cultural and political restrictions of food production. It assumes implementation of the most advanced agricultural technologies throughout the world. Experts who have adopted this narrow definition of carrying capacity estimate the maximum world population that can be sustained indefinitely into the future in the range of 16 to 147 billion people (depending on the specific method applied).

However, a recent FAO study (Alexandratos 1995) offers a more optimistic forecast. Despite numerous pressures, constraints and risks, we will not reach during the next two or three decades insurmountable restrictions on food supply. This optimistic prognosis, however, is only possible under Utopian conditions. The key problem is social, not just economic and technical – the problem of inequality of access. Both within the same society (in the West, generally, socio-economic inequalities are increasing) and between the developed world and the non-developed, there are major social disparities. As those social and economic problems cannot readily be resolved, a population increasingly skewed towards the non-working elderly (especially the elderly without capital investments) places that group at risk, in particular when social values are measured primarily in terms of economic productivity.

The social costs of the increasing elderly dependent population

There are both direct and indirect costs involved in the demographic time bomb. There will be direct impact on the elderly. There will also be indirect consequences for their family relatives and carers, and for voluntary and state agencies.

Within five years, the number of elderly people entering care in Britain is projected to rise from 407,000 to 666,000[9] – a fivefold increase since the beginning of the century. There has been a higher demand for care and nursing home provision in the last decade because of the increasing number of people over retirement age, changes in legislation, and a reduction in local authority residential homes and National Health Service continuing care beds. Inequality pervades. 'It is often the lowest income elderly with no other housing options who are still at risk of being institutionalised' (Heumann and Boldy 1993, p.14).

Nine million people aged over 65 years and one in three of these aged 75 years and over is likely to need some form of long-term care.[10] In 1997, the number of permanent residents in registered care homes was 209,000 of whom approximately 46,000 were in local authority homes, 37,000 were in voluntary homes, and 127,000 were in private homes. The number of beds in nursing homes occupied by older people was 159,000.[11] In England in 1998, the chance of living in a long-stay hospital or care home were 1 per cent for the 65–74 year age group, 5 per cent for those of 75–85 years, and 21.7 per cent for the 85 plus cohort.

About 600,000 people over the age of 65 receive home care from a local authority. Most people (76 per cent) receive some 'care' in an institution during the year before they die. National statistics indicate that most people now die in hospitals or in other institutions for the care of the sick (Royal Commission on Long-Term Care 1999). While 95 per cent of elderly people reside at home in the community at any one time (Walker and Maltby 1997), between 25 per cent and 30 per cent of hospital day beds were occupied by people (mainly elderly) who would be dead within 12 months. Together with care homes for the elderly, hospitals play a key care role. Processing people before their death is a 'normal' part of hospital work. Since most people who die are aged 65 and over, the management of the dying of the elderly is a major function of hospitals and care homes. Of those of 85 years and over, some 37 per cent spent all the last year of their life in a nursing or care home, and a further 19 per cent spent some time in one such institution.

The supply of caregivers to the elderly will not keep pace with the ageing population – a problem of the dependency ratio. During one week in England in 1997, 470,000 households received home help or carer services. Of those who received this help, 79,900 were aged 65–74, 178,600 were aged 75–84, and 155,100 were aged 85 and over (Bureau of Labor Statistics 2000). A diminishing number of workers will care for the greater number of care-requiring young and old. Social carers are now one of the largest growth parts of the labour market but 80 per cent of them have no qualification of any kind.[12] In the United States, more than one-third of the top 30 fastest-growing occupations to 2005 are health-related (Bureau of Labor Statistics 2000). The number of personal and home-care aides, who perform light housekeeping tasks for those in need of home care, may double by 2005.

The carers may have their own problems (Baldwin 1995). In the UK, among the carers in 1995 who spent at least 20 hours a week caring, 47 per cent were aged 45–64, and 27 per cent were aged over 65. The group on which older people are mainly dependent for care often consists of other elderly. In 1995, 53 per cent of carers had dependants over the age of 85 years. Some 800,000 people provide unpaid care for more than 50 hours a week. A survey of members of the

Carers National Association (1998) showed that 65 per cent of them felt that their health had suffered as a result of caring and 47 per cent of carers had suffered financial difficulties. Caring is a 'people industry' – it is labour intensive. The nature of the dominant activities – washing, feeding and taking care of the older person – cannot be replaced by technology or by machine. Being people-intensive, care costs are likely to rise disproportionately – there can be no economies of scale as would occur in Fordist-style industries.

The carer problem is gender-skewed. Working women increasingly take time out from their jobs to care for older parents, even as they become less likely to spend time raising children. Nearly four-fifths of disabled elderly people live outside healthcare institutions. Of those, 70 per cent rely solely on informal caregivers such as spouses and children. Nearly one-third of informal care providers are daughters. As the demands of an ageing parent increase, a daughter's career and lifestyle are likely to suffer. Providing ten or more hours of care per week to a non-resident parent reduces a daughter's waged work by 65 hours during an 18-week period. But a daughter will reduce her full-time work outside the home by 130 hours during the same period to care for a disabled parent who lives with her (Carers' National Association (1998)).

Economic problems of care constitute an emotional drain for older people. A US study shows that most older people are more concerned about financing long-term care (69 per cent) than about paying for retirement (56 per cent). Eighty-seven per cent of respondents claimed that providing long-term care is a very or fairly big problem. Sixty per cent worry they or their spouse will some day need long-term care (Miller 1997).

There are more direct consequences for the elderly than in the provision of long-term care. These occur in the provision of incomes in old age, to healthcare, housing, and transport needs – the facilities for daily life, which everyone takes for granted in their early and middle years (Royal Commission on Long-Term Care 1999). In the UK people over 65 years constitute 14 per cent of the population but account for 47 per cent of Department of Health expenditure (Centre for Health Studies Research 1996) and 48 per cent of local authority services expenditure (Chartered Institute of Public Finance and Accountancy 1996).

The elderly population will be less economically independent. Early retirement is one contributory factor. In the UK in 1971, men aged 60–64 accounted for 8 per cent of the workforce as compared with 4 per cent in 1997. For women, the comparative figures (for those aged 55–59) were 9 per cent and 6 per cent (Social Trends 1999). It is also an unhealthy population. When the welfare state was designed, actuarial projections estimated only three years of life after retirement. In Great Britain in 1996, 55 per cent of people aged 65–74 and 66 per cent of those aged 75 and over in the General Household Survey sample had a longstanding illness, compared with 35 per cent of people of all ages. Fifty-nine per cent of the 65–74 age group, and 66 per cent of those aged 75 and over said that they had a long-standing illness which limited their life style (Office of Population Census and Surveys 1994).

Some 5 per cent of the population aged 65 and over and 20 per cent of the population aged 80 and over suffered from dementia (some 665,000 people in England and Wales in 1995).[13] Health is related to income – the old are peculiarly susceptible to illnesses relating to the absence of necessary physical comforts, and the latter necessarily are related to socio-economic class.

Three to four thousand deaths each year in the UK are attributed to influenza, of which 85 per cent are of people over 65 years. In epidemic years, the virus can account for as many as 30,000 deaths.[14] Of all patients admitted to hospital in 1997 in Great Britain, the average stay was seven nights. However, those aged 75 and over spent on average 12 nights (men) and 13 nights (women) (Social Trends 1999).

The elderly are especially prone to violent deaths. Elderly people are significantly more likely to die from a range of (accidental) violent actions than are younger people. A comparative analysis of mortality in 24 developed countries during the period 1985–89 shows the importance of injuries causing death amongst elderly people. One out of four men and one out of two women who dies from injury is aged 65 and over. Not merely is there an overrepresentation of the elderly among injury-related deaths, but the risk of injury continues to increase after the age of 65 years. The highest proportion of the latter is from accidental falls (Department of Trade and Industry 1999). In 1996, 15.4 per cent of all accidents within the home involved people aged 65 and over (Department of Trade and Industry 1999).

They are also exceptionally susceptible to traffic accidents – more than commensurate with their freedom from accidents at work. In 1997 in Great Britain, of 973 pedestrians fatally injured in road accidents, 437 (45 per cent) were aged over sixty years. A year earlier in a three-month period, 15 per cent of all persons and 24 per cent of those aged 75 and over had attended the casualty or outpatient department of a hospital (DETR 1997).

The cost of care

Supporting such an elderly population represents a major cost for the state (see evidence given by Age Concern to the House of Commons Health Committee, 20 September 1995). According to research at the University of Kent, spending on the costs of the elderly will need to rise by more than 150 per cent over the next 30 years as the cost of services outstrips economic growth – a £14 billion increase. If half of the most dependent elderly have to go into residential care, spending on services would need to rise by almost 200 per cent to £18 billion. The cost of long-term care will rise from 1995 to 2031, when the number of over-65s is projected to rise by 57 per cent and of over 85s by 79 per cent, necessitating a 61 per cent expansion in the cost of care provision assuming an annual increase in the real costs of services. Overall, the cost of care would go up by 153 per cent by 2031, 174 per cent in NHS expenditure, 124 per cent in social services, and 173 per cent in private payments – compared to a forecast rise of 123 per cent in Gross Domestic Product. Nursing home fees average £330 per week (£17,000 p.a.) but can rise to as much as £30.000 p.a. – about 4000 elderly people a year have to sell their homes to pay care fees[15], although proposed financing changes may significantly diminish this figure.

The United States spends approximately 15 per cent of the GDP on healthcare. In 1995, the bill for nursing home care finance by the Medicare and Medicaid programs reached $44 billion, which represents 55 per cent of all spending for nursing home care. By the year 2000, the United States may be spending as much as 20 per cent of its gross domestic product on care provision. Currently, more than one-third of total healthcare expenditure is spent on the 12 per cent of the population aged 65 and over. In the United States, nearly half the people aged 85 and over require help with care. At least four and a half million pensioners (excluding those in nursing homes) use mobility devices such as crutches, canes, Zimmer frames and wheelchairs, a number rising by one-fifth over the last 20 years. Sixty-two per cent of mobility devices such as crutches, canes or walkers are used by people aged 65 and older (Ehrlich and Ehrlich 1996).

Equally, the elderly population is more subject to recorded criminality, both as victims and increasingly as offenders.[16] For example, the prison population is ageing. Longer sentences will bring a long-term increase in older prisoners. Twice as many older prisoners are now held in Britain's jails as ten years ago, and the trend is likely to continue – a combination of longer sentences and increases in particular forms of elderly crime. Special institutions – such as HMP Portsmouth – have been developed to cope with the extra numbers (Brogden and Nijhar 2000).

In the United States, in 1998 there were at least 800 prisoners in their 70s and 13 in their 90s. Langton (1999) notes inmates 'too incapacitated with Alzheimer's to find their way back to their cells'. But the real problem is the mushrooming of the prison population of over-50s, many of whom die prematurely through drug abuse and through the psychological effects of prison – most die in their early 60s. The head of the Wisconsin prison service commented: 'Inmates age much more quickly. Historically, they have not taken good care of themselves. So you see them reaching 70 at 50' (p.75). For example, in 1998 the Huntsville Prison in Texas executed 19 prisoners but buried more than 100. In Florida, the number of inmates dying of 'natural causes' has tripled to more than 200 in ten years. In

North Carolina, the state has converted a former TB hospital to a geriatric prison for 300 of its inmates, many of them almost blind, or partially paralysed from strokes. Wardens organise 'remembrance therapy' sessions to recapture life before prison. Alabama's Hamilton Correction Facility for the Aged and Infirm has 24-hour nursing care for prisoners suffering from diabetes, heart and lung diseases, cancer, and so on. American estimates suggest that it costs three times the average to care for elderly prisoners (Langton 1999).

Finally, included in this category of death-hastening are those cases where the elderly face violent non-consensual death. While criminal action may be the most obvious example, more common is the fact – as we noted above – that the 'normal' victim of a road traffic accident is an elderly person. In a range of contexts, older people die non-consensual deaths as the result of the actions, intended or unintended, of second parties.

Death-hastening by rationing

Early death is promoted by a process of ring fencing of scarce resources in which elderly people may be deemed not worthy of resource commitment. Rationing in healthcare occurs when someone is simply denied (or simply not offered) an intervention that everyone agrees would do them some good and which they would like to have (Age Concern 1999a). While not every withholding of healthcare contributes to an early death, generally mortality becomes a function of organisational and agency need. Death-hastening in nursing and residential homes, as well as among the general elderly population, may be a simple function of prioritising the needs of the working and younger population. In Britain, on one hand, the Patient's Charter is clear: 'You have the right to receive health care on the basis of your clinical need, not on your ability to pay, your lifestyle, or any other factor.'[17] On the other hand, discrimination against older people is widespread. J. Morrow catches the spirit of this discrimination in his drama *The Silver Whistle* (1958) set in a church old people's home. His Reverend Watson unctuously regrets to an elderly female that the parish is unable to pay for a serious operation for her and that it is perhaps unfortunate that some people must die in order for the relatively impoverished parish to continue functioning.

Older people's needs are reportedly systematically neglected in overstretched acute wards in hospitals (the practice of 'bed-blocking' – refusing elderly people admissions until they are at 'death's door' in order to save money). Between a third and a half of cardiac rehabilitation programmes have upper age limits in access to services although two-thirds of heart attack patients are over 65 years. Some 40 per cent of coronary care units attach age restrictions over the clot-busting thrombolytic drug therapy after heart attacks. Kidney dialysis and transplants are regularly refused to 66 per cent of kidney patients aged 70–79 years. Older people with arthritis who visit their GP are often told that their symptoms are simply part of the process of growing old and that they should put up with the pain. Many such people are reportedly too frightened to complain or made to feel that they should not question medical evaluations because 'they've had a good innings' (Age Concern 1998).[18]

Women over 65 are not routinely invited for breast screening although women in this age range are at the highest risk.[18a] There is also clear evidence that in the treatment of breast cancer, younger women get a better deal even though the condition is essentially a disease of older women.[19] The risk of breast cancer for a woman of 20 is one in 43,000. By the time she is 50, the risk has risen to one in 56. At 60 it is one in 25, at 70 one in 16, at 80 one in 12, and at 85 one in 11. In the National Breast Screening programme women are automatically invited for X-rays between 50 and 64. Older women can have this free treatment, but only if they request it. Radiotherapy is not offered to older women after they have had their mastectomy or lumpectomy. Amongst other rationalisations, assumptions are made that it is often too far for elderly women to travel to a treatment centre. The Director of the Breast Cancer Coalition commented that the age limit 'has just given the impression to older women that their risk actually goes down over the age of 64 when in fact it goes up'. When offered such screening, the take-up rate for older women was much the same as for their juniors.

Only 39 per cent of patients over 75 years had active treatment for lung cancer compared with 79 per cent under 65 years.[20] More than half were seen by a geriatrician rather than by a lung cancer expert. Dr Mike Pearson of the British Thoracic Society commented:

> How lung cancer is treated is a particularly good example of how age makes a difference to what you get. The elderly are still less likely to be referred to a lung specialist and more likely to be treated on a geriatric ward. This is good for rehabilitation but not good for the assessment of lung cancer. People are just being written off. There is a difference between a person's biological age and their chronological age. If you are young biologically, you will do just as well from intensive care whether you are 60 or 80. (*Electronic Telegraph,* 6 December 1999)

Elderly people with Alzheimer's disease who lived in a care home were frequently means tested before care was delivered (Royal Commission on Long-Term Care 1999). According to the Chief Executive of the Alzheimer's Disease Society, 'it is unthinkable that a young person with CJD, another form of dementia, would be means tested for their care'.[21] Historically, dementia was portrayed as an inevitable consequence of old age, and attitudes have not changed. The main drug (Aricept) which alleviates Alzheimer symptoms, although licensed for treatment by the NHS, is rarely used because only half the health authorities in the country are prepared to budget for it because of relatively high costs (some £1000 per annum per patient).

Similarly with strokes – up to the age of 44 years, strokes are suffered by an average of fewer than one in a thousand people each year. By the age of 74 years, that figure has risen to 6.9 and by 84 years to 13.39 per 1000. But stroke care is haphazard, unfair, and unequal.[21a] Sue Knight of the Stroke Association: 'Stroke care is neglected just because people are old and there is no miracle cure.'[22] There are major reported failings in stroke care in NHS hospitals (Royal College of Physicians 1999). A recent survey of rationing reported 'hundreds of incidences' of older patients who deteriorated so much while waiting for hip replacement surgery that they became unfit to operate on.[23]

A Gallup survey revealed that one in 20 people over 65 had been refused treatment by the NHS (Age Concern 1999a). Ten per cent of respondents had noticed different treatment from the NHS since their fiftieth birthday. Most people cited GPs, the gatekeepers of the NHS, as the main source of their problems. Comments included: 'I was refused treatment because the money would be better spent on someone younger. It was a new treatment for cancer' and 'I was turned away for being over 65'. Age Concern also cites evidence of local health trust policies which use age as a barrier to receiving health services (Age Concern 1999a).

> I made an appointment with my medical practice to have the flu injection, as advertised and recommended for elderly people. ... Without preamble, the doctor said 'Don't you think you are depriving younger people, particularly young mothers who really need this vital protection?' I replied that I understood that this jab was offered directly to and for the elderly, but he answered that I was greedy and selfish and that he could easily refuse to administer it. (Age Concern 1999a)

Hospital Trusts aim to shift old people into nursing homes where costs are the responsibility of local authorities. As the Chief Executive of a large Trust commented, 'his' hospital was 'compromised' by the presence of elderly patients.

> There should be alternative acute care for the elderly, and there should be more restricted admission criteria. Too many patients only need intravenous feeds of antibiotics ... surgical wards should be ring-fenced to protect them from outlying elderly, medical patients.[24]

Elderly and infirm patients who used to be cared for in long-stay hospitals are now sent to nursing homes where they become the responsibility of the local GP, releasing hospital resources for younger people. Age Concern claimed that such hospital trusts were targeting old people in search of a solution to their funding problems.[25]

The Royal College of Nursing (RCN) Report[26] claimed that 90 per cent of British Health Authorities were liable to be ruled unlawful in charging the elderly for care in homes that should be free. For example, 30,000 elderly people had been wrongly placed in nursing homes when their medical conditions were serious enough to warrant free care under the NHS. Further, several health authorities exclude from NHS care functions (which were clearly nursing duties) especially relevant to the elderly – artificial feeding, pain control, terminal care, catheter and stoma care. The RCN General Secretary stated:

> By making the vast majority of nursing home residents ineligible for long-term nursing care, health authorities have created wholesale rationing within the NHS. This form of rationing is far more significant than excluding specific treatments from NHS funding. It is the exclusion of a whole sector of society from NHS care, which is not only unfair but also unlawful.[27]

The RCN report also noted rationing by postcode lottery – several local authorities refused to pay directly for an elderly patient's nursing home care. Those authorities paid only when patients were so ill that they needed hospital treatment.

A British Geriatric Society survey (1998)[28] revealed that an average of 12 per cent of all mental and geriatric beds were blocked – 42 per cent of these were due to patients waiting for a local authority to find appropriate institutional care. Similarly, an Audit Commission report (1997) claimed that there were areas of the country with severe bed blocking. The elderly in such regions were locked into a cycle of expensive and inadequate care from which they could not escape. Ebrahim and Bennett (1995) noted a significant reduction in the number of rehabilitation beds available to older patients. With a smaller pool of rehabilitation beds, there is increased pressure to withhold rehabilitation from patients with a lower likelihood of 'success'. In the United States, some private nursing homes shift dying elderly patients to public hospitals in order to decrease their own mortality rates.

A further study examined the deaths of patients over 90 years of age after surgery and found that as many as 20 per cent had experienced delay for non-medical reasons. Often the physical status of the elderly was not taken into account in preparing for the operation. Operations on them may be conducted in hospitals without high-dependency units (elderly people are at greater risk of complications after an operation). The most vulnerable patients were often allocated to the least experienced members of ward teams.[28a] The President of the Royal College of Physicians commented: 'We hope the report helps stop the ageist approach to care of the elderly.'

Finally, a recent US study found rationing in terms of pain management for the elderly. Bernabei and Gambassi (1998) found that 25–40 per cent of elderly cancer patients experienced daily pain. Of those patients, 16 per cent received a non-narcotic, 32 per cent received weak opiates and only 26 per cent received morphine or similar substances. More than a quarter of all patients in daily pain did not receive any pain-killing agents. The researchers noted a strong correlation between the presence of pain and increasing age. Financial issues were unlikely to have played a part because all the patients in the sample had health cover – ageist ideology was the problem. In part a function of lack of reporting by the elderly, the medical response to pain also demonstrates age discrimination in its relief. The pressure for euthanasia for such individuals in pain should not be underestimated – it is calculated that 85 per cent of patients in the Netherlands withdrew their requests for euthanasia after receiving better symptom control (Block and Billings 1994).

A Medical Research Council (1994) study documented specific evidence of age-based discrimination. But it also claimed that where old people were not excluded from particular treatments because of their age, they often responded as well as – or even better than – younger people. This is an important finding since justifications for excluding older people from particular treatments are often made on the grounds of reduced effectiveness.

Depression and self-killing amongst the elderly

The elderly are especially susceptible to depressive illnesses and conditions, as measured by the rate of suicide. People of pensionable age have always been the cohort most intent on taking their own lives. For example, though accounting for 13 per cent of the population, older Americans commit nearly one-fifth of all suicides (Pearson et al. 1997). Males aged 75 and over have the highest rate of suicide in nearly all industrialised countries. Suicide rates of the elderly are much higher than amongst other groups and the old-old have even higher rates than the young-old. Suicide is the thirteenth leading cause of death for people aged over 65 – one older American kills himself (normally it is 'he') every 80 minutes (Bauer 1997).

Older men take their lives at four to six times the rate of older women. In Canada, the rate for men over 75 is 26.6 per 100,000 and for women 3.7, with the extreme cases in the United States of 50.7 and 5.6 in Hungary (for men over 75 years) of 168.9 compared with 60 for women.[29] People are more likely to commit suicide if they are isolated, if there is a problem with alcohol abuse, and if there is a physical illness that causes pain. Elderly male vulnerability is claimed to be especially contributory due to a relative lack of social integration.

While males at every age have higher suicide rates than females, the elderly show by far the greatest gender differences – the male–female ratio for the entire United States population is approximately 5:1 for the 65–74 year age group, 8:1 for the 75–84 cohort, and 10:1 for those aged 85 and over. Rates rise constantly for the over 65 group – only in the very oldest group (90 and over) has there not been an appreciable increase (Lindesay 1993).

Most had depressive illnesses prior to death (as compared with drug-related problems and alcoholism amongst younger groups). In the UK, high rates of depression are common amongst elderly suicides. There is also a low ratio of attempted suicides to actual suicides among the elderly. Suicidal behaviour by the elderly tends to be well-planned and highly lethal (Pepe *et al.* 1997) – and sometimes supported.[30] In the UK, the ratio of *attempts* to *completion* amongst the elderly is about 4:1 as compared with from 8:1 to 200:1 amongst younger groups (McDowell 1997). Older adults attempting suicide have greater lethality, greater intentionality, less desire for attention or rescue, and motives not amenable to easy resolution (Bauer 1997). Also common is the degree to which virtually none of these elderly suicide attempters and completers sought mental health services or wider support. Death was intended.

Elderly suicide transcends social change. It appears to be independent of the level of economic development and degree of urbanisation (Stack 1980). Alcoholism and divorce are both related to the propensity to elderly suicide, but this is mainly correlated to the older person's degree of social isolation (Fernquist 1995). Research before the 1990s explained elderly suicide pathologically in terms of variables such as the process of ageing, widowhood, loss of work-role, terminal chronic illness, and depression or impending institutionalisation. But suicide at all stages of the life cycle is better seen as multi-dimensional. Lifespan approaches emphasise the elderly person's unwillingness or inability to cope with central development issues over older adulthood such as retirement, bereavement (especially widowhood), unwanted or unexpected isolation, physical and mental decline, and increased incidence of illness. Analysis of the intentions stated in suicide notes suggests that there are more commonalities than differences in suicidal behaviour across the life span – the young are as likely to cite such factors as isolation as are the elderly. But the person's age determines the life-tasks, which may become the precipitating stressors to suicide in those most vulnerable. These propensities to suicide are only exposed in later years. Major life changes force the issues into the open. Thus for the older individual, inability to cope with the vicissitudes of ageing becomes the primary precipitant of self-killing.

Elderly suicide rates are in any case likely to be underreported due to reliance on less violent 'soft' methods (Carollo and De Leo 1996). The elderly consume the most drugs, often potentially lethal ones, for reasons of survival. Many elderly suicides may therefore not be recognised as they are carried out by 'indirect' methods, such as deliberately taking the wrong amount of drugs or failing to take life-saving drugs. An apparent diminution in soft methods such as gas poisoning is largely due simply to lesser access to toxic gas. Similarly, lack of motorised transport means that, unlike young people, the elderly may not use car exhaust fumes. Old-age suicide commonly features factors of omission or non-performance (failure to use life-saving drugs or to consume food) or 'letting oneself go' rather than being the result of a precise series of preparations. Less access by the elderly to 'soft' methods may mean a move to 'harder' devices and techniques. The suicidal old patient may receive implicit encouragement from others.

Older people contemplating suicide rarely have to confront the 'attention-seeking' or 'manipulative' labels that are frequently applied to their more youthful equivalents... Perhaps some nurses support the idea that the older person's suicide attempt is a sane response to an insane or harsh reality (Bowles 1993, *Nursing Times* p.33).

Moreover, some elderly suicides may wrongly be attributed to secondary diseases or pre-morbid alterations, rather than to self-destructive behaviour. Generally, their techniques are the most invisible to recording and, where suicide is the expression of depression, signify a strong desire by older people to terminate life.

A study of 3000 GPs claimed that tens of thousands of elderly people living in their own homes are not being treated for depression. Most doctors fail to detect this life threatening illness amongst the elderly. Only 6 per cent of doctors had a formal system in place to detect depression in older people and only half had checked for depression in their health assessments of over-75s (quoted in Age Concern 1999a). Sally Greengross of Age Concern commented: 'Depression is too often seen as an inevitable consequence of old age and left untreated'.[31] Depression in itself, however, may be a consequence rather than cause – late onset depression is generally treatable, especially when the sources are structural and psychosocial.

Limitations to the demographic time bomb thesis

We need to be cautious about overstating the demographic time bomb thesis and its implications for the rationing of life-preserving care for the elderly. In Western societies, it ignores the extent to which the future 85 years plus groups may be healthier than their predecessors. Life expectancy is increasing but active life expectancy is growing even faster. People are not only living longer but are enjoying healthier later years. The old may be growing older but not necessarily sicker. Future generations of healthier over 64-year-olds will make relatively few demands on healthcare and other services (Mullan 1999). While old people will require more healthcare, the age at which they are becoming 'old-old' increases with longevity. Elderliness is not necessarily equivalent to illness. For most people, the time when they make their greatest demands on the NHS is in the final six months of their life. It does not matter in terms of costs whether this occurs at 70, 80, or 90 years. Chronic disabilities may decline. Better diets and health education are likely to have an effect on the lifestyle of the elderly. Improved mobility, hearing aids and visual aids will give them a greater degree of independence.

The elderly are not a homogeneous mass but are differentiated in a variety of ways. The dependency ratio can be fed as much by the young as by the old (in Britain the under-16s cost more to sustain than the over-65s). Fertility rates are as important as longevity and cannot be forecast with the same accuracy, being dependent on social factors such as people's confidence in the economy. Dystopian projections are based on what happened in the past. British society aged steadily over the past half century without the economy suffering any evident harm. Medicine can increase longevity, but the major advances may now be over after the successful attack on infectious diseases and improved social conditions. Economic and social factors play a more significant role in longevity. Finally, the dependency ratio emphasis ignores the fact that by no means all those of working age are at work – women bringing up children, the unemployed, and so on. Fluctuations in the non-working adult population may be much more significant than the number of dependent elderly.

While more people are living longer, they are experiencing fewer years of ill health before death, and their incomes are relatively higher than those of previous generations – their need for carers and financial support may not increase proportionately. Where occupational pensions are the norm, people retiring today are relatively less poor than at any time in history.

Not all the elderly are dependent. Pensionable age does not of itself mean economic retirement. During the 1990s in Britain, the fastest growing section of the population in employment has been the over-50s. Since 1992, the number of men aged 50–64 and women aged 50–59 in work has risen by some four million – far exceeding the rise in the proportion of the population in this age group. The rise in employment is evenly split between males and females, although much of it may consist of low-skilled marginal labour.

The growth of an elderly population will also mean an expansion of a consuming market, involving the creation of new jobs and a productive services industry directed towards their paying needs. Featherstone and Hepworth (1989) have documented the growth of an array of retirement magazines targeted at the young-old – constructing an image of the body as a machine that can be serviced and repaired. The advertised products cultivate the hope that late life can be constrained into a future where ultimately even death can be packaged under human control. Elderhood has been reconstructed as a marketable lifestyle with commercial products. Further (as we noted above), the major increases in longevity have already occurred in Western societies. Average life expectancy for men and women born in Britain doubled over the last 150 years. The time bomb is on a slow burner not a fast fuse.

Generally, the apocalyptic view fails to distinguish between well elderly and frail elderly. One theme of this book is that concern with the expansion of the elder population may be limited to the latter rather than to the elderly as a collective notion. The elderly as a political force – epitomised in the notion of the Grey Panthers or the Third Age (Townsend 1963)[32] – may be active in shaping their own destiny, not simply a passive residue to be consigned as human detritus to an earthly garbage tip. Geronticide resulting from demographic factors may be limited to a passive minority of elders.

Responding to the critics

But there are summary responses to that critique of the time bomb thesis. The elderly are not yet safe.

First, it is true that changes in technology and in wealth in Western countries will modify the meaning of age. However, the wealth of the elderly will be unequally distributed – some old people will become frail, independently of their chronological age. The effects of social policies in different Western countries will have differential consequences on elderly populations.

Second, any increase in the employment of the over-65s is in that sector with the lowest wages – principally in retailing. Quantitatively, there has been an increase in that employment but qualitatively it is doubtful whether that growth has more than a marginal input into the quality of life of older people. Third, the increase in the elderly in non-Western countries is unlikely to be accompanied by the same technological and healthcare developments as in the West.

Fourth, while higher productivity from the diminishing workforce may partly compensate for the larger number of elderly, that simplistic view does not take account of the rising expectations of their share of the cake by the remaining workforce. Differentials are likely to increase as they have elsewhere in society between those with and those without. In Britain in 1961 there were almost four people of working age to support each pensioner; by 2041, there will only be two. Even chronologically positioning the age at which the elderly become sick and dependent does not abolish that period – its extent will be greater simply because of the larger number of elderly. In many ways, while the elderly may be becoming healthier – especially with regard to the decrease in the prevalence of disability – the bad news is that the survival of patients with dementia is increasing. Mental impairments put greater strain on domiciliary care than does physical disablement. If strokes and coronary heart disease are replaced by Alzheimer's disease, for example, even if levels of overall disability decline, costs of care may still increase.

Age is only one social factor, although a critical one. Elderliness is a multi-dimensional status. Gender and sexuality, race and ethnicity, and socio-economic class are all factors which cut across the notion of the demographic time bomb. The demographic approach is a necessary but not sufficient basis for the development of a concern with the construction of the elderly as social problem. One result of this may (as in the case of elderly suicide above) be expressed through the rubric of geronticide.

Continuity in geronticide

The conception of the elderly as a problem, as implied in the demographic time bomb thesis, is a social construction. It depends on the valuation placed by others on the quality of life of older people. It relates to the degree of acknowledgement of their rights. It derives in part from the relative political powerlessness of older people to articulate and support their demands for equality of treatment. It is an argument that has its source in social inequality.

Tradition reflects this social construction of the old-old as a hindrance, who should best soon be on their way. As Ashliman (1999) argues, every culture has its own rituals, practices and preparations directed not at the older person's return to 'normal' adulthood but to the termination of life. For example, medieval European superstitions refer to potions intended to help the mortally ill die faster and more easily. Removing roof tiles or opening windows were widely believed to speed death by giving the departing soul an easier exit. Similarly, some advised filling every hollow space in the house, thus denying the reluctant soul a hiding place. Other acts – for example, taking away the dying person's pillow, cutting a scrap from his clothing, or not allowing him to clench his thumb in his fist – were more intrusive.

In contemporary Western societies, a more sophisticated process of death-hastening has largely replaced those practices – a process in which younger people are prioritised in terms of social, economic and health needs. Death-hastening modes may vary from direct neglect – thrusting elderly people out of doors to fend for themselves (across the parish boundary!) – or it may take the less crude form of decisions over surgery priorities that push the elderly to the back of the NHS queue. Ring-fencing and bed-blocking contribute to death-hastening just as much as by the medieval peasant removing tiles from the roof of the elderly parent. In the modern health system, while the elderly are more susceptible to illnesses such as influenza, they are also often deemed not suitable for cost-effective ways of reducing deaths by immunisation processes.

Elderly homicide – from murder through death-hastening to suicidal pressures – is like many taboos easy to associate with untouchable practices, and equally easy to regard as the behaviour of non-humans. Yet geronticide, senecide, fenecide, patricide, matricide, and so on, have taken place in all societies. Styles have changed but purposes often have not in the killing of the elderly. Old people may be buried alive – as with the Australian aborigines, the Tiwi: 'The method was to dig a hole in the ground in some lonely place, put the old woman in the hole and fill it with earth until only her head showed' (Glascock 1987; see Chapter 3). Or it may be by subjecting the elderly poor to the minimal support of the workhouse under the rubric of industrialism and modernisation (see Chapter 4). Present-day elderly death-hastening frequently involves bureaucratic disposal in a so-called care home, a twentieth century impersonal termination process, with the full knowledge that a quarter will be eliminated in their first residential year (see Chapter 5).

Notes

1   For an excellent discussion of the historical arguments regarding overpopulation, see Hutchinson (1967).

2   Leaving out the contributions regarding life-extending preventive medicine, hygiene, and technology.

3   China's population has long encouraged geronticidal proposals by Western academics. Note the stark advice, nearly half a century ago, from G.F. Winfield: 'Existing checks on population growth must not be removed until the controls exerted by direct limitations and industrialisation are well established... The death rate must not be reduced too quickly. I suggest that public health means which can save millions should not be practised in China... (1956, p.344).

4   Some 'less developed' countries, such as Colombia, Costa Rica, Liberia and Venezuela, are expected to experience an increase in the elder population by more than 200 per cent in the next 25 years.

5   Age Concern evidence to the House of Commons Health Committee, 20 September 1995.

6   Derived from an analysis of month of death statistics compiled for 1992–1996.

7   On African American suspicions of terminal healthcare, see Hauser *et al.* (1997).

8   'Dying in Care.' *Detroit Free Press,* 26 February 1997.

9   For domiciliary care the figures are 517,000 to 804,000; and for nursing 444,000 to 717,000. General Household Survey (1998).

10   'Long Term Care Needs of the Elderly.' *Electronic Telegraph,* 11 March 1997.

11   'Lonely Old Age' *The Guardian,* 17 February 1998.

12   'Code to Set Standards for Nursing Home Care.' *Electronic Telegraph,* 26 September 1998.

13   See also *The Observer,* 13 March 2000.

14   Dramatic evidence of the number of elderly deaths from influenza during the winter of 1999/2000 is given in 'Death rates for elderly soar in flu outbreak.' *The Sunday Times,* 9 January 2000.

15   'Dorrell proposes way of insuring home against cost of old age.' *Electronic Telegraph,* 11 March 1997.

16   There is some evidence that elderly offenders are especially likely to be characterised by psychiatric problems – up to 50–60 per cent according to Dr Graeme Yortson (1999).

17   The President of the Royal College of Nursing (commenting on the funding of care for the elderly, children and people with mental health problems) claimed that 90 per cent of health authorities in Britain were acting unlawfully in determining the lack of eligibility for care of those groups ('The Future of the NHS.' *The Guardian,* 4 April 2000). Current state proposals aim to abolish such means testing for nursing home care.

18   Elderly kidney sufferers may be being turned away from dialysis because...they are elderly, have other complications, and a short life expectancy' – Dr Paul Sweeny, consultant nephrologist at the Royal Free Hospital in London, quoted in 'Shortages in NHS: Denying elderly patients dialysis.' *Electronic Telegraph,* 10 March 2000.

18a   Cited in 'Old people are made to pay for care that should be free.' *Electronic Telegraph,* 2 December 1999.

19   'Elderly patients left "starving to death in NHS".' *Electronic Telegraph,* 6 December 1999.

20   *Ibid.*

21   Quoted in 'Shortages in NHS: Denying elderly patients dialysis.' *Electronic Telegraph*, 10 March 2000.

21a   *Electronic Telegraph*, 6 December 1999.

22   *Ibid.*

23   A survey by the Saga insurance group found that the majority of over-50s questioned believed that the National Health Service had a policy of discrimination against people over 60 years – 'Catering for old age.' *The Times*, 15 April 2000.

24   'NHS complaints at record high.' *The Guardian*, 17 January 1999.

25   'GPs will now treat new patients from nursing homes.' *Electronic Telegraph*, 7 November 1996.

26   RCN report 'Rationing by stealth.' *Electronic Telegraph*, 2 December 1999.

27   *Ibid.*

28   Quoted in Age Concern (1999a).

28a   'Elderly patients dying because of bad management.' *Electronic Telegraph*, 18 December 1999.

29   'Older males more likely to kill themselves.' *Toronto Star*, 20 August 1998.

30   'Perhaps some nurses support the idea that an older person's suicide attempt is a sane response to an insane or harsh reality.' – see Bowles, L. (1989) 'Suicide in homes for elderly.' *Nursing Times 31*, p.31.

31   *Electronic Telegraph*, 30 June 1996.

32   Indeed, there is now even talk of a Fourth Age.

CHAPTER 3

Death by Social Obligation
The Political Economy Thesis

A limited number of cultures have seen fit to kill the very old who are no longer useful. It prevails when the climate is especially severe and tribes live a nomadic existence. While it is still unlikely that modern Western societies informed by the Jewish and Christian traditions would make exceptions on the basis of age to the moral rule against killing, it is possible that in our ageing society, pressure will again mount to take the moral guidance from anthropological data. (Simmons 1945)

Political economy: The elderly as non-producers

There is nothing inherently problematic about growing old. Yet in most societies old age is understood in 'social problem' terms. It is contested terrain. Its meaning is given within assumptions about the longer life cycle (Hugman 1998). Similarly, attitudes to the disposal of the elderly cannot be understood without a cross-cultural and historical perspective. Their position is contingent on their relative power. The status of older people is never won but always granted – it depends on the dictates of powerful others in their community. They belong to a supposedly unproductive minority, and their fate frequently depends upon the sectional interests of the active producers.

The political economy approach to geronticide recognises that old age is a social construction, a status that must be understood in terms of both its material and ideological dimensions (Fennell, Phillipson and Evers 1988; Guillemard 1986; Phillipson 1982; Street and Quadagno 1994; Walker 1980). Drawing on a materialist understanding of social structures and relationships, this approach stresses the way in which the treatment of the elderly cannot be understood separately from the social and economic distribution of rewards, and inequalities in power, in that society.

All societies differentiate between the waged and the non-waged, income generators and income disposers, those who work productively and those who are dependent upon the productive. In any society, from the primitive to the modern, there are demarcations between on the one hand those who generate disposable goods or income in order to ensure the sustenance of themselves and others, and on the other hand, those like children and pensioners in modern society who do not. The less functionally differentiated the society, the more direct the link between producing and determination of the use of sustenance. Those who do not labour are at the mercy of those who do (unless the former have some residual powers of coercion or of ideological legitimacy, which binds the labourers to them, as in traditional caste societies).

Minkler and Estes (1984) define political economy as 'the study of the interrelationships between the polity, economy, and society, or more specifically, the reciprocal influences among government...the economy, social classes, state, and status groups.' (p.10–11) Age is essentially a social construction in the sense of having economic foundations (Phillipson 1982). The primary value of the elderly is economically circumscribed. The status and resources of the elderly, and even the existence of old age itself, are conditioned by one's location in the material circumstances of existence (Estes 1979). The treatment of the elderly, and in some societies their disposal at the behest of others, is a consequence of the relationships within that matrix.

The political economy of geronticide suggests that elderly people are often victims, direct or indirect, of economic imperatives outside their own control. It aims to show how ideologies of ageism and social acceptance or rejection of the elderly are constituted through economic exigencies – especially the relative ability to fend for oneself and not to be a burden on others – and how ideologies towards the elderly are transformed into concrete practices. Inequality produced by economic relations is the key to the treatment of older people, although that experience may be mediated by different cultural attitudes (Zelhovitz 1990). Elder victimisation is contextualised within structural imperatives (Phillipson 1982).

Rarely is there a one-to-one relationship between economy and geronticide. In relatively undifferentiated 'primitive' societies the inability of the elderly to produce the necessities of family life was often mediated by other, producing, kin. In so-called 'developing' societies (such as India), economic factors of survival (and of urbanisation) may disrupt traditional affinities with the elderly. Exigencies of economic endurance override cultural tradition. Ideologies of care vary between different societies, and within societies, frequently independently of the economic structure (Mahajan 1992, in a study of family violence in India). Further, from more 'primitive' societies one cannot directly deduce relationships between the economy and quality of care in Western societies. Western societies feature a complex web of state, private and voluntary agencies that mediate between the economy and the elderly experience. Nevertheless, there *are* insights from early studies of relevance to understanding death-hastening behaviour towards older people in modern industrial society.

In this chapter, we explore several of those themes, drawing on a wide range of social anthropological studies.

Many of these accounts rely on deductions from relatively undifferentiated, so-called primitive societies – pastoral versus hunter-gatherers. The hunter-gatherer thesis is simply that where a community is dependent upon mobility and hunting for its livelihood, it is less likely to tolerate those who are less mobile and less capable of obtaining their own sustenance than is a pastoral society which can provide slow repetitive work for the elderly. In hunter-gatherer society, it was typically the old-old who were most likely to suffer geronticide. Where death was determined for the elderly, it was normally characterised by a liminal period and ceremonies in which the old person was transferred from the present world to the next. However, some such societies were less likely to dispose of the elderly because of assumed religious and magical knowledge (which might cause fear as much as respect). They also had a choice in which the extremes of infanticide and geronticide were both possible, geronticide being often the less preferred option. Even in these relatively simple societies, decisions over geronticide were often subject to a complex matrix of factors.

Insights from patriarchy and from Marxist studies

Gender as well as Marxist studies furnish insights that can be applied to the elderly. Kappeler (1995) draws on Mandelian Marxist theory to explain victimisation of women and the elderly. In early modern society, goods produced were essentially for family use – utensils and food. Labour was valued only in terms of the requirements of the kinship structure. Women being bound to the household and to familial obligations only produced goods of *use* value in the home – whether for child rearing, care of the elderly, or general household tasks. Their absence from the public workforce (the market of *exchange* relationships) deprived them of recognition in waged income.

While major changes emerged in industrial society – such as the increase in the number of women in the public workforce (and the revelation of how many women worked outside the home in early Victorian society) – the stereotypical view of women as primary carers of the elderly is maintained. Ideological baggage, derived from an earlier period, has transcended economic transformations. It resulted in women, as producers of use values, retaining the *expressive* care function rather than assuming an *instrumental* function (an exchange value, or public wage).

In Western countries, based on market exchange relationships, private space non-producers (such as housebound women and older people) who have little to exchange (who do not produce goods of market value, are not paid a wage) may be economically victimised. The majority of unpaid carers are female with few waged labour rights. Female status includes care obligations, constructed through historical economic imperatives as mediated by gender-based ideologies. Being a woman, like the concept of ageism, carries ideological trappings, derived from institutionalised economic inequality in Western society.

Ageing is not a fixed status but depends upon social and cultural perceptions, and the economic consequences of those factors upon the lived experience of the elderly. Variables relating to fundamental economic conditions affect the position of older people and in turn determine the degree of maltreatment to which they are subject and to which they may be unable to respond.

A heuristic body of neo-Marxist studies elucidates the political economy argument. In a classic article, Spitzer (1975) discussed the extent to which the market economy under advanced capitalism has created what he called 'problem populations'. Transfer of low-skilled exchange production from advanced capitalist economies to the new so-called 'tiger economies' of the East, together with the automation of unskilled and semi-skilled work (Braverman 1998), and a process of de-industrialisation (Piore 1984), affected financial resources for welfare. The production of exchange values in advanced capitalism has decreased and become concentrated in white-collar occupations (requiring higher skills).

This development had several effects. It diminished demand for the low skills of 'youth' and the elderly. It also decreased the state's revenue capacity to support both *care* (the elderly, the disabled, and children) and *pacification* ('troublesome' youth and the 'under-class'). Spitzer refers to what he calls 'social junk' – the elderly population. The latter are expensive to maintain but generally do not threaten the social order. While there are exceptions to this passivity in Western societies, pensioners have little visible political presence. They can be discarded at minimum cost. Where they 'return to work', they are often confined to low-paid retail employment. Older people are therefore prone to victimisation because they are economically marginal. There is no benefit to the wider society in costly protection. They are cared for at a minimum rate by the cheapest labour – labour that may through incompetence and stress, rather than through intention, react harshly (Brogden and Nijhar 2000).

Geronticide practices may reflect a political economy perspective. Prejudice based on age is the product of the division between public and household (private) production and the structure of social inequality, rather than a natural result of the ageing process. All services for older people (health, social services, provision of pensions) are affected by the commodification process and reinforce the dependency created through wider social and economic trends (Biggs, Phillipson and Kingston 1995).

Such a view is not new. Walker (1980), for example, discussed the 'social creation of old age', the structured dependency of older people which arises from compulsory retirement, poverty, and restricted domestic and community roles. A common theme in many British interpretations of elder victimisation has been the way ageing has been constructed in relation to dependency costs. Nowhere is this truer than in the stark model culled from primitive society.

Nostalgia over primitive society

Much of the debate about present-day treatment of the elderly has been informed by a nostalgic, if unfounded, view of the past. The theme of a golden age of the elderly was most obvious in the Romantic Movement, which reacted against the emphasis on materialism and rationalism that was linked to the new industrial order and sought to replace the emphasis on rational self-interest with a recognition of historically sanctified social obligations and responsibilities.[1] Within the Romantic Movement, there appeared an image of an historical elderly idyll.

Both earlier and subsequent writers noticed variations in the treatment of the aged in 'primitive' as opposed to 'civilised' societies. As early as the eighteenth century, social philosophers believed that the extent of societal development was the key determinant of the status of the aged. In 1776, Adam Smith wrote that among the hunting peoples of North America, age was the sole foundation of rank and precedence, whereas in 'opulent and civilised nations' its role was merely residual, regulating rank 'among those who are in every other respect equal and among whom, therefore, there is nothing else to regulate it' (1880, p.6711). A century later, Emile Durkheim noted the importance of the aged in traditional society. Durkheim viewed the old as the living expression of tradition, unique intermediaries between past and present. Social solidarity was maintained by the 'authority of age, which gives tradition its authority (1964, p.2931). Thus Smyth on aborigines in Victoria:

> Aborigines everywhere and on all occasions pay great respect to old persons...
> (and) the utmost affection...they were always...treated with kindness, fed and
> attended to when decrepit, and never left to die. In contrast, in civilised society,
> old men are pitied more than respected, as ancestral customs lose their predomi-
> nance and the worship of age is steadily weakened. (Cited in Durkheim 1964,
> p.294)

The sociology of Saint-Simon, of Tonnies and of Spencer offered an evolutionary account of human society – developing in social Darwinian fashion from the so-called primitive society to the modern industrial. Social mores are assumed to evolve according with civilisation – or rather the rational basis of social mores – being explicitly a product of the modern industrial bureaucratic society.

In small pre-industrial communities, when the majority wished to avoid lawless rivalry between their members and to maintain the established order, they found it convenient to choose men of a different kind to act as intermediaries, adjudicators or representative figures, men upon whose authority all could agree. The aged fulfilled these conditions. But once the answer had been reached, the problem solved, they were rejected.

Old age was powerful in Confucian China, in Sparta, in the Greek oligarchies, and in Rome up until the second century before Christ. However, it played no evident part in the periods of change, expansion or revolution. Far more than the conflict between the generations, it was the inequality of the elderly that gave the notion of old age its ambivalence, significant in one historical context, cast aside in another. In practice, it was often the crude determinism, the exigencies of economic survival – often mediated by cultural patterns – which determined the degree of acceptance of life termination for older people.

The hunter-gatherer thesis

Early attempts to test the political economy thesis on geronticide entailed comparative examination of different primitive societies. A distinction was drawn between pastoral societies where economic production was based around the stable use of land – whether by tilling the soil and growing crops, or by keeping livestock – and those societies (hunter-gatherers) such as the Namibian bushmen and the Australian aborigines who traversed a cycle of different districts, depending on wildlife and edible plants for their sustenance.

Attitudes to the elderly were frequently determined by the labour power required to sustain them. In hunter-gatherer society, where the community must constantly be on the move, the old and the sick hindered that mobility. Only those who were fleet of foot and agile in the search for food and game were able to feed themselves and avoid depredators. Consequently, geronticide was frequently a means of disposing of those who were relatively immobile and who could not feed themselves. The elderly hindered production and hampered movement.

This view appears in the work of the anarchist Prince Kropotkin in his lyrical essay *Mutual Aid Among Savages* (cited in De Beauvoir 1973)

> When a 'savage' feels that he is a burden to his tribe: when every morning his share of food is taken from the mouths of the children – who every day has to be carried across the stony beach or the virgin forest, on the shoulders of younger people…he begins to repeat what the old Russian peasants say…'I live other people's life. It is time to retire'. And he retires…the old man asks himself to die; he himself insists on this last duty to the community, and obtains the consent of the tribe; he digs out his grave; he invites his kinfolk to the last parting meal. His father has done so, it is now his turn; and then parts with his kinsfolk with marks of affection. The savage so much considers death as a part of his duties towards his community, that he not only refuses to be rescued…the savages as a rule are so reluctant to take anyone's life otherwise than in a fight, that none of them will take it upon himself to shed human blood, and they resort to all kinds of

stratagems. ... In most cases they abandon the old man in the wood, after giving him more than his share of the common food.

Conversely, in the agrarian/pastoral society, little mobility is required. The community is stable and sedentary. Crucially, there are functions which can be fulfilled by the old which require little dexterity and speed. Thus typically, tilling the soil, milling grain and household chores, which require slow repetitive labour, can be delegated to the elderly. They can therefore contribute to their own sustenance. They are not a handicap to the community's safety.

This deterministic view of geronticide in primitive society is more evident in the exception than in the rule. It ignores particular and relatively autonomous cultural factors such as elder deference. It does not recognise the alternative role that elders may carve out for themselves in the household and in developing different – if non-productive – functions in the community. But as a general guide it indicates that older people are especially susceptible to death-hastening responses in contexts where their labour power is not valued and where physical deficiencies threaten the well-being of the larger community.

Reid (1985) examined this thesis in a study of Australian aborigines. On the one hand, aborigines furnish a classic example of a hunter-gatherer society where forms of death-hastening could be expected. On the other hand, they may possess traditions which accord elders wisdom, sanctity, respect and affection by their younger relatives. Ideology is mediated by immediate exigencies.

Simmons (1945) illustrates the first perspective on the practice of elderly homicide amongst the hunter-gatherers. In his study, in over three-quarters of the 71 tribes, elderly males were normally venerated. In some Himalayan tribes, the greatest compliment was to call someone an 'old man'. He reports similar findings from parts of Africa where old people were referred to as the 'Great Ones'.

> However, some Inuit people abandoned their elderly to die on an ice floe. Other North American indigenous people would hold a final feast for the elderly and smoke a pipe of peace. Then the son would kill the father with a single blow to the head. The reindeer herding people of Northeast Siberia, the Chukchee, commonly practised direct killing. Few old Chukchee died a natural death. When an old person was taken ill and became a burden to his surroundings, he or she would ask one of the nearest relatives, to be killed. The oldest son or daughter or son-in-law then stabbed the person through the heart with a knife. (Sverdrup (1938) cited in De Beauvoir 1973, p.54)

De Beauvoir (1973) cites other Siberian examples of direct geronticide. She emphasises that such deaths are constructed within a process of ceremonial ritual, which gives positive meaning to the process of life termination. Most societies do not let their old people die like mere animals. Their death is surrounded by ceremony, with significant others giving some semblance of consent. She notes the case of the Koryak, a North Siberian people who lived in an environment as harsh as that of the Yakut. Their only resource was the herds of reindeer with which they travelled across the steppes. Their winters were extremely severe, and the long marches exhausted the older people. The latter were killed, just as the incurables were discarded. This was innate to Koryak culture, and they would cheerfully boast of their skill, pointing out the places where the thrust of a spear or a knife was fatal. The killing took place in the presence of the whole community after long, complex ceremonies.

One of the Grimms' German legends tells how, in the eighth century, a community fleeing from enemy soldiers buried one of their old women alive to keep her from being taken captive. They carried out the fateful task while chanting 'Creep under, creep under, the world is too sorrowful for you; you can no longer follow the commotion.' In their commentary to this legend, the Grimms document two additional instances of ritualistic killing of the aged. In each of the Grimms' examples the geronticide was accompanied by a ritualistic chant, which appeared to legitimate the killing of their aged (noted in Ashliman 1999).

The young-old versus the old-old

In an apparently more caring society, geronticide features but distinguishes between categories of the elderly. According to De Beauvoir (1973), among the northern Ojibway, before white colonisation, there was a striking contrast between the status of the still vigorous elderly men and those who were broken by age.

The Ojibway endured exceptionally cold winters, but also harvested from rich soil. Children were given a great deal of affection and were rarely punished. In this relatively harmonious society, the sick were tended carefully. Grandparents lived with the parents and advised them, giving the newborn child its name and treating grandchildren as equals. Respect was returned and the young and middle-aged were taught to honour all old people. The old men formed part of the adult council. The elders, who were thought to possess great magical powers and to be potentially dangerous, initiated young men. Length of years was admired, so long as it was accompanied by good health.

However, this respect was often merely superficial. When age and decrepitude combined, there were significant changes in treatment. They had lost their magical powers and were no longer feared. The old were neglected and their food stolen. They might be abandoned in a distant hut or on an uninhabited island. Help from relatives was discouraged. Alternatively, they could be solemnly killed. A pipe of peace, a death-song and a dance followed a feast. While the father was still singing, the son would kill him with a tomahawk.[2]

Calamities could legitimise geronticide (Ashliman 1999). In times of war, forced migration or famine, the temptation to do away with the weakest members of a group would be especially great. A saga contains the following description of a famine in Iceland in the 10th century: 'Men ate ravens and foxes, and many loathsome things were eaten which should not be eaten, and some men had the old and helpless killed and thrown over the cliffs' (quoted in Ashliman 1999).

Glascock (1987) similarly notes much anecdotal information about the killing of the elderly in non-industrial societies. Highly developed societies are not the only ones to grapple with moral objections to death-hastening of the frail elderly.

But two distinctions are crucial. First, most societies, ancient and modern, distinguish between deliberate killing and death-hastening behaviour. Few societies kill their old people deliberately by acts of *commission*; but many others slaughter them by acts of *omission*. Second, a cultural distinction is drawn between the intact, fully functioning aged, and the decrepit minority. Both supportive and death-hastening behaviour can coexist in all societies in later stages of the life cycle.

Death-hastening in primitive society

Geronticide then is too confined a term. The broader concept of death-hastening is more applicable. The latter focuses on abandoning and neglecting the elderly – non-supportive behaviour that leads indirectly to death for aged individuals. A majority of the societies in Glascock's (1987) sample exhibited some form of death-hastening actions, with less than one-third furnishing unconditional support. Ashliman recounts several allegorical stories of the way death-hastening appears as a dominant norm, a process against which the elderly have constantly to struggle.

> A man had a father who had grown too old to do anything but eat and smoke, so the man decided to send him away with nothing but a blanket. 'Just give him half a blanket,' said the man's son from his cradle, 'then I'll have half to give you when you grow old and I send you away.' Upon hearing this, the man quickly reconsidered and allowed his old father to remain after all. ('Half a Blanket' retold from Glassie's *Irish Folktales* in Ashliman 1999)

A modern sardonic version of that death-hastening process appears in Edward Albee's play *The Sand Box* (1960). A grandmother talks sarcastically about being taken in by unwilling relatives. Her final repository is under her son-in-law's stove with an army blanket and her own dish! (pp.15–16). [3]

Levi-Strauss (1936) too notes an almost casual example of death-hastening by abandonment amongst the Amazonian Bororo: '...the old people; after a hunt or successful fishing trip...are brought a piece of meat or a few fish. But also sometimes they are forgotten. The indigent person is then reduced to going without a meal and all night long, utters ritual lamentations.' (p.276)

Abandonment is far more common than outright geronticide. Thus the Lau people in Southern Fiji recounted that 'when the (headman) of the...clan became old and feeble he was taken to Takuma Islet in the lagoon and abandoned. ... There is a cave filled with skeletal remains of old people who die there after leaving the community' (as cited in Simmons 1945). They might also abandon them in huts in the bush.

De Beauvoir (1973) draws on secondary sources. The Bolivian forest-dwelling Siriano tribe would contradictorily never kill their handicapped babies, despite continuing hunger, dearth, and lack of clothes, ornaments and domestic animals. Lack of food was a constant cause for dispute. A few plants might be cultivated but the people were dependent upon gathering and hunting when possible. Consequently, the Siriano were old at 30 and decrepit at 40 years. The old people walked slowly, hindering tribal movements. The children then neglected their parents, overlooking them when food was being shared out. Sick old people could be suddenly abandoned as the tribe moved to new hunting grounds.

Death-hastening was not simply a function of extreme poverty. Amongst the earlier hunting and fishing community of the Gaboon Fang, age was an advantage (although not decrepitude), but not as much as talent. The head of the family was the eldest active male. The old parents lived with him, and retained limited moral authority so long as they remained 'real men' and 'real women'. Women, however, were often mere instruments of production and reproduction, and when past the latter state were regarded as non-persons and could be treated as witches; whereas a man retained status until the birth of grandchildren. When their strength declined, elderly males lost all their status, and led a marginal existence. If they became decrepit, they were so despised that after their death, their skulls could not be used in the religious ceremonies. Like childless elders, they might be abandoned destitute in the forest during migrations. Choice was overcome by the fatalism of tradition (cited in De Beauvoir 1973).

Gender bias in determining unfitness is common. Amongst the Eastern Cape Thonga, many tasks were ritually reserved for women. Independently of resources, the aged came last in the queue – especially elderly women. The old had no economic resources, inspired little affection, despite taking care of the young. The latter were separated from family early in life, and affective bonds sundered, with few mutual obligations recognised. Some elderly women survived through the accretion of apparently magical powers but generally, when no longer able to work the land, they became a burden, and their decrepitude was despised. Aged men often officiated in tribal ceremonies but possessed little status. Social rank and stratification were based on gender, health and wealth. When a man's wives died, and he himself was incapable, he was subject to the same treatment as the elderly women. When a village moved, it left them behind to perish of hunger (cited in De Beauvoir 1973).

Ashliman (1999) uses fables to demonstrate how these two extremes – care for the able-old and geronticide for the old-old – could coexist. He quotes a Chiricahua Indian myth of how tribal members concluded that a certain old woman was 'good for nothing' and decided to abandon her. But her subsequent prayers to the Spirits cured her of her debilitating ailments and she returned to her people.

Many societies respect the old so long as they are clear-minded but dispose of them when they become senile and infirm. De Beauvoir (1973) quotes the semi-nomadic Bushmen of South West Africa. Community bonds were strong – the words 'grandfather' and 'grandmother' were used as honorifics. The elderly were respected and valued for their knowledge and experience, being consulted on key community affairs. The council sought their advice. Being elderly immunised them from the supernatural powers that affected others in the community, and they played a key part in the rituals which encompassed central parts of the community life. Owing to this role of the aged, the tribe maintained its cohesion when under stress. Yet this did not prevent the elderly from being neglected once the loss of their faculties rendered them useless. Sons would consult the community council over their disposal and, if granted, would provide a village feast. All members would say their farewells. The old man was hoisted on to the back of an ox and escorted to a remote hut where he was left to die either of starvation or by beasts of prey. Similar 'death huts' were common amongst the North American Hopi, Creek, and Crow First Peoples.

Where resources were even more meagre, as with the Amassalik Inuit, the decrepit elderly, when perceived as a community burden, could be persuaded to lie in the snow and wait for death, or were abandoned on an ice floe when the tribe was out fishing. A ritual public confession might be made by the elderly person before being placed in a kayak and pushed away from land. Adult children would cooperate in encouraging such an early death. Ethnologists note apparent cooperation by the elderly in such abandonment rituals. Perhaps they themselves had killed their own parents. They felt honoured by the terminal feast (Glascock 1987).

Glascock (1987) illustrates death-hastening through simple abandonment or neglect among the Yakut herders in Siberia. Similarly, 'Aged people are not of favour: they are beaten by their own children and are often forced to leave their dwellings and to beg from house to house' (Jochelson 1933, p.134).

In one of the most sophisticated and recent ethnographic studies of death-hastening by abandonment, in Polynesia, Barker (1990) located that practice in its cultural context. Evidence from the Niue suggests that in that relatively egalitarian society, featuring a flexible social hierarchy and individual achievement, the prevailing ideology worked against elders. Their privileged position was lost once their competence was in any way compromised. Decrepit elders were frequently ignored, even neglected, by kin and by community. If sick, often their relatives could not be bothered to summon medical help. They were left to fend for themselves when no longer possessing the physical or psychological means to succeed.

Abandoning the elderly fits within a long tradition of isolating the sick (for example, those dying from a bout of influenza might have to fend for themselves) to avoid the health of the larger community being contaminated by ghostly influences from beyond. Neglect might allow the decrepit elder to make the transition to the other world as smoothly as possible. Amongst the Niue, illnesses in old age were perceived as punishments for wrongs done when they were children. Accidents to them were not merely mishaps but could be rightful societal retaliation for evils committed at an earlier period of life, and should be regarded not as a source of sympathy but as one of amusement (as illustrated by the case of an elder who had a coconut fall on his head). 'To laugh at decrepit elders, to deride their feeble attempts at being competent humans, to be wary of and distant during interactions with them is not to disrespect an elder but to guard against foreign intrusion' (Barker 1990, p.312).

Barker argues that this indirect geronticide must be connected to a wider constellation of cultural components. He documents a Polynesian culture in which little empathy is displayed for the needs of others. This includes a notion of just desserts – those elderly who had seemed excessively materialistic, individualistic and selfish when young were merely reaping the consequences. Further, emigration had depleted the resources available to any one extended family. Old people were not on the consequent list of domestic priorities. The structural context furnished the seedbed within which geronticidal attitudes could flourish.

Death-hastening behaviour was relatively common in such societies. But where it happened it could paradoxically coexist with support for 'well' elderly – differentiating in the same society between different populations – the frail (the 'grey fish' of the land) as opposed to the healthy, 'grey-haired' ones. Barker also makes this distinction. In Polynesia, he found there was a major difference between the experiences of the intact and the decrepit (minority) elderly.

Ritual demarcation allowing geronticide: Concluding liminal status

In most primitive societies, public ceremonies determined the personhood of individuals – the recognition of them as part of the community or separate from it. These rituals might mark, for example, the baptism of an infant, which affirmed it as a person with communal rights. They would also occur to the frail elderly in a reverse direction.

If marginality due to lack of social contribution is the primary determinant of geronticide, then one can expect similar forms of disposal to occur at the other end of the age spectrum. Glascock (1987) has argued that the killing of surplus and dependent individuals, infants and the elderly is produced by the same forces. In order to reduce stress from the environment or fluctuations in the workload, many societies, from the Arctic to the tropics, when they perceived a resource threat to the communal good, might decide to kill expendable persons, thereby stabilising their conditions. The expendable people were the very young or the very old on the borders of society or the margins of life.

The liminal status passage

The expendables are persons occupying a *liminal* status. To become liminal, to occupy such a marginal position, an individual undergoes several stages and ceremonies, a ritual process, before being socially constructed as dispensable. Turner (1957) speaks of a 'widely prevalent social tendency to make what is fashionable the norm and therefore to destroy the exceptional' (p.72). For example, in the life cycle, the normal healthy adult provides a standard by which others are judged. The old who are past the standard and the young who are incapable of achieving it – the physically, mentally, or socially aberrant who fall to either side of the standard – are both subject to elevation as sacred objects and also vulnerable to their own destruction. The two possibilities may not be exclusive.

This social death does not correspond to biological death. Frequently, a period of dying occurs during which the behaviour of the affected person mutates from the socially alive to the socially dead, a period in which the individual accepts that his or her social role has ceased, a period of dying which includes the liminal process. This social death consists of three major components. First, the dying individual is separated from his or her fellows. This process is similar to the disengagement from the previous status of an individual about to undergo any rite of passage. Second, behaviour by significant others in relation to the dying person slowly comes to resemble the treatment of a corpse – the living becomes the undead becomes the dead. Finally, there is gradual recognition on the part of the dying person that he or she is no longer alive – in the sense of being regarded as a proper member of the community. When the dying person views himself or herself as a corpse and is treated appropriately to that condition, that person has become an outsider. Status transition has been achieved and the individual is placed in a position of 'post-personhood'. This status may actually accelerate biological death. Symbolic killing assumes reality.

Social death is a feature of many primitive societies, as a stage that lies between life and death. Thus in Melanesian culture, this transitional stage complicates crude notions of life and death. This category of the socially dead may include not just the decrepit elderly but also those too handicapped to participate in the normal economic and cultural life of Melanesian society. As Simmons (1945) points out, this final stage of the life cycle is found in a large minority of primitive societies and is clearly distinguished from normal life. The distinction between the intact and decrepit elderly (the socially dead) is demarcated by a variety of linguistic, behavioural and ritual codes.

People at this stage are separated emotionally and often physically from the larger group. Liminality is that juncture at which individuals are perceived as incapacitated by age or illness, or by a combination of these, to a degree that they are living liabilities to the social group. Families and friends do not interact with the individual. Food is denied. Funeral rites are planned, and even begun. Mourning is simply the threshold to this process. Simmons (1945) notes a variety of terms for this liminal period – 'senility', 'over-aged', 'useless stage', 'sleeping period', 'age grading of dying' and the 'already dead'. Most religious systems view death simply as part of the status passage to the after-life. Social death is a crucial stage on the way. Once in the category of social dying, the process cannot be reversed.

The critical stage in this process is therefore the way in which societies decide to move from positively supporting the elderly to death-hastening behaviour or neglect, in which the socially dead liminal status is constructed. In this respect, there are three major response patterns for the aged in non-industrial societies – supportive behaviour, non-death-hastening neglect, and (more frequent than non-death-hastening), death-hastening behaviour. In turn, non-death hastening appears to be more uncommon than supportive behaviour.

Deliberate prolongation of life is actually rarer in such societies than is non-supportive or death-hastening behaviour. The latter relate directly to the transition from the intact to the liminal categories. In only two of the societies in which that division is noted does death-hastening behaviour not appear to occur (Simmons 1945). In other words, normally old people are supported until they become a burden at which point they are socially dead. Once a person is defined as entering the liminal process, he or she is in fact no longer a social person, and the implementation of death-hastening behaviour appears to be relatively non-traumatic. However, it may not be the actual behaviour, mental faculties or appearance of the older person that prompts the transition. Rather, it may be a change in the social environment – in the reaction of proximate others – that results in development of the decrepit label and subsequent death-hastening reaction.

Infanticide and geronticide

Ceremonial delimitation for liminality could occur at both ends of the life cycle. Unwanted infants as well as the elderly could be defined as liminally dead.

Evans-Pritchard in his study of the Nuer (1951), notes that twins are elevated to the sacred because they are symbolically associated with birds. Birds are the products of multiple births and creatures of the 'above' and 'children of God'. Twinship presents the paradox that what is physically doubled is structurally single and what is mysterious as one is empirically two. Many cultures contain these twin mediational figures. While some societies elevate such children, others kill one or all. 'Reports of infanticide are so common over time and place that we assume that some unwanted children are killed or allowed to die in virtually all societies' (Post 1990). The infants that are killed are not yet regarded as full social beings. Correspondingly, the decrepit elderly are ceremonially stripped of their human status before being abandoned.

In Minturn and Stasak's (1982) study, infants were killed before the birth ceremony, a rite of passage that establishes the recognition of the infant as a full social being. Hence the period from birth to social acknowledgement constitutes a liminal stage. At birth, the baby separates from the mother, from the darkness of the unborn status, a stage similar to that of death. Birth itself might be considered as an entry to the liminal process. After birth, the infant may be allowed to progress into becoming a full social person – or it may not. The placement of the infant – as with the elderly – as liminal, is possible because of a close connection between liminality and outsiderhood. With the infants, the common reasons for allocating an outsider category include the viability of the infant, multiple births, irregular paternity, the denial by the mother who decides she doesn't want the child, and physical deformities. For Minturn and Stasak, mixed ancestry or presumed inferior stock is the main reason for infanticide. In most societies where infanticide is practised, the majority of adults will kill the infant outright, while only a minority will exercise the practice of malign neglect.

Infants are liminal partly because of their social invisibility and may be disposed of outside public gaze. In early modern England, the killing of an infant was less than that of a child or adult – the infant's being illegitimate might define that inferior status. Nursing babies could even be regarded as parasites because they drank the 'white blood' of the mother, and kept the latter out of church and out of other public ceremonies. The elimination of the infant would alleviate both the physical and mental stress, or hide the social origins, allowing the woman to maintain her own relationship with her family while simultaneously easing the economic problems of that family. The parallel with the elimination of the elderly is evident.

Young and elderly are killed symbolically through ritual and then re-born in new statuses. The symbol attached to the liminal person is complex and modelled on biological processes. The individual who is liminal may be marked with symbols of birth and death simultaneously. The actual definition of the individual as liminal makes him or her available to be sacrificed at appropriate times. This decision-making about life and death serves to define and redefine individuals under changing circumstances, killed under specific socio-economic conditions that permit the social construction of them as liminal. Structural conditions might precipitate the imposition of liminality. However, some people – perhaps because of physical or mental handicaps – may be permanently in a liminal position.

Criticisms of political economy

There are three problems with the early political economy approach to geronticide. First, there are enough exceptions to prevent any generalised rule. Second, the political economy approach appears uni-causal. Finally, how applicable is such a model drawn from relatively simple forms of social organisation and production relevant to the complex differentiation of post-industrial society? The final caveat – on its relevance today – will be dealt with in our discussion of bureaucratisation in Chapter 5. In this concluding section, the criticisms are limited to the experience of other primitive societies that do not practise geronticide and to the other modes of stratification that may affect the propensity violently to dispose of older people.

The leisure–magic–elder status equation

There are primitive peoples in which the old people – even the very old – are most unlikely to be threatened by geronticide (De Beauvoir 1973). Some hunter-gatherer Chukchee peoples respected the old, unlike the Chukchees described earlier in this chapter. The elderly played a key role in social stability. The eldest male was not so much the owner of the family wealth but the intermediary between the legal inheritors. There was therefore no question of this wealth being snatched from him by any one of his progeny. The possessions that the old man retained conferred high status on him. He might continue to govern the camp even when almost senile – making decisions over migrations and upon the location of the summer camp. When they migrated from one camp to another, the old men sat in the sledges. If there was not enough snow, the young men carried them on their backs. (Older women remain a significant omission from this account.)

De Beauvoir draws similar evidence from the nomadic Yaghan on the coast of Tierra del Fuego, a people she described as 'among the most primitive of all known tribes – no axes, fish-hooks, cooking utensils' (p.95). Strong reciprocal relations were said to exist between all generations within a harmonious whole. The elderly were prioritised in terms of food and accommodation. It was they – especially the elderly women – who passed on respect for the unwritten law. They might carry out euthanasia to shorten the sufferings of a dying man, but his condition had to be hopeless and required general assent.

Similar accounts appear from studies of the Aleuts and of the Kikuyu. If the Aleut treated his parents well and attended to their advice, he would be rewarded. His fishing would be good and he would enjoy a long life. The very old men instructed the young. They were responsible for attending to the calendar (moving the stick that pointed to the day of the month). The old women cared for the sick, were trusted and given credibility (cited in De Beauvoir 1973).

The Kikuyu attached great importance to age cohorts as the basis for social organisation. There were close links between grandparents and grandchildren, and symbolically they belonged to the same age group. A neighbour's children, whom he looked upon as his own, helped a childless old man. The elders ruled over public business. One generation governed for 20 or so years and then ceremonially abdicated in favour of the next. That abdication constituted a movement up the hierarchy rather than down – the eldest were thought to be free of passion and to be capable of impartial decisions. A council of old women enforced moral rules over the young, demonstrating magical powers in that process, and punishing when necessary, a council possessed of magic powers. The Kikuyu had a saying, 'An old goat does not spit without a reason' and 'Old people do not tell lies'. The old women were much respected when they had no teeth left, were thought to be highly intelligent, and their bodies were buried ceremoniously instead of being left to the hyenas. However, De Beauvoir also notes that there was still ranking amongst the elderly based on wealth and ability.

A more recent study by Spenneman (1998) in the Marshall Islands demonstrates that, when faced with survival problems because of the combination of demographic growth and dearth, closed societies have other options than killing the elderly. Historically, the island of Majuro was regularly faced with problems of overpopulation, dilemmas that could not – as in the present day – be solved by migration or by importing food. People could only influence the productivity of the island to a limited extent. Even if as much food as possible was actually stored, the population could reach a ceiling beyond which it could no longer be satisfactorily fed. Each additional person meant less food for everyone else. The human population could not be allowed to exceed the carrying capacity of the island, if the survival of the group as a whole was not to be imperilled.

Four possibilities were available – abortion, infanticide, geronticide and genocide (killing strangers). In such times, abortion was the first remedy; it was not seen as murder because the fetus did not count as a human being. Second, during these periods a family might be allowed to have three children; but subsequent additions were buried alive at birth. Handicapped children in particular were eliminated. Killing strangers was the third preferred option – castaways and refugees from other resource-starved islands were frequently killed. There was no evidence of geronticide being a final resolution, despite the elimination of the other categories.

Surviving geronticide through fear

Similar accounts appear from the Indians of the Grand Chaco – where access to religious powers appeared to be the key ingredient of elderly status. Perversely, magical powers could be utilised malignantly, a capacity that increased with age. When an aged man became decrepit, he was killed with an arrow in the heart and his corpse burnt. This complete destruction of the body served to prevent its mutating into a dangerous ghost. Fear rather than respect can encourage geronticide (cited in De Beauvoir 1973).

In Yolngu society, White (1983) found that certain attributes of the elderly were negotiable, such as the development of a new valued role within the community. Others were ascribed, such as hierarchical membership of a clan or family. The freedom of venerated elderly males from death-hastening behaviour was not simply because of the assumed positive sacred knowledge or mystical powers. It was also because such wisdom – like the physical strength of younger men – was something to be feared. Safety in old age could derive from the acquisition of a different kind of power, one possibly peculiar only to the elderly.

Ashliman (1999) draws a similar moral from a Ukrainian tale of the elderly as the source of essential wisdom. This ritual dominance by elderly males meant that they could maintain care not just through respect but also by fear. They were cared for, not through affection, but because others were fearful of their magical power to do harm.

Studies of the Navaho give the same emphasis to cultural attributes as a way of mediating the effects of non-productivity on status. But in their case, ideals could be differentiated in practice (White 1983). Responsibility for care and discipline over the young was given to the grandparents – a tribute to their magical connections. Society was most attentive to the old even when they were senile. If an old person rambled away from his home, he was fetched back. Yet an underlying resentment was evident. The young and the middle-aged men made fun of the dodderers, if secretly from fear of the old men's vengeance. Further, many of them had no influence whatsoever – they belonged only to the fringe of the community. Access to magical rites, to the role of tribal singer, determined elderly status. Those without this status suffered accordingly. The Navaho showed little respect for an ignorant old man.

In the case of the Navaho, in a rather more differentiated society than those noted earlier, economic life called for more complex knowledge, environmental exigencies were not as severe, and there was space for the development of magic and religion. When primitive society is no longer as harsh, where the demands for daily survival are no longer as extreme, mystical powers develop. Within those cultural artefacts, a space is carved out for those who possess such 'other-worldly' knowledge. Because of their non-working status, they transcend direct economic disputes over sustenance.

A multi-dimensional perspective on geronticide

Early political economy approaches failed to take account of other forms of stratification and of culture that could mediate between economy and decisions over life and death. Victor (1987) furnishes a comparative résumé of anthropological work, noting the wide diversity of responses to old age that have been observed in 'pre-industrial' societies. He claims that the position of older people in these societies was structured around certain key issues. In particular, wealth and social status could override age distinctions. In practice, the mode of production and the subsequent status of the elder are mediated by the interplay of several variables:

- The *type of social organisation* – from hunter-gatherer/nomadic to pastoral.

- The *economic or cultural value of the activity* of older people – the older person's labour constitutes one source of value. We noted above that there may also be valued roles such as the possession of special knowledge with regard to waterhole location, as in the case of the Australian aborigines, or access to specific cultural magic (as in the Nuer).

- The *physical or mental attributes* of the older person – the healthy older person versus the frail elderly. The ideal is compared with the personality features of the elder. For example, a querulous older person might be avoided and hence subject to neglect and death-hastening behaviour. Similarly, the rules of succession to a coveted leadership or sage role might be amended by leadership qualities.

- The *social importance of the experience of older people* – do they carry special knowledge essential to the tribe's survival? In primitive society, the elderly may use varying skills to avoid being classified as decrepit and hence subject to death-hastening behaviour. They could transfer from agricultural work to household chores. They might adopt new social roles such as those of clown, storyteller or healer. Many such frail elderly would survive because they served – in societies without written texts – as the conduits of oral tradition.

- The *extent to which older people maintain the status of activity from which they have now retired* – does the retired chief retain his place in the hierarchy, even though his active participation in the role has now ceased?

- The degree of authority of older people over others through *control of scarce resources or political power* – is ownership held feudally in a person rather than a transferable office?

- The *family situation* – birth or assigned order in the family might be important. For example, a younger wife may not be as important as the first wife. She could gain status only if she became the surviving woman. Similarly, possession of children might be important. Without obligated carers, the elder cannot be tended.

- The *economic structure* – ecology and land use may be critical. Where the land is abundant with food, feeding the elderly is not a problem, but transporting them is. However, in the case of aboriginal peoples, problems of mobility might be mediated (especially for males) in determining death-hastening activities because elderly men might be uniquely familiar with water location and often determined the site of camps on a trek.

- *Social change* – structural factors that could affect changes in attitudes to the elderly amongst the aboriginal communities have been illustrated. For example, white colonisation might drastically affect attitudes (the impact of Christianity and of industrialism in the form of mining enterprises on ancestral aboriginal land). Intrusive social change may have differential effects on various dimensions of status such as health, authority, economic independence, ritual influence and household ranking.

- *Gender* – White (1983) found that the most disadvantaged aboriginal members in the allocation of meat were old women, especially widows and separated women, who received the least nutritious portions of a butchered animal such as a kangaroo. If they were too old or sick to forage with younger women, they would be doubly disadvantaged by missing out on food cooked and eaten during the day and had to rely on that brought home by others. Food intake studies show females declined in weight much faster than males and this may reflect the greater variability in the status and care of older women in aboriginal society. Males through ritual dominance and proximity of kin, were more often assured of attentive care in old age.

- *Cultural definitions of ageing* – for example, the traditional view of Inuit abandonment of the elderly as a consequence of the harsh environment has been challenged. It may be that in Inuit culture death is seen simply as a way station towards a further stage of life. Generations may be linked together in a seamless web that continues after death. Killing the elderly may not be a stoical action in the face of environmental exigencies but an indifference to death when, in Inuit cosmology, the person is the one enduring, immutable substance (Guemple 1990). There is, in effect, life after death.

Each of these factors may contribute to an explanation of the attitudes towards geronticide in different societies. Critically, direct focus on the non-productivity of the elderly ignores the importance of socio-economic stratification. Amongst the Maya, the wealthy aged were favoured by reduced taxation, communal help and stores from the royal storehouse. Select families spent their lives advancing in status so that in later life they achieved high priestly or secular posts. Other Maya records suggest that the low-status aged and the crippled were thrown into the killing pool and sacrificed to the rain god Chac (Freidel 1995).

Silverman and Maxwell (1984) summarise the complexity of the geronticide matrix in their data from 96 societies, noting the wide variation of cultural perspectives concerning the social position and role of older people. Reactions to ageing are positive if older people are socially active, occupying non-trivial roles linked to strong community boundaries and clear social structures. In particular, control by older people over information and resources (whether material or symbolic) is important. They conclude that ageing is gendered almost universally, with power and esteem clearly divided patriarchally in all societies. In short, the thesis that old men are safer from geronticide than old women appears to be a rare example of an anthropological absolute. Even amongst the old-old or decrepit, those cultures might embody quite different treatments of the elderly independently of the healthy/frail division.

The complexity of this matrix can be illustrated in the relationship between gender and decrepitude. In Eastwell's (1994) study of Yolngu society, two distinctions are made within the cohort – between males and females and between the active and the frail elderly. The latter would generally be ascribed to the liminal – the socially dead – *in* but not *of* society. But only if the lives of others were affected would the frail elderly be killed at their own request. Chaseling (1957) notes distinctions amongst the Yolngu between old women and old men. The position of women itself may be contradictory. On the one hand, because men not women are perceived as the transmitters of sacred knowledge, older women suffer correspondingly and are more subject to death-hastening behaviour, 'women live a much harder life than men and are neglected and unwanted as they grow old before their time' (p.65).[5] Other writers quote stereotypes used amongst aborigines regarding old women – old crones, ancient widows, gossips, and so on. On the other hand, some Yolngu studies show certain elderly women to be powerful because of their leadership of polygamous families. Further, and ironically, being women and inferior in status they – unlike men – may have little to fear from the supernatural, and they preside over important rites in relation to birth and puberty. Generally, women who have specialist knowledge of religious matters are valued but elderly women without that knowledge are not. In other words, death-hastening susceptibility varies within Yolngu society from low-status elderly women without family membership, and access to particular knowledge, to high status men within family structures who possess sacred oral knowledge. Geronticide was aimed at specific categories of the elderly, not at the frail elderly in themselves.

Kaberry (1939) documented similar evidence on the Tiwi aborigines. In that society, only a minority of the elderly was treated with reverence. This was the small group of highly prestigious polygamous and powerful 'old men' of 60 years or more. Those with fewer wives, and old men devoid of power, were given much less prestige. Similarly, the care of an old woman was dependent on whether she was the wife of a polygamous male. Propensity to death-hastening behaviour depended on whether there was a competent relation to assume the caring role. Widows, widowers, elderly bachelors and spinsters were liable to geronticide when they were no longer sufficiently ambulatory to travel with the tribe.

The ability to control, to contribute and to advise are critical factors mediating the effects of social change on the elderly (Amoss 1981). For example, Coast Salish elders had access to all three of these prestige-generating components because of their command of traditional ritual knowledge in a context where the culture was being revived. Conversely, the Asmat of New Guinea were in a 'ritual void' stranded by the disintegration of their society's complex religious system within two decades of exposure to European society, and bypassed by contemporary opportunities.

Such modernisation exposure could have complex effects. For example, the allocation of pensions to aboriginal elders resulted in the elder becoming a resource rather than a drain. Pensions contribute to the family income – indeed may be the primary source of it. But pensioners may be forced to rely on the literate young to translate and explain the pension requirements and to count money. At the same time, the children constitute a drain on elderly resources demanding a share of their meagre income for other innovations such as commercial entertainment and for alcohol.

Ashliman (1999) furnishes a medieval folk story 'The Old Father's Pretended Treasure', to illustrate how survival may depend upon financial rewards. In that account, an old man nearing death divides his property amongst his sons. However, failing to die and having passed over the inheritance to his sons, he found the latter treating him cruelly – no longer as an object of worth. To remedy this harsh treatment he pretended that he still possessed several bags of money (actually filled with stones). Consequently, his sons reacted to their better future prospects by restoring him to favour. Survival could depend upon the cash nexus.

The consequences of social change – benefits and ill effects – do not impinge equally. They intersect with other influences and may be manipulated by the elderly to ward off poverty and neglect. The process is not uniform. There is no one-to-one relation between the primitive mode of production and attitudes to elderly people. Old people in different situations have unequal opportunities to negotiate status and to influence the balance between market costs and the contributions they can make. The treatment and status of the elderly is probably no more uniform in aboriginal society than it is in Western societies. Differences between the fortunes of individual elders largely reflect their capacities, their differential location in the economic, political and social structures, and changes within the social environment.

But what appears from this account of primitive society is a rebuttal of a notional golden age. It also demonstrates that in some such societies, attitudes to the disposal of the elderly were socially sanctified and legitimised by custom. The collectivity rather than the individual came first in that disposal process;[6] there was reportedly an unspoken acceptance of that tradition by the person who was being subject to such life termination. Furthermore, the more recent development of a broad political economy approach recognises that other factors may mediate between fundamental needs for sustenance and the extent to which the elderly may be exposed to death-hastening practices. In particular, under the generic rubric of 'critical gerontology' other perspectives can link with that political economy path – especially those drawing on emergent feminist perspectives on ageing (Cool and McCabe 1990) and (as in Chapter 4) humanistic orientations that appreciate the relative autonomy of an ageist ideology (Minkler 1996).

Notes

1   Among those who rejected the new cult of reason and rationality were Thomas Carlyle, Charles Dickens, John Ruskin and William Morris.
2   Other examples of such outright killings are drawn from studies in northern Brazil and amongst the Lapps.
3   A similar account appears in the Grimms' tale 'The Old Grandfather and His Grandson'.
4   Drawing on the work of Tokarev and Gurvich (1964), cited in De Beauvoir (1973).
5   Chaseling reports finding the bodies of two aged women, one of whom was blind, who had been left to perish in the sand-hills as the tribe moved to fresh hunting grounds.
6   But see the emphatic point made by Maxwell, Silverman and Maxwell (1990): '...geronticide is usually a family affair. It is the result of decisions made by an intimate group of kinsmen, often jointly with the old person. We have never encountered...any instances of the mass execution of old people. They tend to be dispatched singly...' (p.77)

CHAPTER 4

Death by Attrition

Modernisation and the Workhouse

There is one incident in the Bible (Daniel 13)[1] that associates not virtue with old age but vice. It is the story of Susannah and the two elders. These men, who were judges and who were respected by the master of the house, fell in love with the beauty of his wife. One afternoon they hid in the garden to watch her taking a bath. She refused them her favours and in revenge they said they had seen her lying with a young man. They were believed and Susannah was condemned to death. But Daniel, still a youth, saved her by questioning the two judges separately. Their evidence was contradictory, and it was they who were sentenced to death.

> Rattle his bones
> Over the stones
> He's only a pauper
> Whom nobody owns.
> (Old English saying)[2]

Introduction

Historical accounts of geronticide are subject to reconstruction. As the first quotation indicates, the social history of the elderly often represents simply the views of those who hold power in that recounting. Many of the proverbs passed down from generation to generation restate the importance of preserving the elderly as a valuable resource. Proverbs representing a different point of view are notable by their absence.

Killing elderly people is rarely a fixed procedure. Rather it represents one end of a continuum of care and rejection. It is often the end result of a trajectory of inter-personal violence and neglect. One cannot easily separate geronticide as a single act from the more general mistreatment of elderly people, especially given the frequency of death-hastening behaviour. As in the field of criminal punishment, the ceremonial executions of the elderly in primitive society were later replaced by the long-drawn-out slaughter through transportation and abandonment. Negative attitudes to older people only occasionally resulted in life-threatening actions. But throughout social history, we have evidence of behaviour that often resulted in termination – although normally stopping short of direct violence. Death-hastening as a gradual form of attritional geronticide represents the motif of this chapter.

In the following pages, we explore the explanations of attitudes towards the elderly within the industrial modernisation process. A classic body of sociological theories (generally located under the 'logic of industrialism' or 'convergence' rubric) allows us to consider related approaches that seek to demonstrate that social history has been intermittently accompanied by a deterioration in respect. The venerated elder of the past (a view severely doubted in the last chapter), under the impact of industrialism, increasingly encountered neglect and varied death-hastening procedures. Nowhere is that process more obvious in British history than in the system of Poor Law control in the nineteenth century – principally, the system of 'indoor relief' by the workhouse.

We explore the four dominant sociological and historical approaches to the estrangement of the elderly before illustrating the fact that, whatever the flaws with such theories, the evidence of industrial Victorian society details a miserable dispatch for the elderly poor.

- *Modernisation theory* suggests that in pre-industrial society the elderly were part of the organic affective community. But industrialism requires individualism, and social atomism, which means that the elderly who rely on collective relations are now discarded.

- *Functionalist sociology* – principally the thesis that the extended pre-industrial family took care of the old but the nuclear family structure of industrial society no longer required that contribution. The elderly lose necessary expressive contact with their younger kin. Social and geographical mobility casts off the elderly into the isolated familial wilderness.

- *Convergence theory* sees all societies eventually following the same path, one feature of which is the separation of home and work. Where work was home-based, there was a place for the elderly to contribute. But complex industrialism concentrated newly skilled work elsewhere. Sophisticated new skills could not be acquired by older people, who were consequently marginalised from social and economic life as non-producers and of little value.

- *Ageist ideology approaches* suggest that the estrangement of the elderly occurs largely independently of economic forces – the growing culture of individualism and of 'youth' replaces the veneration of the old with a quite different ideology which has no place for those who do not meet the new social values.

But the death-hastening consequences of the above did not affect all the elderly equally. They affected principally the elderly poor, especially elderly females. The primary example of such death-hastening with the progress of industrialism was the Victorian workhouse which regularly consigned the poor elderly to a liminal status in which they were designed to die as soon as possible and to lessen the charge to local ratepayers.

The modernisation process

The modernisation approach to old age posits a relatively straightforward trajectory of economic and social history (Stearns 1986). The thesis overlaps with the other three approaches – the demographic, that of political economy, and bureaucratisation (as in the following chapter). But there are certain unique features of the modernisation approaches that offer an even more deterministic picture of the attitudes to, and treatment of, the elderly than in the other cases.

Gerontologists have long been interested in the effect of modernisation on the status of the elderly (Gilliland and Jimenez 1996). Modernisation theory explains the history of the aged in terms of the structural differences between traditional and modern societies. Societies are arranged on a continuum, and those that exhibit certain qualities of social structure are termed 'modern' (Smith 1973). Its appeal to historians of old age is the presumed ability to highlight how a wide range of significant long-term developments – including declining fertility rates, induced changes in familial and community structures and secularisation (all within the larger forces of industrialism) – have affected the elderly.

Commentators (such as Plath (1984) and De Beauvoir (1973)) had argued persuasively that industrial society inevitably led to a degraded position for the aged. They were joined by modernisation and sociological functionalist theorists (Cowgill and Holmes 1972) who claimed that the treatment of the elderly will decline as societies industrialise. Lower status was an inevitable consequence.

The reasons include the loss of economic sources of power held by the elderly (such as land passed down to the children when parents can no longer work) and critically, from functionalist theory, the effects of social and geographical mobility. Industrialisation is presumed to impose a meritocracy in which extended family structures dissolve as the new recruits achieve occupational promotion and higher socio-economic status than their aged kin, consequently losing contact and retreating from affective support. The educational qualifications intrinsic to the new meritocracy ensure that the values and norms of the new nuclear family are substantially different from those of the older extended kinship structure.

Cowgill (1986) regards ageing trends as a primary indicator of human progress. Certain value systems are favourable to high-status and active roles for the elderly – especially filial piety and familism. When these values prevail, they promote ascendancy of elders and appear to inhibit the reverse tendency of modernisation. Another set of contributing values, however, often accompanies modernisation and accelerates its downgrading momentum – the work ethic, egalitarianism, individualism, and the cult of youth. In all societies, people have sought to provide for security in their old age; only in pastoral and agrarian societies (before the days of state and private pensions) in which private property exists in reasonably durable form, such as cattle or land, was this a viable possibility. In collective economies and among hunters and fishers, in the absence of technology for long-term preservation of produce, older people and other marginal groups who cannot provide for themselves depend upon the productivity of others, usually members of their families, to accumulate surplus resources for their support.

In a peasant agrarian economy, production tends to be family-based and unspecialised with little labour mobility. The young follow the parental occupations, and children of both sexes learn their economic roles by working along with their parents. Because the latter usually have more accumulated work-related experience and knowledge than their adult children, they may retain respect and authority in their old age. Co-residence of elderly parents and adult children, supported by norms of filial piety, underlie economic integration.

However, in an urban industrial economy, production is no longer family-based, occupations are more specialised, and labour is mobile. Jobs are obtained through a labour market that treats kin as atomised agents not as members of a family. The separation of work from family life fosters a degree of individualism (self-interest and preservation) not only in the labour market but also in kinship relations. Ideologies inherent in late industrialism, such as consumerism, accentuate differences between the generations in lifestyle and outlook. Sons may not follow the occupations of their fathers. Women may also work outside the household. Parents and adult children often reside in different localities. In the early years of industrialism, physical migration may accentuate this separation.

Where co-residence arrangements exist, parental authority is culturally endowed but rarely economically supported, thereby increasing the potential for intergenerational conflict and the relative abandonment of the elderly non-working. Under these circumstances, both adult children and elderly parents often prefer, if possible, to maintain at least partial independence by separate residences (Davis and van den Oever, 1981). If they can establish individual or group property rights and maintain those rights into old age, the elderly have a safety margin. But because this has been feasible only for herders and farmers, it is in these societies that we find the highest status, the greatest power and the most prestige of the elderly. It is also in these societies that we find the greatest tendency towards a pattern of age structuring in which each higher age bracket represents a higher status and increased power. This constantly changing pattern stands in contrast to the modern pattern of disengagement and discontinuity in roles.

The converse approach to modernisation theory espoused here is not the dichotomy of human betterment and barbarous decline. Instead, it has two key themes – discontinuity for some and continuity for others, often differentiated by social stratification. It is a story of inconsistencies, in which veneration could be accompanied by a variety of extreme forms of death-hastening behaviour. From the eighteenth century onwards, with the onset of industrialism, attitudes have moved backwards and forwards – from scapegoating of the destitute in periods of economic dearth to the provision of almshouses and other forms of charitable giving in more prosperous periods (Biggs, Phillipson and Kingston 1995). Diversity rather than unilinear change appears to have been the situation with regard to the treatment and experience of the elderly. Since the onset of industrialism, attitudes to the elderly mixed official respect, some real power, considerable economic and physical degradation, and cultural derision. Where improvements occurred relatively, the traditional demarcation of social stratification was the key guide.

But there were also continuities, as the workhouse material illustrates. The elderly poor and especially elderly women, when they also showed physical and mental frailty, were always those most exposed to abandonment and disposal. All modernisation (where it was consistent) offered the social residuum as a different process of death-hastening.

Modernisation and social differentiation

Under the modernisation rubric, gerontological studies have traditionally operated with a golden age perspective – that some time in the past, stable families of all social classes, ethnicities and political persuasions took care of their aged. There were no ostracised elderly poor. The old were as functionally integrated as the young, and accorded due respect as the sagacious cornerstone of the traditional household. Abandonment or harsh treatment in the household would have breached key social norms and values.

In recent pre-industrial history, central to that golden age thesis in those sources, is a vision of the family strongly but kindly disciplined by the patriarch, where the woman of the household dealt with the chores and cared for the children, and where the granny figure was given an honoured family status. This Utopia embodies notions of a pre-industrial family life in which the elderly were incorporated functionally with familial relatives, and three or more generations lived harmoniously in extended family structures. As members of these family units, the aged were lovingly cared for, and reciprocally assisted in household chores. Laslett (1985) identifies this view as the 'world we have lost syndrome' which involves the sense that a 'before' period exists in which the elderly were revered and played valuable roles, and an 'after' period in which the aged became scorned and abused.

Contrary to the social Darwinian approach, which suggests that history was characterised by progress in morality and in perception of 'marginal' members of society, modernisation theory offers a gloomier prognosis. Social change, especially between pre-industrial and industrial society, involves an inexorable hardening of attitudes to the elderly. Social extermination of the elderly may be the price paid for economic progress. As Stearns (1986) phrases it, 'gerontological interest in history has too often been confined to a "tradition is good, modern is worse" conviction' (p.3).

The thesis overrides traditional social science and social Darwinism in its accounts of that progression, replacing affective relations and functional homogeneity with patterns of instrumental contracts, and of functional interdependence. The nineteenth century philosopher Herbert Spencer, for example, viewed primitive humans as basically predatory and warlike and therefore amenable only to an autocratic military form of social organisation. But a more highly differentiated and interdependent society was evolving based upon peaceful cooperation of enlightened individuals who, in seeking their own interest, also served the higher forms of society. Such rationality under the Enlightenment provided the ideological foundations for the new industrialism.

The tradition encompasses the concepts of *Gemeinschaft* (community) and *Gesellschaft* (variously translated as 'society,' organisation,' or 'association', from Ferdinand Tonnies (1955)). *Gemeinschaft* extended beyond a purely local community to include any set of relationships characterised by emotional cohesion, depth, continuity and fulfilment. In contrast, *Gesellschaft* referred to the impersonal, the contractual, and the rational aspects of human association. Tonnies grounded these types of relationships in patterns of settlement and in particular geographical locales. Adopting the prevailing idealised views of traditional rural society, Tonnies believed the village to represent *Gemeinschaft*, and modern urban communities, *Gesellschaft*. From a typology of social relationships, Tonnies' concepts became a taxonomy of settlement patterns, fitting with prevailing cultural views of urban and rural ways of life (Newby 1977). Affective morality bound the elder to the community in the rural village to be replaced by instrumental neutrality in the industrial society.

Similarly, Max Weber (1964) discussed domination by 'honoratoires' whose authority in olden times was based on age:

> In all communities which orient their social conduct toward tradition, i.e., towards convention, customary law or sacred law, the elders are, so to speak, the natural honoratoires not only because of their prestige of wider experience, but also because they know the traditions (p.950).

However, Weber also recognised that even in traditional society the power and prestige of the aged were subject to change under certain conditions, such as in periods of dearth, when those who could no longer work became burdensome, or under conditions of warfare when the prestige of older men was likely to sink below that of warriors. Inevitably, the status of the aged was lower in mass society, as the growing complexity of administrative tasks led to the rise of technical superiority among those with training and experience.

Evidence of familial disintegration and loss of reciprocal obligations support this orthodox thesis on the apparent increase in maltreatment of the elderly and elderly victimisation. The institutionalisation of retirement with pension support in the twentieth century, while it reduced the stresses produced by the growing economic dependency of the elderly (now living longer), sundered them from conventions of family support. Independent economic sustenance had the contrary effect of apparently making the younger adults no longer sentiently responsible for the maintenance of their elders.[3]

Modernisation and convergence

Industrialism and sociological functionalism link with a further component – convergence theory – accounting for the changing status of the elderly. Convergence posits modernisation as an inevitable universalising process.

The initial statement of modernisation theory drew upon the Western experiences through a notion of unilateral social change. In Daniel Lerner (1964), for example:

> The Western model of modernisation exhibits certain components and sequences whose resonance is global ... the same basic model reappears in virtually all modernising societies on all continents of the world, regardless of variations in race, colour, or creed. (p.75)

In pre-modern industrial societies, older people continued their normal work activities as long as they were physically able. Only in modern industrialised society has retirement become a prevalent practice, and only in those societies does one find a general withdrawal from work processes by the elderly. That disengagement coincided with the universal development of novel pension and social security schemes.

Cowgill (1986) expanded the analysis to include societies at different stages of development, in the unilinear model. Societies were arrayed on a continuum according to the degree of modernisation. Pre-literate societies were equated with pre-industrial Western societies. 'The status of the aged is high in preliterate societies and is lower and more ambiguous in modern societies' (Cowgill and Holmes 1972, p.101).

Cowgill focused on four variables – health science, economic technology, urbanisation, and mass education – which inexorably contributed to a loss of status for the aged. Modern health science multiplies the numbers of elderly and contributes to the ageing of the population and its work force. As the lives of workers are prolonged, death no longer creates openings in the labour force as rapidly as in the past, and competitive pressures are generated between generations. Eventually, retirement is initiated as a social substitute for death. In a society that highly values a work ethic and allocates material and nonmaterial rewards accordingly, 'retirement from this most valued and status-giving role is accompanied by a reduction in rewards, including monetary income and psychologically satisfying status' (Cowgill 1986, p.27). Modern economic technology also 'creates new occupations and transforms most of the old ones' (p.168), which means loss of jobs, income and status by the aged. At the same time, urbanisation attracts the young to the cities, breaking up the extended family as a household unit. Finally, the growth of mass education and literacy means there can be no 'mystique of age' based on the superior knowledge and wisdom of older people.

A key contribution to the transition from tradition to modernity in the treatment of the aged appears in Burgess (as discussed in Quadagno (1982)). The universalising features of convergence and industrialisation had contributed to a decline in the status of the elderly. Migration, urbanisation and the mass production of commodities undermined the economic basis of the extended family and decreased the number of self-employed entrepreneurs. Industrialisation destroyed the economic basis of the extended family by removing production from the home. Family members no longer worked together in agriculture or in household. Factory production accelerated the process of urbanisation, and younger family members migrated to the cities, diminishing the likelihood that an aged parent would be taken into a child's home. The nuclear family unit composed solely of parents and children replaced the extended family. Extended family isolation was coupled with a loss of decision-making power in the workplace creating pressures for retirement. As the quality of life for older people declined, improvements in life expectancy increased their proportion in society with many elderly ending their lives without spouse or family support. The loss of family forced the aged to rely upon the state in a new instrumental dependency relationship.

Palmore and Manton (1974) elaborated the convergence implications of the modernisation thesis. They were concerned with three questions. First, does the status of the aged decline with modernisation? Second, if the status of the aged declines, which aspects of modernisation best account for it? Third, is this decline linear, or is a point reached when the decline stops and status increases? Three measures of socio-economic status were used – employment status (whether or not the aged are economically active), the prestige of the occupation of those economically active, and education. Using an equality index to compare the status of the aged with the non-aged, Palmore and Manton drew two conclusions. First, they determined that the two most important factors in reducing aged status were the shift from agriculture to manufacturing and increased education. Second, they found that the relationship between modernisation and the status of the aged was not linear but J-shaped. In the early stages of modernisation, the status of the aged was reduced. However, as societies matured, the differences between the aged and non-aged in education and occupation tended to level off, and discrepancies in status decreased.

Similar evidence appears in Cohn's (1980) comparison of 30 countries at varying levels of economic development and rates of economic growth. He hypothesised that the demands of increased technology associated with societal development as well as cohort differences in education in a rapidly growing society would create age differences in occupational distribution. Relating the rate of economic growth and the extent of development to the proportion of older workers in prestigious occupations, Cohn concluded that the faster the rate of growth, the fewer older workers are found in higher-status occupations. Thus, economic growth and development led to a loss of occupational status for older workers.

In sum, modernisation appears to affect the status of the aged in four ways, leading to consequent estrangement and susceptibility to social disposal. First is the decline in domestic production that abolished work that older workers traditionally performed. Second, the shift from domestic production to factory production eliminated autonomy in the workplace, and consequently constrained older workers' power to determine their own time of retirement from producing exchange values. Third, the demographic factors explored in Chapter 2, especially life expectancy increases, led to increased intergenerational competition for jobs, with technological changes making the skills of the aged less valuable. Finally, modernisation theory also predicts that a decline in agriculture, which represents a predominant form of domestic production, would be accompanied by higher rates of retirement. Deterministic rules subjected the elderly to marginalisation.

Ageist ideology's contribution to death-hastening

A similar approach to the decline in elderly status appears in the work of several recent historians. However, it breaks with the determinism of modernisation theory by emphasising ideological and cultural, rather than industrial, forces (Achenbaum 1987). Their work emphasises attitudinal, not structural, change, in the denigration and degradation of the elderly – that history is informed by the image of ageism as an independent force, that 'culture' powerfully influences the status of the aged irrespective of the forces of modernisation.

On the one hand, these historians generally agree with the modernisation view that there has been an increase in elderly death-hastening. On the other hand, they explain it not in terms of economic forces but rather through free-floating cultural change (Gratton 1986). Cultural forces might overcome the impact of industrialisation. The discovery that the nuclear household was the predominant form in pre-industrial Western societies undermined the unilinear model. The aged could not have exercised power through an extended family. Acknowledging the finding that the elderly in modern societies may also maintain close contact with their kin makes the modernisation claim of a sharp break between past and present seem implausible.

These histories regard the structural change from farm to factory as of little consequence. The decline in the elderly's status is connected to an independent force, ageism. Fischer (1978) argued that American history demonstrated the failure of modernisation theory because the decline in the status of the aged occurred before industrialisation, urbanisation and the growth of mass education. He criticised the sociological reliance on changes in social and geographical mobility in contributing to a decline in the elder's status.

He argued that the aged were venerated in the past and that status decreased. However, the decline occurred much earlier, before industrialisation or modernisation had any impact. Using data such as age of property ownership and household composition, he concluded that a 'cult of age' existed in early America but disappeared between 1770 and 1820 due to the influence of the ideals of equality and liberty spread by the French Revolution. Egalitarian ideology destroyed the hierarchical conception of society on which the authority of age had rested, and the growth of the ideal of liberty dissolved the communal base of power. Since the authority of elders had depended upon the submergence of individuality, social atomism gradually dissolved the ties of obligation between generations as well as those between classes (Fischer 1978).

Throughout the nineteenth and into the twentieth century, attitudes toward the aged became increasingly negative. Social commentators spoke of the uselessness of the old, and the belief that men made their greatest contributions to society while still young was promulgated. It was this attitude, combined with a rise in the median age of the workforce, that led to the growth of retirement.

Increased retirement, in turn, brought about a rapid increase in poverty among the aged. Changes in attitudes toward the aged could not have been caused by industrialisation, urbanisation, demography, bureaucratisation or rationalisation, because all of these trends occurred after the demise of the exaltation of age and were secondary in importance to the ideals of equality and liberty (Fischer 1978). Thus, changes in ideals rather than in material life, led to the marginalisation of the elderly.

Like Fischer, Achenbaum (1987) found a historical dichotomy in views of old age. In the late nineteenth century, a decisive break occurred – a broad denial of age and a new cult of youth – with hostility to age manifest in perceptions of the aged worker. His argument that the attitudinal shift occurred independently of structural change draws on an analysis of labour force participation rates. Between 1790 and 1860, the elderly were perceived as indispensable, providing valuable insights about healthful longevity and serving as moral exemplars. By the outbreak of the First World War, most Americans affirmed the obsolescence of respect for old age.

Achenbaum identified three possible relationships between the rhetoric and reality of age. First, the modernisation thesis – that changes in the position of the aged associated with industrialisation and urbanisation could have precipitated unfavourable evaluations about the usefulness of the elderly. Significant increases in the numbers of older persons in the population, reductions in employment opportunities, and changes in the plight of dependants may have made Americans revise their opinions about growing old. A second possibility is that changes in conceptions of the aged and changes in their actual position in society occurred simultaneously. Finally, Achenbaum conceives of a third relationship – that Americans may have perceived the aged as obsolete burdens before their position in society warranted such a verdict. Achenbaum examines each of these hypotheses with regard to demographic change, to work opportunities, and to old age dependency.

He eliminates demographic pressures as a causal factor on the grounds that the growth of the aged population was slow and undetectable until after 1920, when negative ideas were already widespread. In the late nineteenth century, employers frequently justified the discharge of older employees by denigrating the value of their work. Thus, negative ideas about the aged became a source of discrimination in the marketplace. However, the greatest withdrawal of the elderly from the labour force has occurred since 1930, long after unfavourable notions about the aged were already commonplace. In neither case did increased retirement cause a loss of prestige.

Achenbaum also asks whether developments in old age dependency before 1914 could have caused a re-evaluation of the elderly's status. He notes the proliferation of private institutions, and retirement programmes for the aged in the late nineteenth century, but claims that these innovations were piecemeal and had negligible effect. Changes in popular conceptions of the aged between 1790 and 1914 were unrelated to observable shifts in older Americans' actual position in society. Therefore, ideas about the worth and functions of the elderly have a life of their own, independently of the structural changes of modernisation. Although the turning point for Achenbaum is later, his basic theme is similar to Fischer's – agreeing with the modernisation view on marginalisation, but attributing it to ideological factors.

Haber (1994) offers a different interpretation, one that has resonances in the work of Illich, and which is developed further in Chapter 5. The abandonment of the elderly was a function of the pathologising of old age as a medical condition in the late nineteenth century. Old age was equated with sickness and was the province therefore of specialised geriatricians. Cultural prejudices of ageism developed with the simultaneous advance of science and medicine. The result was the segregation of the aged in a 'postclimacteric' medical category that labelled old age as illness but offered no cure. Bureaucratisation and centrification led to increased discard of older people. In a clear break with the attitudinal school, she connects the new discriminatory practices directly to structural change in economic and familial relations – recognition of the reciprocal relationship between increasing structural poverty among older people and the bureaucratic response to it by the 'helping professionals' in the production of ageism. Unlike the earlier histories, she links this process with economic factors such as the introduction of mandatory retirement and the new concept of the 'work cycle'.

Other historians (e.g. Cole 1992) argue that denigration of the elderly is primarily a function of changes in religious ideas. The impact of fundamentalist Protestantism with its emphasis on the values of individuality and entrepreneurship worked heavily to the detriment of the elderly, whose security rested on collective rather than individualistic ties. Individual assessments of worth led to the discard of those who did not measure up. In emphasising self-discipline and self-control, a 'rigid form of moral self government', the evangelical ministers connected age with decay and dependency; and 'old age emerged as the most poignant and loathsome symbol of the decline of bourgeois self-reliance.' (p.73–4)

These accounts share with the modernisation approach the thesis that the elderly are increasingly open to social disposal. They suggest a measure of agreement with the dystopian view of Garvin and Burger (1965): 'It is difficult to imagine a time in history when a group of people was subjected to such violent extremes of living conditions as are the aged in twentieth century America.' (p.9) Their explanations and timing of that transition vary. Both approaches posit that the abandonment of elderly people is a relatively new phenomenon. They concur with the view that the advent of industrialism coincided to a varying extent with a decline in elderly status. The old could be discarded in the late nineteenth and twentieth centuries in a manner that was not feasible a century earlier. The question is whether the catalyst was one of economic change or whether ageism represents an independent cultural force.

The critique: Social history as uneven

In Chapter 3, we demonstrated that – as opposed to the modernisation thesis – there was no golden age in primitive society, in which old people were held in social esteem. In this section, we are concerned with two further criticisms of that approach and of that of the social historians cited above.[4]

Modernisation theory fails to recognise that ageism, as an ideology, has been present in all societies, past and present. The first section of this response draws on a variety of more recent social historical work to illustrate the continuity rather than discontinuity of ageist practices, and of procedures for the disposal of the elderly.

Perhaps more importantly, that ideology of dispensability did not encompass all the elderly. It was demarcated by socio-economic stratification and by gender. Similarly, socio-economic status was also a key indicator – the elderly poor were always much more susceptible to death-hastening practices. Drawing mainly on the experience of the nineteenth century workhouse, the second section of this critique demonstrates the way geronticide practice bore most heavily upon the poor. At all historical periods, elderly women were more exposed to geronticide practice. In an addendum, the particular experience of elderly women is noted through the application of a witchcraft label.

Continuity and discontinuity in the disposal of the elderly

Social history demonstrates unevenness in its treatment of the elderly rather than a unilinear process. The complexities of social change throw doubt on the possibilities of a model in which attitudes to the elderly have been one-directional, uniform and irreversible. Disposal practices in relation to older people characterised many different societies at varying historical periods. There never was a golden age. Elders were never automatically granted positions of authority or admiration in Western civilisation. Whatever the formal records, practice could be different. Modernisation theorists often mistake ideal and normative statements about old people for their real condition, confusing ritual deference with actual practice.

Stearns (1978) argues that the golden age approach makes its subjects seem like helpless pawns. In exploring views about the aged in France, he found not traditional veneration but rather unmitigated disdain, a disrespect that has persisted well into the contemporary era. From the eighteenth century to the inter-war periods, the outlook towards old age has remained unchanged. Thomas (1976), in a discussion of old age in early modern England, also rejects the idea that there was once a golden age. Although a considerable body of literature venerates a gerontocratic ideal, rulers in the past were middle-aged, not old. Most seventeenth- and eighteenth-century writers took it for granted that 'old age was a wretched time of physical deterioration' and portrayed the aged as peevish, forgetful, covetous, garrulous, and dirty (Thomas 1976, p.244). He concludes that there is no reason to look back wistfully to this period, for once health and mind had started to decay, wealth was the only source of respect. There was little community respect for the elderly in the absence of wealth or hierarchical prestige. The status of the aged in western Europe was related primarily to their economic value (Stearns 1978).

Steinmetz (1988) draws on varied sources (such as property transfer and migration records of young immigrants who had left their elderly in Europe) to document the mistreatment of the elderly in early America. From her exegesis of that pre-industrial context, it seems that the elderly, far from being respected as sources of sagacity (especially amongst the poorer classes), were wished well on their way to the other world as burdens on the local community.

In early Western societies, the elderly were located at the hub of property relationships, a status that had wide and unfavourable effects on younger family members. Ashliman (1999), for example, quotes an Austrian farm rhyme to symbolise the need for the father to move over so that his son can provide for his own children. These tensions often had deleterious effects on the treatment of the older members (Stearns 1986). Steinmetz (1988) furnishes a wealth of documentation on disputes over property transference between old and young. The use of parental control of economic resources to command their adult children could have negative consequences. Abuse and maltreatment might result from conflicts over property rights, over the failure of the elderly to 'move over' and to surrender their ownership of the household property and chattels when they were infirm (Stearns 1986). One Cotton Mather, writing in 1726, illustrates the leitmotif: 'Old folks often can't endure to be judged less able than ever they were for public appearances, nor to be put out of offices. But, good sir, be so wise as to disappear of your own accord, as soon and as far as you lawfully may' (cited in Steinmetz 1988).

Frequent conflict occurred over property inheritance, as sons waited eagerly for their parents to die so that they could inherit their land (Biggs et al. 1995). Elder control of property frustrated the aspirations of the young (Stearns 1986; Thomas 1976); an unmarried daughter faced pressures when left to care for her parents (Bardwell 1976); crises were generated through economic recession and through the contradictions of meeting the care needs of both older and young generations (Murphy 1931). The stress laid upon carers in physical strength and in bodily vigour was not unique to twentieth century care systems (Minois 1989).

One myth relates to the assumption of the localised integrity of the family unit – that increased geographical mobility cuts the elderly off from their roots and from care. But over the last two hundred years there have been vast migrations by the young away from the elderly. The migration from Europe to the New World, as well as the internal migration from countryside to the new industrial cities, were a phenomenon that sundered family structures long before the rise of the modern period. The elderly were as likely to be abandoned through that process as they were through any social and geographical mobility under advanced industrialism.

Further, the three-generation family pictured as a rural idyll is a common misapprehension. Blythe (1979) found that

> ...people like to think now that grandfathers and grandmothers had an honoured place in the cottage. In fact, when they got old, they were just neglected, pushed away into corners. I even found them in cupboards! Even in fairly clean and respectable houses, you often found an old man or woman shoved out of sight in a dark niche. (p.231)

In rural society, the elderly were often regarded as an economic hindrance and irrelevance. All the evidence indicates that in western Europe the three-generational family was exceptional, and certainly not idyllic (Laslett 1985). In pre-industrial society, fewer children survived to adulthood and fewer parents survived to old age. Where possible, the elderly preferred to live separately in nineteenth century Britain and America, and only remained with their adult children when forced to for economic reasons.

Discarding the elders as social junk was not a uniform process or one characterised by a direct trajectory. Instead, as we suggest below, the one constant in the history of the elderly is that the poor elderly and especially female elderly, were always regarded as socially disposable and treated differentially worse than their socio-economic betters. Generally, the work of the aged was marginal and sporadic, as in the following account:

> An old lady still living in the village used to scare crows for the whole of the harvest holidays: she was paid six shillings. She was given a wooden clapper and had to keep making noise with it: if she once stopped and the clapper was silent, the man who hired her would look out of his house to see what she was doing. (From Evans (1957) quoted by Quadagno 1982, p.47)

Modernisation theory is, in any case, too ethnocentric, based largely round the experiences of the USA. There are major problems in attempting to understand procedures for the disposal of the elderly in non-industrial and developing countries from the modernisation perspective. Linking such diverse nation states as nineteenth-century Russia, India and China in the present day, and western Europe in the Middle Ages, because they fit into the same slot on the continuum, ignores the immense differences between them. The criteria for the classification of the peoples and cultures of the world become the qualities of Western society – of 'care', indeed of being elderly in itself. Similarly, definitions of the elderly differ. In the United States, 35 years may be seen as the onset of deterioration. However, in Nigeria, old age equals the time of the menopause – the only function of a retiring age may be that it simply clears jobs for the younger generation. Any different or unique qualities of non-Western societies are simply ignored. Societies that seem superficially similar on some 'variable', such as the proportion of the population engaged in farming, may exhibit different demographic, economic and social patterns.

There is an unfounded assumption that the extended family cares for the elderly in a generalised 'Third World' (Tout 1989). For example, the lower status of the elderly may result from direct political intervention independent of other modernising forces. But in China, revolution brought legal action abolishing the previous privileges of the elderly and raising those of the young. Political action in the promulgation of the one-child policy affected attitudes to the elderly.

In India, overall status may vary according to caste, gender and work status. A significant reduction in mortality and increase in fertility is likely to have major economic and social consequences. In rural areas, increases in life expectancy are indicative of improvement in health condition and living standards on the one hand. On the other, endemic poverty, illiteracy and general lack of basic amenities constitute a major problem for rural elderly. Life for them becomes increasingly stressful as a result of the ageing process; the old person in the developing countries may become a liability, rather than an asset, to families and community.

Within necessary restraints, it has been possible to demonstrate that there are many examples of mistreatment of older people in pre-industrial and non-industrial society. As we illustrate further, from literary sources, in Chapter 6, elderly death-hastening was not an invention of modernisation and industrialism. Both in western Europe and elsewhere, older people have long been on the receiving end of final disposal techniques in order to make way for their younger kin.

Social stratification and the poor elderly: Death hastening in the workhouse

> A poor old man when he reaches four-score,
> And has done all he can, can do no more;
> To ask for relief, it makes him afraid,
> Since they took up with this body-snatching way,
> He must go and die in the union! (cited in Longmate 1974, p.63)

Irrespective of variations in attitudes towards older people, the poor elderly were always subject to arbitrary discard, often within institutional contexts intended to ease them invisibly on their way. A history of the elderly is indistinguishable in England from a history of poverty and the workhouse (Biggs *et al.* 1995), especially given the requirement for any person on relief to receive it through the workhouse system. The availability of domiciliary homes for the indigent elderly goes back to sixteenth century 'almshouses' in England and on the continent.

In the United States, from colonial times, caring for the elderly poor was a responsibility of government. This aid took the form of shelter in an almshouse, where 'unfortunate' and feeble old people could be forwarded quietly to death.[5] Fischer (1978) notes that by far the majority of those registered as inmates of pauper institutions into the twentieth century were elderly. Throughout the nineteenth century, the proportion of almshouse residents who were old increased sharply, and after 1860 the number and variety of private institutions for the aged increased rapidly as well. At first 'officials tried not only to pass the buck but also to make a few as well' (Bates 1999, p.12). Until the 1820s, villages and cities confronted with growing numbers of impoverished elderly routinely auctioned them off to families who provided squalid accommodation in return for gruelling work. An observer at one Saturday night auction at a village tavern noted that citizens 'could speculate upon the bodily vigour and the probable capacity for hard labour of a half-witted boy, a forlorn-looking widow, or a tottering old man' (Bates 1999, p.12). But as demand – and profits – mounted, cities and counties began to operate their own poorhouses.[6] There was continuity into the twentieth century in dumping the elderly in those institutions. After the First World War, public protest grew over overcrowding and conditions but reformers were mainly concerned with issues of social class. For example:

> Worthy people are thrown together with derelicts, with dope addicts, with prostitutes, bums, drunks – with whatever dregs of society happen to need the institution's shelter at the moment – people of culture and refinement were forced to live with the 'crude and ignorant and feebleminded'. (New York Commission on Old Age Security 1930, cited in Bates 1999, p.12)

In England, the Poor Relief Act of 1601 settled the responsibility of caring for the poor and infirm on the shoulders of each community. Based on a localised system of taxation, the law was intended to equalise the burdens of supportive services by requiring each community to contribute only its proportionate share of money and assistance.

Many of the inmates of the poorhouse and workhouse were elderly. This occupancy was ensconced with the Poor Law Amendment Act of 1834 which was designed to be repressive against the so-called 'able-bodied pauper'. Consequently, by the mid-nineteenth century, the majority receiving any kind of relief – outdoor or indoor – were either aged or infirm.

In traditional English society, according to the romantic view, each individual from the highest to the lowest had a position in the social order and an accompanying set of responsibilities. Among the responsibilities of the upper classes was the care in old age of those below them in the social hierarchy. As the demands of industrial capitalism for labour at open market values became the sole criterion of worth, older workers lost protection in their final years.

In pre-pension Britain (i.e. before 1908), the main source of financial aid for the destitute aged was the poor law. State policy toward the aged was comparatively lenient until 1871, when policies were implemented that reduced payments to them and forced children to maintain their aged parents. The threat of the workhouse loomed for those older people whose children refused to help maintain them. In Edwardian Britain, one in ten of the population aged over 75 would end their life in the workhouse, although the fear of incarceration in it affected a much larger number (Thompson, in Pelling and Smith 1991). Ironically, the caring, sharing, Victorian family coincided with an institutionalisation of the elderly as never before. The workhouse was designed with penality in mind, as a deliberate deterrent. That nineteenth century version of institutional care for the elderly was hardly a model of benefaction. It distinguished the deserving from the undeserving elderly, and generally treated even the former objects with minimal care and responsibility.

> ...with regard to the treatment of the aged and deserving poor, it has been felt that persons who have habitually led decent and deserving lives should, if they require relief in their old age, receive different treatment from those whose previous habits and character have been unsatisfactory and who have failed to exercise thrift. (Local Government Board Advice on the Treatment of Old People 1895)

In a review of mid-nineteenth century reform movements and charitable associations, Haber (1983) notes that the ideologically justified refusal of these organisations to help the old were based on several factors. The old were intractable – they would never change and therefore would never be worthy of instrumental charity. They had outlived their years of maximum productivity; thus charity would not restore them to productive, worthwhile lives. Many older people were forced into dying in institutions such as the almshouse and workhouse, even though they were not expressly designed for them.

During most of the nineteenth century in England, some 5 per cent of the over-65s received daily relief from residence in such institutions, and 20 per cent received outdoor support. But the problem of elderly poverty was much more extensive. Apart from those receiving private, charitable or religious assistance, in any one year some one-third of the 65-year-olds and over would be in receipt of some form of state subsidy. The major proportion were women: 'they are seldom in a position to make unaided an adequate provision for old age, the thought of which is present with them even in youth (Royal Commission on the Aged Poor 1895, pp.xvi–xvii).

The old and infirm formed the largest single workhouse group. But their special needs were rarely recognised, even though the 1834 Royal Commission on the Poor had recommended that 'the old might enjoy their indulgences'. As it was, they tended to be treated like other inmates, different from them chiefly in that only death would give them their discharge. Mere age was not usually interpreted as infirmity. Relief was divided into sustenance for those who could be kept in their own homes, and a workhouse minority who did not even have the basic resources of sustainable home or relatives. Outdoor relief was intended to keep the elderly half-dead as much as half-alive. Subsistence was defined in terms of rate-payers' needs rather than in terms of those of the elderly.

> His wife cannot be away from him long because he is an ill man. Five years ago he had been ill for seven years. It is eleven years by that date since he left off work and this man made an application to the Board. And he was defeated on the Board by one vote. It was a very hard case – allows him 1s and 6d a week: and the woman has to go about trying to get a few jobs in the week to help, then at night she has to be up a good part of the night along with the man: for a good many nights she does not get any sleep at all. The man has been a straightforward, honest, working man: he did his best, and he saved a little money, and he lived on it. He did his best and he made no application for relief till seven years afterwards; and when he has spent all, he made application and he was refused and it is impossible to pay his rent and live on 1s and 6d a week; or even if the sons should give a 1s it would take all their time; it would be like robbing their own families to do it.

> Qu. Except for the great dislike that all these honest men have to go in the workhouse, he would be better off in the workhouse than in a cottage, having that disease? No doubt he might but I believe he would rather die first. (Royal Commission on the Aged Poor 1895, para. 15634–15637)

> Mary Haines, all she was able to earn was 1s a week, going in next door to do a bit of waging for them. They took her for charity. Out of that 1s she had to pay 9d with her sister 1s 6d rent. If they did not give her anything, she had to go without. She was in a terrible state but...made application. Mr Bury allowed her 1s 6d a week but she was unable to get washing because she got older and weaker. That was all she got to live on. She is dead now and I believe there is a good many people would have been living today if it had not been for the policy of the Board. (Royal Commission on the Aged Poor 1895, para.5673)

Cuttle (1934) documented several cases of death-hastening through lack of outdoor relief, in recounting Essex experiences of the elderly at the turn of the century

1. December, 1889, Boreham, man, 73, lived twenty years on his own, called each morning by neighbour; on Christmas Eve not satisfied with reply, and later forced door. Man quite naked, on bundle of rags, very weak, cottage...most filthy; no furniture. Attended by neighbours, died next morning.

2. February 1910, Chignall, widow, 71, eccentric, feeble, alcoholic; lived nineteen years with son, sister visited weekly; would not have doctor. Had fallen on fender, so son tied her in chair. Constable found chest and neck bare, quite black, also hands, hair matted; room full of rags and rubbish; told son go get help, which he did; died five days later.

3. October, 1906, Vange, man, 70, cut throat; four shillings Relief; according to widow, four days together no food. Sons would help parents if lived in small cottage.

4. May 1908, High Ongar, woman, 85, in caravan many years, part-paralysed, refused enter infirmary; found dead.

5. September 1898, Margaret Rooshing, widow, 83, on Relief, refused enter Infirmary, fell downstairs. Three days later son visited her, next day found her dead by bedside; jury thought Guardians should have provided nurse.

6. March, 1899, Hatfield Peverel, woman, 81, house most filthy, death from fire, small lamp on bed. (p.363–365)

Policing of the elderly on behalf of the ratepayers, not supporting them, was the function of the overseer, as George Lansbury (a respondent to the Commission) points out:

Relieving officers, we do not need them. Their (function) is to make enquiries. If an applicant is three miles away, the relieving officer does not care about the journey.

Qu. Does the relieving officer carry the money to the old men? Decidedly not. They have to go for it. Three miles. They have to creep as well as they can. I have seen them on the road when I have been out with my cart, when they could scarcely get along; it was a great pity to see them out, let alone going to crawl along. (Royal Commission on the Aged Poor 1895, para. 15280–15288)

The workhouse, so-called 'indoor relief', was the final dumping ground for the elderly, the ossuary where they were supposed to die, out of sight. Sir George Crewe in an 1843 pamphlet describes it graphically: 'It is a melancholy sight to see the aged collected from thirty or forty parishes like a heap of cast-off, worn-out tools, to be buried alive in the solitude of a workhouse.' The workhouse was geronticide by degrees, death-hastening on a large scale, with the elderly poor segregated in a living charnel house.

I can never forget my first impression when I sat down among the old and infirm...the listless look, the dull vacuity – the lack of all interest except for the petty details of tea versus gruel, potatoes versus rice, the only object from their windows of moving interest, the parish hearse preparing to take away their former companions. There were several old women; all between 70 and 90, crouching round the fire, full of complainings of rheumatism-ache and that friends outside had forgotten them... (Quoted in Cuttle 1934)

For many the reward for a lifetime's labouring was the final indignity of waiting to die under a strict financial and physical regime imposed by their betters.

There is Thomas Dicken, a man about 73 or 74 years of age: he has been in a village club for 59 years; he has been an honest man and he did his best, and there is not a man living in the village who could say that he has squandered his money and his daughter has to keep him; she has to go out nursing and then when he is taken very ill, they have to send for her to go home. She is spending all the little she gets on her father, and they have nothing, only the workhouse to look forward to. He has outrun his club. It is over 18 months since he went to work. ...when he has been coming home from the Ironstone Pits; he has had to stand for three or four minutes to get his breath, and if you speak to him, he could not answer for a minute or two. He suffers from asthma and can only do certain things. He tried to work while it was cruel for him to go.

...the case of Richard Mill and wife? I was with her several nights. I sat up several nights with her before she died. They live in a cottage. They made application, but they had a paper left for to go into the house. The Relieving Officer came and took the particulars. She says 'I hope God will take me; I hope I shall never have to leave my cottage to go into the workhouse. We have been living together all these years and I do not want to be parted. I believe it is nothing only my being in want last winter'.

Qu: Are husband and wife parted in the workhouse? No. They never went. The woman died. (Royal Commission on the Aged Poor 1895, para.156545–156568)

Residing in the Workhouse meant being subject to a totally degrading experience. As in the case of primitive society geronticide (Chapter 3), rituals created liminal non-social persons, ready for physical death. Staff were taught to deny humanity – to create a liminal status – in that process.

The class of officials we have at workhouses – naturally they degenerate into a very bad kind of man and woman. These men consider that the inmates are a nuisance, and that they are to be treated as nuisances, and are to be made to feel that they are something else than other men and women. (*ibid.* para.13771)

Uniform clothing was of the cheapest variety, intended to deny individuality and personhood.

> They have no flannel, unless the doctor orders it, which he does not do, cotton shirts, in winter that is all. Qu. …materials not very thick or warm? Not at all thick, the same dress winter and summer. Qu. Do they have an overcoat in winter? No, Sir. Qu. A comforter? A neckerchief, that is all. Qu. Made of wool I suppose? No it would not be wool – cotton. The women will tell you that their clothing is grossly insufficient.

> The poor old folk are as plainly branded by their dress and in many cases more ashamed of it than a felon would be. … Even if they have decent clothes on entering, or should friends supply them, they are only permitted to wear parochial clothing and must walk about the streets labelled as paupers. I have known many refuse to avail themselves of the monthly holiday because they were ashamed to be seen so dressed. … The garb varies with the taste of the Guardians. In some unions a dirty brown is the colour…with brass or bone buttons; in others a gray not unlike that worn in our prisons and convict settlements. The clothes of the women fulfil the same purpose, a gray shawl, a black or brown straw bonnet, with parochial trimming, a dress which in material is generally unfit for the season…with comfortless shoes with little regard to fit. (*ibid.* para.753)

A variation on the convict theme was to provide shirts and dresses printed with broad vertical stripes in colour on a gray or dingy white background. One rural union (see Cuttle 1934) 'clothed all the inmates of the workhouse in a pronounced livery for their Sunday best, the men in white fustian and the women in blue serge, and expected them to go to church or chapel in procession'. Although the Poor Law Commissioners had told the unions as early as 1842 that workhouse uniform was not compulsory so long as the inmates' own clothes were removed, few Boards took advantage of the concession. Just as the elderly were expected to wear the same clothes as other inmates, so, too, few concessions were made over workhouse food. The only distinction was between the healthy, who received the standard 'house diet', and the sick, who could only receive extras prescribed by the doctor, no allowance being made for the failing digestions, crumbling teeth and fluctuating appetites of old age.

Medical advice was often ignored. In one workhouse (an anti-workhouse meeting was told in 1839), the doctor ordered port wine and sago for an elderly inmate with a bowel complaint, but 'the port was considered too dear and gooseberry wine was given' instead. Soon afterwards the patient died (cited in Cuttle 1934). A former workhouse employee described in 1872: 'Although old people needed frequent, small meals, "The last meal of the day" takes place at 5 p.m. and until 8 the next morning the majority, many of them more than 80 years of age, have to go without any nourishment.'

For most of the century there was a hard-fought campaign, waged on behalf of the inmates, to possess tea and sugar, to enable them to brew a hot drink. However, water was the principal, or sole, workhouse beverage. One regular visitor to a Devon workhouse described in 1857 how she had pleaded 'that there should be a cup and saucer and spoon allowed them, to take the place of the one tin, which looks more fit for my dog to drink its water from than for decent old folk to be reduced to use'. But the crockery and spoons she had sent to the workhouse had been 'returned to me as against the rules of the Poor Law to receive them' (Quoted in Longmate 1974). Workhouse tea, when supplied at all, was so often barely drinkable: the same container was used for it 'which has held gruel, suet pudding, meat or rice'.

A speaker at an 1857 Social Science conference described seeing an old, bedridden woman pick up the potatoes on her plate and gnaw them by hand as there was no one to cut them up for her, while the broth consisted of little more than hot water with oatmeal floating in it *(Social Science Conference* on the effects of the Poor Law, Birmingham, 1857, quoted in Cuttle (1934)). Four years later, in 1861, the medical officer of the Strand Union wrote to the Guardians reporting that 'large quantities of pudding and pea soup are left untouched, and subsequently thrown into the pig-tub' since 'very many of the aged and infirm' could not eat them (Quoted in Cuttle 1934). As late as 1900, one Poor Law Inspector recalled a workhouse where a visitor told him:

> They had two coppers so set that their tops were separated only by three inches. When I was there they were boiling clothes in one and soup in the other; and there were no lids on them. When the soup boiled over into the clothes I made no objection, but when the clothes boiled over into the soup, I would not stay to dinner. (Quoted in Longmate 1974)

Bureaucratic regulation snuffed out the person before the body, subtracting all individuality:

> I cannot conceive of anything more likely to rob a man of any individual feeling that may be left in him, after the age of sixty, than to be taken into a workhouse, and there drilled into the regulations and discipline that are carried on there. There is a strong dislike on the part of the poor to live by strict rules, having to regulate their life by bellcall; to have each day exactly mapped out for them, and every day exactly the same. (Royal Commission on the Aged Poor 1895, para.670)

All activities were public activities:

> Another cause of the dislike of inmates to enter the workhouse is the absolute want of privacy. The whole of a person's life must necessarily be lived in public and it is impossible for a man to get away from his companions in the workhouse. (*ibid.* para.675)

Living in a public space contained its own problems as opposed to the privacy of the household:

> There had been no alternative for him but going into the workhouse. That man had suffered from bronchitis and influenza, and he suffered very much from coughing, and he disturbed the inmates, and they threatened to throw him out of bed, and very much abused him; and he told me himself he would sooner go and die in a ditch than he would stop there in the house. (*ibid.* para.1607)

The deliberately degrading regime was intended to discourage elderly paupers, while simultaneously denying their personhood, encouraging them to be ready for death. As with clothing and food, the authorities were loath to make the old people's quarters more comfortable for fear that the idea of 'pampering the paupers' might spread like an epidemic.

> Parish overseers who visited the Holborn workhouse during the 1830s...found forty females, of ages varying from forty to eighty, confined in a small room, seven feet nine inches in height, several feet below the surface of the earth, and built over a large sewer, the smell from which was very offensive. The room was...exceedingly dark, and these aged females were confined eleven hours out of the twenty-four, at very severe work, pulling wool for mattresses. (Quoted in Longmate 1974)

There was little change over the century as conditions in 1872 made plain:

> Some are set to pick oakum, to sweep yards, peel potatoes, etc. Whilst others congregate in the day rooms which are provided... These rooms are occasionally below ground, dark, damp and dismal...one of which I had charge for six months contained fifty beds and was more like an immense barn than anything else... Many of the occupants of this room were bedridden and, to shelter themselves from the cold winds, I have often seen them huddle themselves under the clothes; the variety of coughs was quite a study; not only were the sufferers kept awake, but from the incessant and various noises produced by the arthritic and bronchitic others were prevented from sleeping. (Quoted in Longmate 1974)

The Birmingham conference 1857 heard of workhouses where there were still no seats in the wards and where, after working all day, the old people had to sit in the yard or on the stairs. Those patients able to 'sit round the walls, vacant and dreary'. 'None of these poor had even a box or drawer to call their own.' (Quoted in Cuttle 1934) Conditions had not changed much by the early 1900s:

> At Chelmsford the old people were, after 1901, allowed to walk in the garden until 5 pm, but they still had to go to bed at 7 pm and the first garden seats were not provided until 1905. At Ongar, free access to the garden was not allowed until 1907. At Maldon, in 1901, an inspector found the old men still sitting 'bolt upright' on hard forms. (Quoted in Quadagno 1982, p.73)

These conditions were not an accident, but functioned to discourage some and to pass other elderly quickly, on their way to the other side, at minimum effort and expense.

Hatred of the workhouse was intense. Many preferred their own choice of death to workhouse immolation.

> Robert Smith, 71, and his wife, 67, were forced through hunger to go into the workhouse, because they had got no means of living. Friends kept the cottage on in the hope that the Guardians would reconsider the cases, as they were respected in Draughton, and the people felt that it was too hard for them to break up the home and go into the workhouse, but as they had nothing to eat, they were glad to go, and after a time they came back to see if they could do, and in the two times of their going into the workhouse, they were not in above nine months, and they both died, and they said before they went in, they dreaded leaving their own home to go in, but they were forced to do it. (Royal Commission on the Aged Poor 1895, para.15688)

> She said 'I would rather die in the street than I will go back to their union'. The farmer kept her all night and fixed her to go back, drive her over in the trap on Sunday morning, it was hardly so long as a fortnight before they took her as a corpse to her own village. (*ibid.* para.15680)

> There was an old man who applied for relief there, and the Chairman of the Board of Guardians said he would not allow him any relief. [A farmer] said that the man could do part work for him and with some outdoor relief, could manage comfortably. The chairman said he would not allow any relief and told the old man he should go to the workhouse, and he refused to go. So the chairman said he would have to go in by such a morning, they would fetch him at nine o'clock, and he was to be ready; and they went to the man. And he had hanged himself at the back of the premise. (*ibid.* para.15187)

Even in death, the elderly poor were often regarded as a possible charge on the rates, as waste material, detritus that needed disposal with the garbage.

> Samuel Brain died in Northampton Infirmary. His friends were unable to bury him. They applied to the receiving officer for a coffin but were refused. The corpse lay in Northampton Infirmary for a week and they were requested to fetch it away. The relieving officer, when the daughter asked what was she to do, said that she might get a sheet and sew it up in it. (*ibid.* para.15696)

> Symonds was unable to bury his wife, did not know what to do. He had not got any money. The relieving officer said he could not do anything and could not give him any advice what to do. He went back to the Guardians and the Guardians said they did not know what to do, and he made application to the magistrates and the magistrates told him they were unable to assist him. But he had better make another application to the sanitary inspector (who) wrote back that he was

unable to do anything because while the body was in the house, it was a private nuisance and not a public nuisance. He said that if the corpse were lifted out in the street, he could give order for it to be buried. (*ibid.* para.15701)

Attitudes to elderly parents in the labouring class may have contained sympathy. But they were driven also by hard economics. It was not a change in attitudes to their kin that may have affected the disposal of the elderly – attitudes were one thing, financial exigencies another.

> The Guardians having in many instances the greatest difficulty in obtaining contributions from their sons towards the maintenance of their pauper parents, the money often being given in a grudging spirit, because it merely saved the rates. (*ibid.* para.17564)

Attitudes of those who controlled the destiny of the elderly poor contained a mixture of supercilious patronage and rare insights into their structural location. Ageist pathologising contrasted with a recognition that the position of the elderly was structurally created.

> In case of a number who apply for relief the factor is attributable to a lack of mental vigour, to a lack of mental power, to a lack of self-reliance, attributable to improvident habits and a want of training in early life. (*ibid.* para.3249)

> Old age brings with it that lack of power and lack of will, which is necessary to keep people away from the workhouse. (*ibid.* para.3250)

The discovery that at least one in three citizens reaching the age of 70 had to seek relief finally convinced most Guardians that it was not only the thriftless elderly who became 'indoor paupers' and there were some minor reforms. In 1893, the Local Government Board advised the Workhouse Guardians that they could allow elderly inmates 'dry tea', with milk and sugar, to brew their own drinks. In 1895 and 1896 there were more radical reforms. Workhouses were instructed that the elderly should not be regulated in the same way as other inmates: the workhouse uniform would not be required, and that most old people should be allowed to go out for walks. By the 1900s, the workhouses allowed those over 65 to get up and go to bed when they liked, and provided them with locked cupboards for their possessions. Finally, elderly men and women were allowed to mix (Longmate 1974).

Anderson (1980), in his discussion of changes in the British family life cycle from the mid-eighteenth century to the mid-twentieth century, has noted that increased dependency was correlated with conflict between young and old. By the 1900s, the elderly comprised a larger share of the total population and were living longer. They had also had fewer children to look after them. The potential burden of elder care for individual children increased substantially. But, as we illustrate above, while economic exigencies might increase the burden of a grand-parent, this in itself is not indicative of attitude change. Reductions in support to the aged coupled with the threat of the workhouse increased the number of institutionalised aged, and forcing kin to contribute to the support of an aged parent raised family tensions. When the Old Age Pensions Act was passed in 1906, it reduced interfamilial tension by allowing the generations to function on the basis of mutual interdependency rather than one-sided dependency. Anderson concluded that the view that state-provided income maintenance undermines family relationships is false and that defining strong family relationships in terms of financial assistance demonstrates a lack of understanding of the basis of kinship interaction.

Witchcraft: An illustration of the treatment of elderly poor women

Poverty was one major schism that ensured continuity in the disposal of part of the elderly population historically. As noted in Chapter 3, gender – when coupled with the above – was a second. Gender had differential effects historically (Pelling and Smith 1991). Images of them stem from the benign ('dear old thing') to the malign ('scheming hag'). But they were often not the powerless submissive creatures that have often been portrayed in the literature. Indeed, there is some evidence that historically a woman's power may sometimes have increased rather than decreased as she grew older – especially in the practice as opposed to the principle of authority and power (Cool and McCabe 1990).

But older women present a historical paradox of survival. Women can appear as lonely survivors, an effect of unequal ages of marriage, or a result of the internal migration processes which disturbed local sex ratios with the loss of male support. There is evidence from the seventeenth century onwards of women surviving longer than men and therefore becoming more potentially subject to maltreatment, and to encouragement to seek an alternative world.

Nowhere is this clearer than in the phenomenon of witchcraft. In the sixteenth and seventeenth centuries, elderly women were especially vulnerable to accusations of witchcraft. As the work of historians from the early modern period onwards has shown, the rural elderly (especially elderly women) were prone to systematic violence and neglect. Rural elderly were generally socially disposable. But when they were female they could have a more deadly label applied.

Witchcraft records from both Britain and America provide harsh accounts of the victimisation of elderly indigent females. Allegations of witchcraft were an early form of marginalisation, offering easy scapegoating during times of natural disaster. McFarland's (1970) description of the experience of single elderly women in an Essex village demonstrates the extent to which such women were readily blamed by local communities for their calamities. Denunciations escalated during times of economic dearth. They were the most dependent upon community support and therefore, contrarily, the most subject to victimisation.

On one side, a person's reputation for witchcraft might be crucial in ensuring that she received relief. On the other, allegations could be used as a means of denying relief to the old and infirm.

Fischer (1978) notes that such treatment could also affect elderly men. But the majority of those killed during witchcraft epidemics in Europe between the thirteenth and fifteenth centuries were middle aged and older females (Bever 1984). The sinister nature of old women is reflected in numerous folktales.

> An old woman, promised a pair of shoes by the devil if she could bring discord to a happily married couple, told the wife that she could increase her husband's love by cutting a few hairs from his chin. She then told the husband that his wife was plotting to cut his throat while he slept. The man pretended to sleep. Seeing his wife silently approaching with a razor, he struck her dead with a stick. ('An Old Woman Sows Discord', quoted in Ashliman 1999)

Elderly women were the particular victims of pauperism, neglect and death-hastening. In their later years, when not hounded as witches, unless they possessed some family means of sustenance they would normally be shipped over the parish boundaries. 'When the status from being married was lost, the effects were often devastating.' (Steinmetz 1988 p.42) Even when the witchcraft panics died out, more specific hostilities existed, as in the frequent cases in which older widows who managed to remarry were attacked or shamed by gangs of youths.

Gender exacerbated socio-economic divisions. There was no golden age for the poverty-stricken elder woman. While direct killings – such as drowning witches on the ducking stool or immolation on a ceremonial pyre – may have been uncommon, less direct forms of cruelty contributed to lives that were nasty, brutish, and often foreshortened.

Inequality and uneven exposure to geronticide

It is possible that the well-being of the prosperous elderly may have increased throughout the process of industrialisation. The evidence is that from primitive society onwards, being relatively wealthy and being male were often primary determinants of a secure long life. There were exceptions, as in the cases of women with special powers and status. But generally, the continuity of social history reflects that marginalised elderly have always been the subject of geronticidal practices, direct or indirect. Veneration in old age in pre-industrial Western culture was generally reserved for a wealthy masculine elite.

Changing attitudes towards the elderly as a result of modernisation have sometimes been presented as an irresistible, and irreversible process, that once set in motion pushes relentlessly onwards, overwhelming rural peasant societies, transforming them into a uniform urban stereotype. This is far too simple a presentation. No one believes that all peasant societies were the same. There will always be lags and stops, perhaps even reversals. There are considerable differ-ences in the speed of social change in different societies, and there are wide differ-ences within societies varying by region, social class, by gender, and often by ethnic identity. Similarly, in industrial society, the experience of the elderly is not homogeneous – the elderly poor as we consider in today's care institutions (Chapter 5) have constantly been subject to the death-hastening process. Inde-pendently of any postulated changes in attitudes towards the elderly generally, those without an independent income and property were dependent structurally on historical process and on the behaviour of others (Biggs *et al.* 1995) and frequently condemned to an isolated wasting death.

Modernisation may be irrelevant to the status of the old-old, while in other ways it worsens their plight (Logue 1990). There seems to have been a remarkable consistency in how society deals with dependency in old age. Death-hastening by direct means may not be preferred but happens relatively often nonetheless, while more passive indirect forms of death-hastening are apparently timeless and universal (Logue 1990).[7] The fatal exposure of the elderly in any one period depends on a cluster of institutional factors. First, those who control material resources, unless open to serious challenge, can withstand being pushed aside better than those without such resources. Second, from primitive times to the present, some power was maintained by elderly people in possession of strategic knowledge – from aboriginal erudition on the location of waterholes, through the soothsayers of ancient Rome and Greece, to the elderly hermit sage of medieval England. This was especially the case where traditional religion was strong and emphasised elements such as ancestor worship. Third, it relates to the predomi-nant modes and styles of economic productivity. As we argued in the last chapter, there is an indirect relationship between the mode of production and exposure to geronticide. Fourth, bonds of mutual interdependence are guaranteed. Thus in the example quoted by De Beauvoir (1973), where children were treated as unwanted by their elders, reciprocation may be the result. The exposure to geronticide also depended upon the degree of exposure to intra-familial conflict within the wider social and community controls.

Notes

1   This episode appears in an addition to the book of Daniel in the Old Testament Apocrypha.

2   Quoted by Pat Barker in *Union Street* (1982).

3   A contrary view of relative financial independence is also possible. Elders moved out of the households of younger kin and into households of their own, reducing daily contact between the generations and (hypothetically) the possibilities of conflict.

4   For a concise critique of the modernisation thesis approach to the elderly, see Gratton (1986).

5   For a detailed discussion of the experiences of the elderly in the United States poorhouse and almshouse systems, see Haber (1983, 1994) and Dahlin (1994).

6   The expression 'over the hill' comes from Will M. Carleton's ballad (1871) that depicts the plight of an old woman cast out by her children to live in a government-run workhouse. A revised

version (1874) concludes with an old man's lament: *For I'm old and I'm helpless and feeble, / The days of my youth have gone by, / Then over the hill to the poorhouse, / I wander alone there to die.* (Quoted in Scott and Wishy 1975).

7   Logue (1990) also notes that one paradox of modernisation has been that medical technology may have increased the lifespan of many elderly, at the cost of a decrease in the quality of their final days. Perhaps, she argues, the unforeseen cost of technological intrusion may be one of increasing the perception of the elderly as a burden.

CHAPTER FIVE

Death by Degrees
Bureaucratisation in Care Institutions

Swan visited the county records office to review the woman's death certificate and those of others who had died while residing at Creekside and other nearby nursing homes. She was startled to find ten questionable causes of death listed on the first 30 she reviewed. 'They'd listed malnutrition, dehydration, bedsores and urinary-tract infections as causes of death,' Swan says. 'These nursing homes were killing people.' Nearly 22,000 of the nursing-home deaths were attributed to lack of food or water, infections or internal obstructions – all preventable (excluding deaths if the deceased suffered from other ailments that exacerbated those four causes). ('In possibly thousands of cases, nursing home residents are dying from lack of food and water and the most basic level of hygiene.' *Time Magazine,* 27 October 1997)

The owner of a private nursing home has been told that he should pay for an extension to a local graveyard before being granted permission to take on more elderly residents. Parish councillors feared that more elderly residents in the village would place a strain on the church cemetery. Jeremy Chamberlayne, the parish council chairman, said, 'This is not some grisly tax'. ('Nursing home strains graveyard.' *Electronic Telegraph,* 19 October 1995)

The foreword to Diamond's ethnographic study notes no evidence of malignancy in the death-hastening process. In the nursing home, Charon, the ferryman, has a smiling face.

As a participant-observer, he did not discover a melodramatic snake-pit of violence and corruption. Residents have birthday parties. Nice people do volunteer work. Doctors ask kindly questions when they check patients and their charts on a monthly visit. Rather than hell (the author) finds a bureaucratic purgatory run for profit. (Diamond 1992, pp.ix–x)

Other commentaries handle the resort to the care and nursing home for the elderly with a grisly humour.

CUT THE HIGH COST OF DISPOSING OF YOUR LOVED ONES

Our philosophy of loving care is not based on antiseptic floors, lily-white linen, fancy china, or the chilly outdoors, but on giving the old folks what's good for them. After all, you would just as soon not have them around *your* house, and we constantly try to keep them uppermost in mind. You want to keep the cost down, don't you? The old folks are content with just getting by – they wouldn't want to be a burden on you. Think how happy it makes them when they receive their knockout drugs at night. When they wake up in the morning, they realize they've spared you the costs of an all-night nurse. And when they feel those bedsores…it's a sharp reminder of the money it's saving you for a nurse to turn them over. We keep supplied with A & D Ointment – tests have shown that it can pull the old flesh back over those exposed bones in a matter of a few months. They really don't mind the spankings for their bed-wettings. After all, it's a form of personal care and involvement. Loneliness is something you won't have to worry about, either. It's always been our policy to keep several of the old folks in a room. This way, they share their experiences with each other, the little coughings and sneezings, the use of the bedpans, etc. Yes, you'll find peace of mind when you take the high cost out of providing living care, here at the Restful Arms Home in Golden Sunny Acres. (Quoted from Garvin and Burger 1965, pp.43–44)

Though grown-up now, the kids still loved their father…a wise and noble man, versed in the ways of the world, knowing and understanding. But they decided to put him in a home anyway because he smelt funny. (Popular story, source unknown)

Introduction: The bureaucratisation of death

The final approach to explaining the attitudes towards the treatment of the elderly draws on sociological theories of organisation and of bureaucratisation. Within the rule-bound context, the disposal of the elderly has simply come to be itemised as a logistical problem to be dealt with efficiently through fixed procedures. Disposing of older people in Western society in the year 2000 has been reduced to a function of the machinery of state and private institutional 'care' facilities – the approved organisational wastebins for the aged. Death hastening within this perspective has little to do with the exigencies of the demographic time bomb. It is only indirectly related to economic pressures. Nor does it fit neatly within explanations of wider social and industrial change. Geronticide, today, is the way complex organisations in advanced society dispose of the elderly in terms of the criteria of efficiency and of organisational effectiveness clinically, in non-partisan fashion, without regard to human selves.

When organisations grow in complexity, when role differentiation extends, and when tasks become routinised, mechanised and simplified, the elderly are disposed of without any evaluation of their social worth. Aged death is a product of industrial society and has to be dealt with by bureaucratic and effective procedures. W.H. Auden (1969) has noted in rhyme how the new cohorts of elderly are stowed away, anonymous, numerically defined, as surplus baggage, not wanted on the final voyage (p.645).

This chapter documents the way this process of bureaucratisation and routinisation has created a process of clinical death-hastening in care institutions. While no evil or selfish intent by others may be a part of modern care, nursing and care institutions routinely condemn the elderly to an early, sometimes painful, and normally isolated, early death. Their liminal status is beyond the primary institutional function of medicine. Hospitals are about curing people; death and chronic illness represent failure. The care of the dying and of the elderly may be left out of the equation when decisions are made. Few care institutions are staffed by ogres. Presumably rarely is death a result of ill intent. What indeed, the question is asked, are the alternatives?

However, in this chapter we demonstrate that a key feature of elderly care and nursing homes, as well as of the funeral industry, is the way they make death ordinary and banal. Elderly death is not allowed to interrupt the business of life. The liminal elderly has already lost personhood and is to be transformed into a burial or crematorium residuum. We also hope to show that entering the institution means losing all those features of self that allow elderly persons some individuality, and to be a member of humankind. He or she, by the bureaucratic process innate to the total institution, is transformed into a numbered bed or room, and loses most decision-making rights. Several ethnographic studies document this transformation process as the elder undergoes the status passage from person to liminal to deceased.

In any case, being in care is being subject to a range of other death-hastening experiences. The elder may enter with second-hand memories of the workhouse – furnishings and resources may have changed, but its function of preparing the elder to die has not. Few doctors deliberately kill the elderly, few nurses and care assistants, private owners and state home managers contribute directly to death – but sins of omission (death-hastening) are routine.

Also in this chapter we see how regulatory and inspection agencies ensure the efficiency of disposal by the institution in processing the elderly according to hygienic and medical rules, into losing their remaining personhood. Abuse from physical injury (with the best of intentions as the elderly person is breakfasted for his or her own good, or strapped to the bed to avoid night-time perambulations) may occur, but together with other forms of criminal victimisation of residents it is rarely subject to criminal justice processes.

Finally, we discover how bureaucratisation can be conflated with political economy. Care institutions are frequently profit-making agencies. Elderly persons are units on a financial calculus.

Modern societies mediate elderly deaths through bureaucratisation. A central principle of that schema is the ordering of regularly occurring events, as well as extraordinary ones, into predictable and routinised procedures. Max Weber (1968) described how bureaucratisation in the West proceeded by removing the social functions from the family and household and implanting them in specialised institutions autonomous of kinship considerations. Thus, amongst other functions, the modern care home is an organisation committed to the specialist handling of death. It contains through isolation and reduces through orderly procedures, the disturbance and disruption that are associated with the death crisis. The affairs of death, like other societal disruptions, are transferred to science and its representatives – the medical profession and the rationalised, organised hospital and care home. Illich (1991) has sardonically described the recent history of such institutions. The hospital, he says, which at the very beginning of the nineteenth century had become a place for diagnosis, was now turned into a place for teaching. Soon it would become a laboratory for experimenting with treatments and towards the turn of the century a place concerned with therapy. Later still, 'the pesthouse has been transformed into a compartmentalised repair shop. (p.163)

When this repair function failed, it developed techniques for disposing of those it deemed too costly to restore.

Care of the dying, the liminal, the nearly-dead, and especially the elderly who are concluding their life course, is allocated to specialist institutions in the same way that the eventual death and body disposal is handled clinically and efficiently by the 'funeral industry'. As Jessica Mitford demonstrates in her sardonic critique of that industry in the United States, we seek to make sense of the way elderly people are dispatched without emotion as the embodiment of machine produced and terminated products. Death has become one of the great taboos of the twentieth century, but is to be handled by appropriate consumer mechanisms. Hence an advert for funeral services (quoted in Mitford (1978)):

> Chambers' caskets are just fun,
> Made of sandalwood and pine
> If your loved ones have to go,
> Call Columbus 690.
> If your loved ones pass away,
> Have them pass the Chambers' way.
> Chambers' customers all sing:
> 'Death, oh death, where is thy sting?'

'Unlike the distortion and vulgarities of the funeral-home industry, the "before-funeral home industry" raises issues that go to the very roots of social justice.' (Garvin and Burger 1965, p.12) We do our best to immunise ourselves from the brutal facts of dying, death and disposal. Euphemisms abound. A pet, too old and frail to live much longer, is 'put to sleep'. Few people die at home. Funeral 'homes' turn the act of mourning a 'departed' loved one into a sanitised reunion of family and friends. The deceased are not 'dead', they have merely 'passed on' (Mitford 1978). Whereas only a few generations ago most people died at home or were brought into the home if they died elsewhere, today hospices 'care' for the terminally ill, and care homes and nursing homes process those near the end of life.

Aldous Huxley satirically captures the way in which elderly deaths are concealed behind more 'positive' images with his description of a Hollywood cemetery full of statues of young, vital female nudes (in *After Many a Summer* (1965)):

The elderly are more and more segregated from communities and located in institutions for their age group such as day centres, and care and nursing homes, where death can be re-moulded for the consumer. As with other forms of production, dying and death industries (increasingly corporate bureaucracies) are based on the separation of the workplace from the household. Together, they manage the crisis of dying. The mortuary industry (whose establishments are normally called 'homes' in deference to past tradition) prepares the waste product – the elderly body – for cremation or burial and makes many of the funeral arrangements. But often disposal may be out of sight, out of mind, as institutions designed for other purposes are cheaply modified to serve as human dustbins. Buildings devised for different purposes, and awkwardly updated for the new safety and hygiene standards, are frequently the final resting place for those for whom there is no economic product in the dying process (Help the Aged 1999). There are still several Victorian workhouses operating as care homes for the elderly.

> What were older people to do if there comes a time when, even though they are not seriously ill, they can no longer fend for themselves? For those who have families or financial reserves they can draw upon, there are a number of alternatives that may be pursued. There is, however, an undeniable segment of the older population who has neither family ties nor adequate resources. For them, entering an institution may be the only possible way of getting the help they need. (Stannard 1978, p.121)

The elderly may be unable to absorb without trauma the tedium of demographically unprecedented decades of isolated companionship, which makes them more and more dependent on large, impersonal, bureaucratic institutions for even the minimal amounts of that needed support (Stannard 1978). But machines break down. The brand new world of clinical machinery is not infallible. It may, in fact, create its own dichotomies – as in the 'care versus profit' debate and the dichotomy between healing and managing dying. Death can be expedited for many organisational reasons, factors related to the distribution of power and resources in care agencies.

Some elderly have worse experiences than do others. Changes in life-extending technology, the severity of illness concentrated in particular local authority homes, a dearth of physicians sensitive to elderly needs, and bureaucratic rules over timetables and procedures that are efficient for the institution but irrelevant to client needs – all contribute to an unequal processing of the elderly (Bennett and Kingston 1993).

Dying in 'care'

A lingering death in a nursing home remains one of the biggest fears of the elderly. Alice Bell, the elderly widow in Pat Barker's *Union Street*, had no doubt about her fate. Faced with imminent transfer from the terraced house that she had lived in for many years and where she was in increasing need of personal care, she made her own decision. For her, institutional care 'would always be the workhouse: the place paupers' funerals started from' (1983, p.233). While she had breath in her body, she would resist ending up in a pauper's coffin, let them talk her into the workhouse. A lonely death on the town moor was preferable.

Opposition to residential care is in part a recognition of their bureaucratic function of disposal. In a 1997 survey, 30 per cent of those polled said they would rather perish than live in a nursing home.[1] A UK survey reflects the same views. A third of people over 50 years fear going into a residential home 'under any circumstances'. Only 7 per cent said they would expect their children to care for them and 59 per cent stated that the elderly should only go into care homes if they suffered from dementia or were too frail to care for themselves. A third said they would only enter a residential home if their partners could go with them and 47 per cent that they would go only if they became a burden to their children.[2] Elderly people could not normally be expected to live reasonable lives in such places; and few actually want to go into residential care (Wagner Report 1988), a view reinforced by reports of poor practice and standards of care (United Kingdom Central Council 1994).[3] In Britain, some 70 per cent of all deaths now occur in hospital or care home (Biggs 1996).

Death-hastening by illness is much more common amongst the residential population. Elderly people in care are twice as likely to suffer from depression as those living in their own homes.[4] Around 5 per cent of the population suffer from depression rising to 15 per cent of older people and more than 30 per cent in care homes.[5] Further, the Secretary of State for Health, Frank Dobson, said:

Frail old people are vulnerable to catch anything that is going and we know that 20% of elderly people in hospital suffer from something they catch while they are there…because hospitals are dangerous places full of people exuding germs.[6]

Elderly patients may become even more ill than before they went in for treatment simply because they have been in hospital (wrongly prescribed drugs, hospital-borne infection, and personnel mistakes.)[7] They are also peculiarly susceptible to be targeted by depredators. Patients in residential and nursing homes are easy victims.

A Danish nurse was charged with murdering 22 nursing home patients between 1994 and 1997. Police say the alleged victims, fifteen women and seven men aged between 65 and 97, died after overdose of Kettogan, a morphine-based painkiller used to make terminally ill patients more comfortable. The nurse had originally been sacked on the basis of allegations of theft of £60,000.[8]

In the United States, although only 4–5 per cent of the elder population will be in a nursing home at any one time, they accounted for about 20 per cent of all deaths in that age group. In 1996, about 16 million people received care in some 16,800 nursing homes. Approximately 48 per cent of residents have dementia, and 83 per cent are extremely impaired needing help with three or more activities of daily living (e.g. using toilet, dressing and mobility). Just 45 per cent of deaths of those aged 85 and older took place in a hospital. But these old-old were less likely than the average to die at home too, because 39 per cent died in a nursing home.

Of all Californians who died in nursing homes from 1986 to 1993, more than 7 per cent had died of neglect – lack of food, water, untreated bedsores or other generally preventable ailments, as in the following UK example:

Henry Baker, 89, transferred to a geriatric ward at Thanet General Hospital in Margate from the medical ward. According to his daughter, 'when we arrived on the ward, we were shocked by the conditions. The filth and the neglect was truly awful. My father was in great distress; he was unable to attract anyone's attention because the bell was out of reach. He was lying in a soaking wet bed and had been so for some time. He was freezing cold; when he asked for an extra blanket, he had been snapped at and told "I'm too busy, you'll have to wait". There were soiled pyjamas left on the end of the bed and there were dozens of soiled tissues by the locker where he had tried to mop up because he was wetting himself.'

She claimed that the severe infection which was the main cause of her father's death was caused or exacerbated by the unhygienic conditions: 'I believe these patients were the forgotten people, they were dumped there and treated as subhuman'.[9]

If the rest of America's 1.6 million nursing home residents are dying at the same rate as those in the Californian homes, 35,000 are dying prematurely or in unnecessary pain or both every year. A study by the Food and Drug Administration (cited in *Times Magazine* 1997) found that while nursing home residents account for just 2.4 per cent of cases of food-borne illness in the United States, they accounted for 19.4 per cent of deaths from those illnesses. The report also noted that more than a hundred deaths occurred each year in nursing homes, hospitals and private homes due to improper use of patient restraints.

Making ready for death: the community–institution divide

There has been limited research on the institutional handling of death since Goffman's (1961) pioneering account on dehumanising relations in 'total institutions'. Nursing and care homes may include several total institution features, peculiarities that frequently render the resident powerless (Rich 1996). Such institutional features for the elderly may include:

- entry rituals that strip an individual's private identity, and categorise and process an individual's life

- all aspects of life conducted in the same place – from toileting to recreation

- a single, non-specific authority that creates a command/obey dichotomy

- phases of daily life conducted in the company of others who are treated alike – residents treated as residents independent of individuality

- frequent violations of individual privacy – restricted space and time leading to degradations

- small group of staff whose primary duty is to ensure compliance with institutional rules, regulations and policies – organisations functioning by rules, not by principles of care

- activities brought together into a single plan designed to fulfil the official aim of the institution.

Entry rituals that strip an individual's private identity

De Beauvoir (1973) describes this process as the compulsory metamorphosis from human being to liminal object. Nurse and care workers often talk to new residents in ways that foster dependence rather than independence. A kind of 'baby-talk' is introduced – caregivers often believe that non-baby-talk or a typical adult interaction pattern is not as effective as baby-talk in achieving nurturing goals. Although elderly residents may find such patronising speech demeaning, they may accommodate it by eventually responding to it in dependent ways –

such as passively accepting the demands of the carers (Petronio and Kovachls 1997). Such dependent behaviour from elders is frequently perceived by carers as supportive behaviour; whereas independent actions by elders may be disregarded by caregivers. This dependency discourse and script is the norm rather than the exception to which a new entrant must be socialised. Identity disappears and dehumanising categories are imposed. 'Go to 246 and make sure it's clean. His family is on its way.'[10]

One social anthropological study (Maxwell 1979) considers the ecological segregation of supposedly hopelessly impaired old people in total institutions. It suggests that their isolation in care and nursing homes consigns them to a doomed role, rather than a sick role. Maxwell caricatures this dying process for an elderly man referred to hospital for observation.

> The long-term elderly resident has been in the ward for some time, without incurring official notice. One day, complaining of chest pain, the patient is suddenly at the centre of official attention. He is wheeled into a smaller room whose walls are lined with complicated electronic equipment, and finds himself in an oxygen tent with strange suction cups attached to various parts of his body. Medical staff constantly interrupt him by listening to his heartbeat and give bland answers to his increasingly urgent requests for information. Nurses stare at him through a window, obviously discussing him. The other patients in his room, one by one, disappear from sight behind a crowd of strangers dressed in green or white, and are finally wheeled out, covered by sheets. Once in a while, a nurse leans in and asks our patient 'Are you still feeling OK?'. (Maxwell 1979, p.7)

How impaired does an old person need to be before he is unable to realise that – when he or she is transferred to an obscure back area, away from the busy ward routine and to the company of others who cannot speak, walk, groom or toilet themselves – his assigned status is hopeless? The dying person learns his or her role on entering the dying institution. He or she rapidly becomes exempt from such normal role responsibilities as dressing himself, toileting routines and so on. Behaviour and attitudes change as the elderly person is passed into the liminal state (Diamond 1992).

All aspects of life conducted in the same place

Privacy disappears. 'Elders often have to give up privacy of their bodies to accommodate health conditions.' (Petronio and Kovachls 1997, p.115) Free movement – for those who can – is discouraged as an encumbrance to institutional exigencies. De Beauvoir quotes an earlier Paris establishment:

> Each inmate had a bed, a bedside table, an armchair and a little locker. It was there that the inmates spent the whole of their day. They did not even have a refectory. Their meals were served on a little table next to the bed. There was no liv-

ing-room apart from a little place so uncomfortable that nobody went there, not even to see their visitors. (De Beauvoir 1973, p.145)

A single, non-specific authority

In Diamond's (1992) ethnographic study of an old people's home, minute, often unwritten, rules detailed the authority structure. One learns the skills and efforts required to practise a life of patienthood. People had to learn to eat on schedule food that had been planned and prepared elsewhere.

> If the butter was missing, the coffee cold or the milk warm, they had to learn the chain of command to request corrective action. 'Nurse I didn't get any hot dog in my bun.' 'Nurse...got any second helpings?' 'Just wait a minute, will you.' was the regular response from nursing assistants, themselves enwrapped in a tight chain of command and having little say in the production of meals, or in the number of people hired to help serve them. (p.95)

Residents could not decline food out of choice – they could only 'refuse to eat', a medical category and to be recorded as such. In the process, residents were transformed from acting beings into beings acted-upon, defined in terms of the institution's needs rather than of their own. Food may be 'dumped' on lockers and out of reach only to be taken away by assistants or catering staff with a bright 'Not feeling hungry today, again then?'[11] (Diamond 1992, p.145).

Authorities that are not present may prescribe drugs, and the nursing role is to dispense the drugs. Both parties to the exchange have to disregard the practical needs of the situation and figure out how to live and work around the documents that determine elderly care (Diamond 1992). In the UK, there are reports[12] of old people being given drugs to counteract side-effects of other drugs which they should not have been given in the first place. Elderly people in nursing or residential homes were prescribed an average of three to four drugs but some took as many as ten a day. When they were admitted to hospital it was found that one in three drugs could be stopped without detriment to the patient (*ibid.*).

In the Diamond (1992) study, staff schedule daily tightly routines with little variation permitted – duty labour rotas determine care process. The organisation derives part of its legitimacy from bureaucratic timetabling – such as 'rising' at 7am, because this is the hospital-like notion of order. Breakfast, for example, is fixed according to time of shift changeover but patients are persuaded that the fixed time of rising – no matter how early – is for their own good.

Medical and organisational discourse ritually passes the resident on to death not to health. Practitioners appear on set dates for specific rituals.

> The heart doctor came to check the hearts [on one particular day], on another the foot doctor to see the feet, and on a third the dentist to survey the teeth. They signed the charts, having visited the heart, the feet, and the teeth. 'Minor'

incidents were kept minor otherwise a formal report had to be written for which the home might be liable. Residents had to be confirmed as role players in a dying institution. 'Frances, the new admission, is having delusions again. I want one of you aides to keep checking her reality orientation, and try to calm her down.' Disease labels, such as Alzheimer's, were readily applied to those who did not adapt to the institutional roles. Medications were dealt at fixed intervals and could not be refused – every resident had a drug regimen. Records of such drug requirements, like records of their eating and sleeping, came to constitute the patient on the conveyor line to death. (Diamond 1992 p.104)

Daily life conducted in the company of others who are treated alike

The 'new girl' is seized with horror at the idea that she will never have a moment to herself again. 'I have always hated having people look at me,' she says to herself. 'Being stared at was always a torment to me.' From now on all the actions of her life, including dying, are to be carried out before witnesses, often unkind or at least critical. 'Never alone – it's dreadful.'[13]

Violations of individual privacy

Entry to nursing or care home is a loss of self-determination. Once in the institution, elders may be subject to non-negotiable restrictions on almost every activity of their daily lives. Eating, sleeping and going outside are timetabled – little privacy or control over who enters rooms, no choice of who helps them to toilet (Bould, Sanborn and Reif 1990). Elders often have to give up privacy for their bodies to accommodate health conditions (Petronio and Kovachls 1997). Residents often find that they need help from caregivers to use the bathroom, get dressed and bath – to obtain any privacy they must depend on the caregivers to allow them the means of maintaining privacy control. They may be assigned a roommate necessitating the negotiation of chosen seclusion.

They lose intimacy because they may require nurses to read their correspondence aloud. They must select only cherished possessions to bring with them. But keeping them safe may mean that the caregiver has to assume joint responsibility with the elder. Room space, living space, and other territories defined as belonging to the elder are dependent on the caregiver (Petronio and Kovachls 1997). The denial of dignity is common.

A young woman finds her grandmother uncovered on the floor on a thin mattress, a strongly religious woman is left in the last hours of life with a transistor radio blaring pop music at her head, another woman dying in full view on an open ward.[14]

Organisations functioning by rules not by principles of care

Rules are flexible and can be interpreted according to the needs of those in charge. Medications for example, can be transformed into rule-enforcement devices.

> The manageress allegedly silenced disruptive residents by spiking their drinks with a drug, which is used to treat schizophrenia. She also arranged for staff to lace their drinks. When employees expressed concern, she assured them that the residents' doctors had prescribed the tranquilliser. One of the victims was a noisy resident whose bedroom was directly above the manager's sitting room and she would regularly ring a bell or strike her walking stick on the floor. But she would fall asleep after drinking her bedtime Horlicks, which was laced with the drug. Another woman slept for two days after being given the tranquilliser, while some residents would be locked in their rooms after being unwittingly sedated.[15]

Rules may become ritualistic, taking on a life of their own. In Diamond's (1992) study, residents were required to undertake a twice-daily course of hand and neck exercises, even where it was recognisably irrelevant to their physical ailments.

Individuals have little or no influence over the course of their lives while in the institution. Residents are an organisational unit to be managed as passive objects.

Fulfilling the official aim of the institution

> Three meals and two snacks were served each day, all scientifically designed for adequate nutrition. From the standpoint of living out this scheduled and documented design, the result was often hunger. ... 'They give us our three meals all right, but they don't understand that it's fourteen or fifteen hours between the close of dinner and the beginning of breakfast. By the time breakfast comes around, we're weak with hunger.' (Diamond 1992, p.77)

The residents are reconstructed as liminal persons within the hierarchy of organisational goals through a specialised language. They are pathologised by a reconstruction of ordinary discourse. In Diamond, 'vital signs' (blood pressure, pulse, temperature and respiration) were taken frequently during the day. Personal biography and individuality was calculated from the sum of such physical indicators. Residents were introduced to new staff in terms of their chart records.

Abuse in institutional settings

Care and nursing homes are criminogenic contexts. Crime from fraud to physical violence is common although largely unrecorded (Brogden and Nijhar 2000). Elder abuse may take many forms in institutional settings – physical, misuse of restraints, physical neglect, medical neglect, verbal/emotional neglect, and personal property abuse.[16] All contribute to lowering the quality of life of the older person and assisting in consigning them to a liminal non-person existence, to which – unlike with 'normal persons' – the criminal justice system has no access. Abuse in care and nursing homes for the elderly are regularly featured in the media. For example:

> A nursing home worker was jailed for four years in July for abusing eight women in his care. 21-year-old Simon Hack admitted one charge of causing GBH, three indecent assaults on women in their 80s and 90s and four of common assault in a nursing home in Aldershot. ...he poured cold water over a 78-year-old woman and put a stocking over her head, grabbed a 92-year-old woman's breasts, force fed a 96-year-old and poured sherry down the throat of an 81-year-old, causing her to choke. Over 100 complaints about him – many of his victims suffered from senile dementia and were wheelchair bound. Some were unable to tell other staff of the abuse and at least one suffered psychological trauma as a result of the abuse.[17]

External factors contributing to that criminogenic context include the supply and demand of beds and the local unemployment rate. If the area has a bed surplus, patients may be accepted without adequate assessment, resulting in misplacement. Where there is a shortage of beds, patients may be forced into institutions with reputations for poor care.

> A council placed an elderly Indian man in a residential home, where he spent twelve years with nobody able to speak his language. The man, who spoke no English, suffered a breakdown because there was no one he could converse with and he was sent to a nursing home. But he did not need nursing care.[18]

The unemployment rate, along with rates of pay, affects the qualifications, quality, quantity, and turnover of staffing. A 1997 inquiry (Health Advisory Service 2000) found deficiencies in admission procedures and in the physical fabric; shortages of basic equipment; major problems in obtaining qualified staff and in giving appropriate food and drink; a denial of personal dignity and privacy in relation to hygiene and dressing; little information for patients and visitors; shortages of basic equipment; lack of toilets; and the sexes mixed without consent. Hospital routines and interpretations of health and safety regulations may be inflexible (for example, over the time which food could be left in front of a patient and access to food supplements other than expensive tinned foods). Most patients over 70 years of age claimed that 'nurses did not seem to know about eating/drinking and did not seem to care'. Only a quarter of the wards were in good repair. They were badly designed for older people, as was much of the furniture and many of the bathroom fittings. Lifting equipment was often broken. Days and mealtimes were rigidly timetabled, with resulting tedium (*ibid.*).

> Lynn Sheridan was found guilty of cruelty to patients at her former County Down nursing home and struck off the Register. She was found guilty of eleven charges including – smacking a resident and making her stand in a corner until she

stopped crying; striking another resident a number of times on the face; shouting at her in an abusive manner; and making a resident stand naked in a corner of her bedroom as punishment.[19]

Ginny Jenkins of Action on Elder Abuse has argued that abuse is especially prevalent in private care homes, which require stricter regulation:

We hear of short-changing when shopping has been done, of carers ingratiating themselves into people's affection and getting jewellery or that 'nice vase'. People can be subtly threatened and demands are made for money. Physically carers can be rough and not respect the dignity of those in their charge.[20]

Other examples are given of 'straightforward theft' and cases of residents being given overdoses by their carers.[21] Similar stories are reported from the United States. Thus one Marie Espinoza, who

was suffering from a degenerative brain disease, had bruises, bedsores, and a broken pelvis within months after her arrival at the Orangetree Convalescent Hospital. Food was often left at the foot of her bed, out of her reach. She began to lose weight. 'She always seemed to be starving or begging for water.' Espinoza suffered severe dehydration and bedsores and died from choking on food. Oliva says that she was supposed to be fed through a tube.[22]

Unwanted deaths are relatively common – Orville Lynn Majors, an Indiana nurse, was charged with killing six of his patients between 1993 and 1995 by injecting them with potassium chloride. He was on duty during some 130 deaths in the hospital.[23] In Versailles, a 30-year-old nurse was charged with killing some 30 elderly patients over an 18-month period. Her alleged victims, aged between 72 and 88 years, were all in the terminal phase of incurable lung diseases, and had apparently been put to death at their own request or that of their relatives. However, a prosecutor commented that her practices had been from sympathy with the elderly: 'She cannot be compared to the criminal and sadistic nurses who sometimes get the headlines.'[24]

Making death 'ordinary'

In the care home or hospital, staff learn to handle elderly deaths according to normative procedures which reconstitute the person as waste products (Chambliss 1996). Death is routinised by the bureaucratic machine, ironically to make it more 'people-friendly'. Three features enable this normalisation process – repeatability, profanation, and existentiality.

Elderly deaths are a normal feature of the care home and nursing home. Deaths may occur several times a week. What the staff see, they have seen many times. These repeated events take place against the even less dramatic repeated daily aspects of care practices – taking blood pressures, checking for 'vital signs', writing progress reports, changing bedpans. Death is slotted into the continuing banality of the work-life of the institutions – the TV provides the backcloth, meals are served and sometimes eaten, and residents are washed and bathed. The abnormality of death is nullified by the ordinariness of the continuing context.

Second, deaths occur within a 'profane' experience. To the healthy person, the body is inviolate – physical contact is emotional, good and bad. But for the dying elder resident, the body is drastically profaned. It is exposed to strangers, male and female, often in groups; the body may be pierced; intimate bathing and toileting may depend upon the intrusions of others. It loses its privacy and intimacy on the way to death. It is no longer the possession of the individual but is reconstructed as an object within the routine.

Third, there is a process of existentiality. The routinisation of the abnormal involves not so much a mental leap as an existential action. Creating a routine in the dying process is not some trick of the unconscious but rather a whole way of acting that involves physical as well as mental components. It comprises embodied habits, a 'matter of factness'. The dying person may be shifted to a single room; his or her diet is no longer monitored; special supplements no longer added. The care problem now is one of easing dying rather than one of sustaining health and the staff routinely moves into a dying mode of practice. External contact is minimised rather than encouraged – 'let the patients rest'. A 'black' humour allows the staff to distance themselves from the passage onwards – making the tragic amusing and understandable through a different discourse.

> [A] staff member taped a stick to the door…symbolising for them 'The Stake' a sign of some form of euthanasia. Periodically, the word went round that a resident had just won the 'Golden Stake Award', meaning that he or she had, for the first time, allowed or helped a patient to die. (Chambliss 1996, p.48)

Elderly death, voluntary and involuntary, is subject to bureaucratic structures (Glaser and Strauss 1965). In hospital, the elderly patient is deconstructed from human patient to waste detritus. A series of cues – physical and temporal – are developed as doctors signify the changed status, and in doing so have a major effect on the perceived role and treatment of the patient. The process operates through the activation of emergency team and the withdrawal of community support. It results in the death of the individual, partly by means of suggestion (Maxwell 1979).

In this 'nothing more to do' liminal status, the fundamental goal for the patient changes from recovery to comfort. Once the doctor is convinced that return to health is not possible, the problem becomes one of spending clinical time legiti-mately, according to professional values. Scarce skills must be reserved for the patients who can recover. The 'nothing more to do' elderly has a less valid claim on professional time. The increasing absence of the doctor gives cues to patient and to other medical staff. The standard mechanism for handling this dilemma is to 'send the elderly patient home' – hospital services are reserved for people who can recover. If the dying elderly person remains in the hospital, he or she may get special privileges – for example, excused from being ritually turned or washed. A primary nursing function is now to develop painless comfort for the patient in order that other patients will not be disturbed.

If both doctor and nurse are agreed that the patient is in the 'nothing more to do' phase, then the former's instructions are very likely to allow the nurse to use discretion on the dosage necessary to keep the patient free of pain. They may even risk lethal dosages: 'None of the [nurses] believe in euthanasia, but it's just as you give these heavy doses of narcotics, you think it may be that last one they can take' (Quoted in Maxwell 1979, p.18). A collective mood develops amongst the nursing staff as they discover their new function is 'there is nothing more to be done'. The alternative is to put the patient into a living sleep – a social death – a belief that the patient should be allowed to die quickly. Structural factors encourage that status passage. Hospital policy may state that extraordinary efforts are not to be made with patients of the 'nothing more to do' variety. Nurses may not be allowed to use certain resuscitation techniques without the doctor's permission.

There may be tacit allowance for auto-euthanasia by leaving the patient's pills at the bedside, by removing constraints, or by leaving the patient alone in the bedroom or bathroom. The nurses will have a general idea of the death ratio on the ward – the proportion of patients expected to die each week – and will make mental allowances for that reconstruction of their patients.

Doctors tend to view the medical problems of the elderly as a problem of ageing rather than of health: inevitable, and not to be cured. 'Doctors did not consider it their job to ease the process of dying beyond prescribing pain-killing drugs. As far as possible they avoided dying patients, embarrassed by what they saw as failure' (Seale 1989).[25] Ageist ideology plays a role in this process. Hockey (1986), for example, in a comparative study of hospices and old people's homes, suggests that 'normal' dying, such as of cancer patients, involves a clearly designated right of entry into a sick role but the 'very aged' have a 'sometimes stigmatised social role' in entering the liminal process.

Bureaucratisation of elderly death therefore stems in part from this perception of death as an inevitable consequence of ageing rather than of ill health. Death in modern society has become increasingly a phenomenon of the old, who are usually retired from work and finished with their parental responsibilities (Blauner 1965).

Death by care is subtly bureaucratically managed. Personal interest will be subsumed within the normality required by the bureaucratic norms of an institution designed to assist those who 'can become well' and to process smoothly those for whom 'nothing more can be done'.

> A nurse was observed spending two or three minutes trying to close the eyelids of a woman patient. The nurse explained that the woman was dying. She was trying to get the lids to remain in a closed position. After several unsuccessful attempts, the nurse got them shut and said, with a sigh of accomplishment, 'Now they're right.' When questioned about what she was doing, she said that a patient's eyes must be closed after death, so that the body will resemble a sleeping person. It was more difficult to accomplish this, she explained, after the muscles and skin had begun to stiffen. She always tried, she said, to close them before death. This made for greater efficiency when it came time for ward personnel to wrap the body. It was a matter of consideration towards those workers who preferred to handle dead bodies as little as possible. (Sudnow 1967, pp.191–3)

Malignancy is removed from the death-hastening process by the requirements of the bureaucratic machine. Given the stereotypes of the elderly, one of the consequences of the devaluation of the old in modern society is the minimisation of the disruption and moral shock that death ordinarily brings about.

> Staff members wish wholeheartedly for the death of incontinent or otherwise troublesome residents. My fear that a woman left sleeping with her face buried in her pillow might suffocate was met with a straightforward reply 'What difference does that make? That much less for us to do.' (Vesperi 1990, p.236)[26]

Mortality in modern society is rarely allowed to disturb the business of life. This separation of the handling of illness and death from the family limits the average person's exposure to death and its disruption of the social process. When the dying are segregated among the specialists for whom contact with death has become routine, and even somewhat impersonal, neither their presence while alive nor as corpses interferes greatly with the mainstream of life.

> If there was a death, it was noted in the nursing home in a very subdued way, often not announced at all. It might have been recognized silently, known by staff and residents alike, but unspoken, except in whispers. 'The Spanish man must have died last night,' Flora Dobbins observed. 'They've got the doors closed today. That's the only time they close the doors during the day.' Beyond that there was no recognition, no formal observance, no ceremony or public ritual. (Diamond 1992, p.118)

Ethnography of elderly death-hastening

Two classic studies focused on this bureaucratisation process with regard to institutional death (Glaser and Strauss 1965; Sudnow 1967) and several more recent ones (e.g. Chambliss 1996; Diamond 1992).[27] They documented the dominance of impersonal routines over personalised care, associated with the needs of medical and nursing staff to control and suppress the expression of emotion. Imposing order on the potentially chaotic and disruptive event of death involved care processes (especially in Sudnow's study) that were normally callous and occasionally brutal.

Sudnow argued that hospitals are organised to hide the facts of death and dying from patients as well as from visitors. As agencies formally charged with the production of health and cures, hospitals have a particular problem when the result is death rather than health. Within the value hierarchy of hospital (the National *Health* Service), handling a corpse is dirty, low-caste work, which ideally should be left to the next shift. The hospital and care institution therefore develop depersonalising procedures, techniques and discourses to conceal the reality of the process of dying and of the disposal of corpses.

For example, patients are moved to a private room when death is near. Bodies are not removed during visiting hours. The hospital morgue is located on the ground floor or in the basement in an area inaccessible to the general public with a suitable exit leading on to a loading platform which is concealed from hospital patients and the public. Death is rationalised through standard rules ordering the covering of corpses, identifying the deceased, informing relatives, and completing death certificates and autopsy permits.

Diamond's ethnographic study of care homes details the routinisation of death of the liminal person. Market forces swept people out of the care home. When they were gone they were replaced. In a profit-making industry defined by bed occupancy, an empty bed was economically unproductive.

> At the first sign of imminent death an ambulance was called, but often it was too late. 'Is there anything you would like?' I once asked Nancy Block, as she lay nearly powerless from a stroke. 'Yes,' she responded immediately, 'to die.' Two nights later she got her wish. Whether or not the ambulance attendants had arrived before the moment of death, the person was whisked away to the hospital, where death would be formally pronounced. (Diamond 1992, p.83)

In the county hospital studied by Glaser and Strauss, three-quarters of the patients were over 60 years old. The hospital was the setting for a 'concentration of death' – one in 25 persons died each day. The nurses and doctors viewed death as an inconvenience and managed interaction so as to minimise emotional reactions and fuss.[28] Medical staff attempted to avoid unexpected deaths because of possible distraught reactions by relatives. They preferred to let family members know that the patient had taken a 'turn for the worse' so that they could modulate their response, in keeping with the hospital's needs for order. Tranquillisers and pain-killing drugs were given to patients to minimise the disruption of passing, even when there was no need for this in terms of treatment or in the reduction of pain.

Because doctors avoid the terminally ill (there is no performance rating for dealing with the dying) and nurses, care assistants and relatives are rarely able to talk about death, patients suffer psychological isolation, experiencing a sense of meaninglessness because they are typically kept unaware of their condition and of their impending fate. They are not in a position to understand or challenge the medical and other routines carried out on their behalf because the medical staff and care agencies tend to programme deaths in keeping with their organisational and professional needs: control over one's death seems to be even more difficult to achieve than control over one's life. Thus the geriatric ward in the modern hospital – which is formally devoted to the preservation of life and the reduction of pain – tends to become a 'mass reduction' system undermining the subjecthood of dying patients.

While Sudnow's and Glaser and Strauss's studies are now relatively dated, the more recent work of Diamond (1992) and Chambliss (1996) convey much the same message. Pain control and symptom control become routinised and clinical while 'emotional' care – the recognition of a self in the elderly patient – is 'submerged'.

The British Medical Association (BMA) acknowledged that social isolation and the denial of individuality resulting from bureaucratisation lead to pressures for life termination:

> Some elderly people, however, feel that they have outlived their usefulness and are a burden to others and hope that death will not be unduly prolonged by modern medical developments without the patient having any choice in the matter. The majority would not make any deliberate attempt to hasten death but there is no doubt that some may desire it especially if denied the support of relatives and friends. (BMA 1988, p.17)

Direct death-hastening: 'Do not resuscitate'

In the care home, elderly people perceived to have little prospect of survival might be subject to involuntary euthanasia – often by starvation. Recent BMA guidelines stated that doctors should be allowed to authorise withdrawal of food and water by tube for stroke victims and the confused elderly, even when the patient is not terminally ill. But such guidance may be honoured in the breach rather than in the practice.[29]

> In May last year, an inquest was told that Mrs Ormerod, 85, died weighing less than four stone, two months after a doctor ordered her food supplement to be stopped and only liquids to be administered. One nurse told the hearing that Mrs Ormerod was 'skin and bone' when she died of pneumonia. A Home Office pathologist said, 'I don't think I have ever seen anyone who was reduced to this weight'. Although Mrs Ormerod's food was formally stopped, nurses continued

to feed her until supplies ran out. Dr X was arrested when the coroner referred the case to the police but after a seven-month investigation the case was dropped. Dr X said Mrs Ormerod was weak and semi-conscious after a series of strokes. He had told nurses to stop feeding her, believing that she had little consciousness and her life expectancy was poor. ... In Leeds, seven residents were discovered to be so underweight that a doctor contacted Social Services.[30]

Elderly patients were dying because of an unspoken policy of 'involuntary euthanasia' designed to relieve pressure on the NHS, according to senior consultant Dr Adrian Treloar at Greenwich Hospital. Police investigated 60 cases of pensioners who died after allegedly being deprived of food and water by hospital staff, following complaints from families, from NHS staff and pressure groups. Dr Treloar said: 'There are severe pressures on beds and in order to resolve this there may be a tendency to limit care inappropriately where you feel doubtful about the outcome. ... If old people start to resist early discharge they are seen as an encumbrance.'[31]

A similar case was reported from the Royal Oldham Hospital where, it was alleged, an elderly man was being starved. The pensioner was admitted suffering from severe dehydration and undernourishment to be renourished and rehydrated. Later, a nurse claimed that he had not been fed or given a drink for two weeks. An 84-year-old woman died three weeks after going into hospital with an arthritic knee. The son claimed that doctors had issued a 'do not resuscitate' order. In the alleged case of Olwen Gibbings, aged 96, at the Cardiff Royal Infirmary, the death certificate listed septicaemia as principal cause of death but her medical notes were marked 'not for resuscitation', indicating that she was dosed with 4mg per hour infusions of diamorphine, the heroin-based painkiller. A daughter, to her amazement, discovered amongst her father's case notes 'not for resuscitation'. She was told by the nursing staff that this was standard procedure.[32] The Chair of Doctors for Assisted Dying claimed that this constituted involuntary euthanasia.

> She was supposedly put down as 'NFR', not for resuscitation, on the orders of a nurse and/or doctor...this information was revealed to us at the independent review, together with the information that her ulcer had burst prior to her admittance but was not picked up by the doctors or nurses attending to her. She died, we believe, through mis-diagnosis, lack of care and neglect – just because of her age.[33]

To Age Concern's subsequent calls for new legislation, a government minister replied: '...this is scaremongering. This is effectively saying that elderly people are being murdered by doctors and nurses. It is completely without foundation.' The Chair of the British Medical Association responded that he believed that the elderly did receive lower standards of care – 'That is a problem of ageism in society and result of the huge pressure in the system.'[34]

Regulation and inspection

In Britain, the Registered Homes Act 1984 and later amendments cover residential and nursing homes. Part I of the Act requires that a 'residential care home' be registered with the local social services department. Residential care is defined as providing board and personal care. The NHS and Community Care Act 1990 influences the way in which older people access care homes and the way in which funding is provided. But regulation by rules may not mean regulation for care practice.

Annual certificates are issued to the registered home covering resident details and requirements. Registering authorities may also access police records in respect of applicants for registration. Inspections may be conducted without prior appointment. In nursing homes, an authorised inspector may interview independently any patient residing in the home to investigate a complaint or where the person has reason to believe that the patient is not receiving proper care. Inspectors may require independent examination of the resident and the production of any medical records relating to treatment in the home. Many health authorities authorise a pharmaceutical officer to inspect nursing homes to cover all aspects of medication, storage facilities, administration and record keeping.

However, inspection is not a scientific practice. There may be pressure from 'would-be' contractors to ensure that favourable reports are submitted (Royal College of Nursing 1974). There appears to be no standardised approach to ascertain fitness and for the protection of vulnerable people. Checks on owners and persons in charge of registered and nursing care homes may be conducted in an *ad hoc* manner. Visits are often announced beforehand preventing inspectors from ascertaining the real picture. There is no consistent approach in the way in which inspectors are trained or the way in which inspections are carried out. For example, one authority carries out only 45 per cent of its statutory inspection of care homes for adults compared to a national average of 92 per cent.[35] Reporting of abuse by junior staff may encounter major obstacles.

Different values of the local registering authorities may be reflected in the inspections and in refusal or cancellation of a registration. Minimum standards become the norm, concerned with adequacy rather than quality. Disparities occur over a range of matters – from requesting references to checking finances.[36] A person whose application for registration is refused or revoked in one area can simply apply to another local authority or health authority.

The Patient's Charter, produced by the Department of Health in 1991, details what consumers may expect in the delivery of health services. It established national standards including access to information, reduced waiting time and access to services. The 'named nurse' concept requires that a named qualified nurse, health visitor or midwife will assume responsibility for an elder's care. But older people may be refused care by local authorities who have run out of community care funds or by a health authority if they do not meet the eligibility criteria. The latter may be set according to the funding and resources allocated to health and local authorities, rather than being based upon need and demand. If a local authority places its contracts for long-term care with independent residential or nursing homes, older people will be subject to means testing. Consequently, care may be purchased on the basis of cost rather than quality, given funding limitations. The current system of medical inspection reacts passively to the demands of residents, whose expectations are low because they equate disability and ill health with normal old age. Most GPs do not review residents routinely but only when a problem occurs (British Geriatric Society 1998).

Inspection is to be tightened. In 1998, the Health Secretary proposed to give inspectors new powers to investigate nursing homes and residential homes.[37] But the registration authorities are aware that closing a private home as a sanction will put them in the unmanageable position of having to offer alternative places in their own premises, and these may simply not be available. There are several reports of the inadequacy of the complaints system in relation to domiciliary care.

At the cheapest end of the market, patients are often reluctant to complain because of their dependency status. Surveys of complaints may therefore underestimate the true degree of patients' (and relatives') concerns. 'Older people have few of the rights of commercial consumers as they lack purchasing power and are subject to contracts negotiated on their behalf by the purchasing authorities.'[38] After several apparent cases of involuntary euthanasia and subsequent complaints, SOS NHS – Patients in Danger claimed that the 'NHS complaint system is a farce... It sends people on a cruel and cynical merry-go-round. It is designed to find out just how much a relative knows and how damaging that information may be to the doctor, rather than to get at the truth and answer legitimate questions.'[39] In the United States, recent revelations have shown dramatic failures in the system of inspecting care and nursing homes for the elderly. As death disposal units, they have often been immune from external scrutiny. The General Accounting Report submitted to Congress in 1997 found that more than a quarter of the nation's 17,000-plus nursing homes harmed residents or put them in danger. Forty per cent of 74 nursing homes cited for patient abuse and neglect in four states were repeat offenders. For example, an elderly man wandered away from his Detroit nursing home unnoticed and was later found stabbed to death. The nursing home involved in the incident did not notify police of the man's disappearance, paid a $16,000 fine, suffered a temporary ban on new admissions and remained open. 'The result is a "yo-yo" pattern of compliance: a nursing facility is found deficient, the facility corrects the problem temporarily and the facility once again slips into non-compliance', said Representative John Dingell. Inspections are in any case extremely weak. Conditions in facilities could change just before the predictable visits of the inspectors. Inspections were rarely conducted at stress times outside daylight hours and at weekends. An inspector charged with visiting California nursing homes claimed that her complaints were regularly ignored because of 'the "cronyism" that exists between state overseers and nursing home operators. We write down violations, the nursing homes complain, and our superiors keep us from going back or else they dismiss our citations.'[40]

Diamond's (1992) ethnographic study furnishes an illustration of one such inspection. He assumed that because residents and staff often commented negatively on the food, the inspectors would be especially interested in nutrition. On inspection day, he was surprised to learn that the staff who had worked during the day did not know whether the inspection had occurred. None of the officials had come to the floor.

> 'Someone said we passed.' The inspectors came to the offices downstairs, where they inspected the records… Since all of the meal cards had been carefully collected, alphabetized, coded, and entered into the computer, the officials' job was made easier. After a glance through the kitchen and a fleeting exchange with a few residents, they simply had to look at the records to see that proper nutrition had been delivered. In the process, the tomato soup and cheese sandwich became something other than what they were when mocked and left half-eaten upstairs. Downstairs they became units of nutrition; coded sustenance for the administrators and state officials to agree in their shared language that food service was adequate and certifiable. Through the new technologies and codes of this emerging industry, 'look at' came to mean inspect the records and rendered superfluous the need to look at the food or the people who ate it. [It] represented not just a recording of the events and the food, but a transformation of them. All along the bureaucratic hierarchy, beginning with inspection, state officials define reports as the reality. Reports are what they pay for, the entities they recognize for money exchanges. It made the events of everyday life countable. (Diamond 1992, p.102)[41]

In 1996, a quarter of the United States nursing homes failed to assess each patient's needs or develop individual care plans.[42] That year, 10,000 of the nursing homes inspected had violations noted. Many were forwarded to the federal government with recommended penalties for confirmation. But fines were inflicted in only 2 per cent of the cases. State inspectors recommended that 5458 homes (one in three) be barred from receiving money for new patients. Washington reduced the figure to 156. Inspectors recommended special training for staff in 3039 homes; the federal government cut this to 103. Inspectors wanted fines for 2395 for violations; but the federal government only fined 228 and those that paid without appealing only had to pay 65 per cent of the fines.

Government officials were unable to justify these decisions, apart from claiming that nursing homes 'have a right' to correct problems before penalties are imposed. The main sanction against the homes is to threaten to terminate the provider's contract, a threat rarely acted upon.

> A nurse found about forty maggots in a bedsore in the left heel of an 87-year-old man. State inspectors recommended a $24,000 fine but the nursing home appealed, saying that the wriggling larvae didn't constitute evidence of poor care. Beside, the nursing home contended, maggots are good for eating away dead tissue inside a wound. The state hearing officer agreed with the nursing home and threw out the fine. The Licensing Deputy Director echoed the nursing home's account. 'In an era of alternative medicine, maggots are being used for the debridement of dead tissue…the fact that these sorts of eggs and maggots can hatch in a 24-hour period may not even mean there was improvident wound care.'[43]

State reports noted a catalogue of problems with care homes that could affect the lifespan of the elderly – major financial improprieties; inadequate specialised staffing and turnover; theft from residents; inappropriate discharges or transfers; breaking of diet rules; inadequate provision of laundry; and drugs administered for discipline or convenience. Between one-quarter and one-third of all residents had body mass problems resulting from incompetent or inadequate nutritional practices; and employment procedures that resulted in individuals with a history of violent criminal behaviour being routinely employed as direct caregivers.[44]

One resident lost a third of his body weight over seven weeks, the nursing home failing to weigh him during that period, give prescribed painkillers, or alert his doctor. Another resident had a bedsore and, despite medical orders, the bandage was unchanged for two weeks instead of being changed twice a day. A third resident was brought to a hospital, where he was found to have had a broken leg for at least three weeks.[45]

A further ethnographic study showed that surveyors spent little time assessing quality of life issues or observing clinical treatments and care delivery. Little time was spent with the residents. Only one inspector compared the formal charts with direct observation (Weissert 1998). Early complaints about the use of 'over-drugging' and using psychopharmacologic medications as 'chemical strait-jackets' had given rise to new regulations in 1987. The only consequence was that over the following decade, while there had been a decrease from 34 per cent to 16 per cent in the resort to antipsychotics, this had been accompanied by a 97 per cent increase in the use of antidepressants.

Elderly care as a business enterprise: 'Culling sheep or cattle'[46]

The political economy approach (Chapter 3) combines with the arguments about bureaucratisation and geronticide in decisions regarding the increased entry of the private sector to the care of the elderly. Profit-making requirements converge with dysfunctional institutional rules in sacrificing elderly residents.

In the private care home, healthcare is commercialised. It conforms to the process of commodity production, in making patients into itemised goods and services (Diamond 1992). Residents as consumers are removed from participation in bargaining over costs for their residency, as are their family members. Fundamental to that bargaining process between the state and the care industry is the ideology that the elderly are not citizens or consumers but a cost drain on the public purse. Personal savings became – together with the state payments – the basis of private investment. Long-term nursing home residence has come to mean pauperisation. The elderly that do not die 'on time' may inconvenience profit. They create problems for the bureaucratic order. In effect, systemic and ideological factors may be much more important in producing the death-hastening process than inter-personal relationships.

Glaser and Strauss (1965) cite the case of a private elderly patient who was expected to die within four hours. He needed a special machine to ease his last day but had now run out of funds. The private hospital at which he had been a frequent paying patient for 30 years agreed to receive him as a charity patient. He did not die immediately but started to linger indefinitely. This new problem however created much concern to the administrators and to his family. Paradoxically, the doctor had to keep reassuring both parties that his patient, who actually lasted six weeks, would soon die – trying to change their expectations that he would 'die on time'.

In the UK, problems have been exacerbated for certain parts of the profit-making sector,[47] especially for small private nursing homes, because of a decreasing occupancy rate (despite the demographic explosion). Five years earlier, the occupancy rate (measured like commercial hotel beds) was well above 90 per cent and is now in the low 80s. The main reason for this trend away from institutional care is that local authorities now have to assess more economically who goes into care. Further, staff costs for care assistants may be rising due to the introduction of a national minimum wage. Any home with fewer than 15 beds may be vulnerable to closure. However, the trend to monopolisation is not affected, with large companies able to avoid the problem by leasing homes rather than owning them.

The expansion of the private sector in Britain under the Conservative government of the 1980s was partly welcomed by local authorities, relieved that commercial homes were able to take the pressure off their own waiting lists for places. Unlike local authority homes, which serve a poor and relatively homogeneous population of frail old people, private homes exist in great variety. The law has been inadequate to stem growth even where it has been considered undesirable.

One new owner, wishing to fill his beds, recently advertised a free weekend trial stay for elderly people. When the rested carers came to collect their equally satisfied elderly parents, lamenting that it would be nice to continue the arrangement except for the money, the proprietor had a solution. He had a supply of SB [Supplementary Benefit] forms to hand, and rapidly filled his beds. (Brogden and Nijhar 2000, p.121)

Public funds are such a large part of the income of these businesses that nursing homes constitute a major industry drawing for its profits mainly on state subvention. In the emerging relations of ownership, care has been continually reinvested as a premium, a privilege for those who can pay the price, rather than being a right of citizenship (Diamond 1992).

Because of various scandals, US federal lawmakers decided in 1935 to hand the elderly over to private industry. The Social Security Act specifically said that inmates should not receive cash payments and the state bypassed the elderly in paying the new private investors. The creation of Medicaid in 1955 to assist the elderly poor through provision of health insurance, meant a huge infusion of public money into private nursing homes with few strings attached. In essence (Bates 1999), the new owners were given a blank cheque that virtually guaranteed them a profit on their investment. Hence the entry of global corporations like ITT into that market.

That was when nursing homes moved away from mom-and-pop operations to large for-profit enterprises. They were more interested in real estate transactions than in health-care; they shifted properties back and forth between subsidiaries, jacking up property costs to increase reimbursement. Those real estate ventures become the source of corporate empires.[48]

Most homes in the United States are owned by corporations, three-quarters of which are run for profit, with increasing control in the hands of investor-owned chains.[49] They are arenas of caregiving, but they are also bureaucratic organisations founded on specific relations of ownership and control. Caregiving becomes something that is bought and sold. This process involves the construction of goods and services that can be measured and priced. It entails the enforcement of power relations and means of production so that those who live in nursing and care homes and those who tend to them can be made into commodities and cost-accountable units.

Over the last two decades, elder care has become an excellent area for investment with a guaranteed cash flow consisting almost entirely of government funds. The federal government gives more than $45 billion to nursing homes annually.[49a] Corporate chains boost profits by laying off staff members, cutting wages (two out of every three dollars paid goes on payrolls, so nursing homes wanting increased profits have to shed staff) and doubling patient loads. The two major chains are now worth some $23 billion with annual revenues of $3 billion each – seven chains now collect 20 cents of every dollar spent on supporting homes nationwide. The industry in the United States is worth more than $87 billion a year. It gives millions in lobbying funds to state and federal officials in order to ensure weak oversight (Bates 1999).

Phillips[50] claims that the homes have directed as much money as possible into property, administrative salaries and ancillary services like drugs and physio-therapy, while cutting corners on patient care and staff wages. Many facilities have only one registered nurse on duty, relying on a skeleton staff of nurses' aides to provide almost all the hands-on care for dozens of patients – most of these staff on little more than the minimum wage and receiving only very limited training for difficult jobs that require them to monitor and feed patients, and move ill and disabled residents. Caregivers are often overworked and grossly underpaid, a situation which often results in rude and abusive behaviour to vulnerable residents who beg them for simple needs such as water or to be taken to the bathroom.

A Case Study of Profiteering through Death-Hastening

Sarah Duggan went to work at the William and Mary nursing home for $5 dollars an hour. Being unskilled, she felt she was lucky to get the post. Elsie Claus, 89, was a resident. She simply couldn't support herself any more. Her memory was failing, and she barely walked. A Maryland psychiatrist was the new owner. In ten years, [he] built a $2 billion company while Sarah Duggan (eight to twelve hours a day) changed Elsie Claus' sheets, helped her to the bathroom, lifted her patients out of bed, filled water pitchers and handed out evening snacks. During that ten years…conditions became disorganised, schedules changed constantly, fewer supplies. Staff came and went. [Duggan] began bringing her own lotion and soap for residents. Across the country [the corporate combine] continued to grow and stock analysts cheered – throughout 1997 [it] took on a heavy debt to buy a collection of companies that provide nursing care. One transaction cost 600 jobs. [The owner] explained in a news release '[the company] intends to profit as Medicare changes the rule on payment'. In September 1997, state inspectors found many problems at the home … residents were being left wet, languishing with bedsores. A year later, conditions were approved although they remained unsatisfactory. 'They were so budget-minded in the kitchen, we couldn't get anything special. There was no supervision, no training. I'd complain but nothing would happen' (Duggan). She had four bosses in two years. Elsie lost her hearing and sight and developed dementia disabling her ability to eat safely – she would stuff food into her mouth and try to swallow without chewing. Her doctor gave her a liquid diet, which she hated. So she was assigned to special therapy that allowed her to eat soft solid foods, but continually reminded her of the dentures in her mouth and to take small bites. These instructions were not written into her care plan. An 18-year-old kitchen attendant by mistake made her a solid sandwich, which Duggan fed to Elsie without knowing. They found Elsie turning blue and she choked to death on the peanut sandwich. Duggan was blamed and fired. The first call from the home was not to the police but for the doctor to release the body for cremation. The doctor did not ask how Elsie died and the nurse did not give any information. No one called the police or state officials.[51]

Overview

Bizarrely, even the timing of such deaths seems to be subject to the bureaucratisation process. In a curious paper, Matcha and Hutchinson (1997) have documented how it varies between institutionalised and non-institutionalised elderly. Deaths amongst the elderly in hospitals and nursing homes are more likely to occur during the week, whereas deaths among the elderly at home are more likely to occur at weekends. Death amongst the elderly occurs mainly within institutional structures. The elderly are more likely to die on a Tuesday regardless of location of death, their gender, or marital status. Institutional exigencies do not merely affect the frequency of elderly deaths; they also appear to determine their timetable.

However, this bureaucratic approach has two general defects that it shares with the cruder versions of the modernisation, demographic and political economy perspectives. First, it fails to take account of the extent to which residents may be active rather than passive in that process. It treats them as dummy figures. But as Diamond (1992) has shown, even in the conveyor belt private nursing home, some form of independence is exerted. That autonomy may be exerted in the direction of staying alive – of bucking the system. But it may also be directed at speeding up one's personal termination.

Second, other explanations of death-hastening in care institutions have denied the importance of both the structural factors, as noted above, and its being a product of inter-personal dynamics ('staff burn-out'). Instead, they have emphasised the central contribution to that brutalisation process of the continuity of a historically shaped ageist ideology (Vesperi 1990).

In their work on primitive society, Maxwell, Silverman and Maxwell (1982) comment '...it may be that geronticide...is now routinely practiced, perhaps to a greater extent than ever. It is impossible to know precisely how frequent geronticide is in modern hospital settings...' (p.82).

Notes

1   Cited in *Times Magazine*, 27 October 1997.
2   'Survey reveals opposition, to entering care homes.' *Electronic Telegraph*, 14 December 1997.

3   See the White Paper *Caring for People* (Home Office 1989) and the subsequent *NHS and Community Care 1990* (Home Office 1990).

4   As we noted in Chapter 1, suicide rates after depression amongst the over-65s are the highest for any age group in the UK.

5   'Charity offers haven of care and respect for old and dying.' *Electronic Telegraph*, 10 December 1999.

6   'Dobson puts accent on home care.' *Electronic Telegraph*, 22 October 1997.

7   Cited in 'Thousands in worse health after hospital.' *Electronic Telegraph*, 8 November 1999.

8   'Nurse accused of killing 22 elderly patients.' *Electronic Telegraph*, 22 October 1997.

9   Cited in 'Thousands in worse health after hospital'. *Electronic Telegraph*, 8 November 1999.

10 Quoted in Diamond (1992).

11 Similar accounts are furnished in 'Charity offers haven of care and respect for old and dying.' *Electronic Telegraph*, 10 December 1999 and 'In possibly thousands of cases, nursing home residents are dying from a lack of food and water, and the most basic level of hygiene.' *Time Magazine*, 27 October 1997.

12 Royal College of Physicians Report, 'Hundreds abused in care home.' *Electronic Telegraph*, 20 June 1996.

13 Quoted in De Beauvoir (1973).

14 *Electronic Telegraph*, 10 December 1999.

15 'Nursing home manager "drugged" resident.' *Electronic Telegraph*, 11 July 1997.

16 See *inter alia* the *Sunday Times* account 'Revealed: Cruelty of staff in NHS hospitals.' (12 March 2000) of a secret investigation at two London hospitals which revealed varied forms of abuse of elderly patients (including a patient being left bleeding profusely when the doctor was summoned to a meeting; nurses mocking an elderly woman who had become incontinent; threats of incarceration for a 'difficult' patient; theft by a porter; and drug abuse and drug theft by care staff) relating to elderly patients.

17 'Care abuse worker jailed.' *BBC News Online*, 7 February 2000.

18 'Community care putting lives at risk.' *Electronic Telegraph*, 25 November 1998.

19 'Nursing home manager abused patients.' *Sunday Life*, 23 May 1999.

20 Quoted in Age Concern 1999a.

21 'Lack of care rules put elderly at risk.' *Electronic Telegraph*, 27 February 1996.

22 Evidence to the Senate Special Committee on Ageing. Cited in *Times Magazine*, 27 October 1997.

23 'Hospital nurse accused of killing elderly patients.' *US News*, 30 December 1997.

24 24 July Adult Federal Protection (AFP).

25 Quoting Saunders, founder of the hospice movement.

26 See the allegations of bureaucratic disposal of the elderly in NHS hospitals by Dr Rita Pal ('Elderly are helped to die to clear beds, claims doctor.' *The Sunday Times*, 2 April 2000). Dr Pal quotes examples of a diabetic patient being deprived of basic medical attention ('she will die anyway,' a nurse reportedly commented); and a doctor who, when told about a patient dying from a liver complaint, allegedly said 'Well, he is over 60.' and made no effort to administer medical attention; and life-saving medication was withdrawn from a third on the principle that the hospital needed beds. Similar allegations appear from a paramedic of regularly witnessing elderly people being condemned to death on arrival at hospital before they had undergone a full medical assessment ('Paramedic tells of hospital leaving patients to die.' *The Sunday Times*, 16 April 2000).

27 See also the review of hospice studies by Seale (1989).

28 Illich (1991) has argued that a primary function of twentieth century medical practitioners is the role of 'managing' death effectively.

29 See Chapter 8. The guidelines say doctors should be authorised to withdraw food and water from stroke victims and the confused elderly, even when the patient is not terminally ill. ('Doctors to decide right to die.' *Guardian*, 24 June 1999).

30 'Hospital accused of letting patients die.' *Electronic Telegraph*, 1 December 1998.

31 'Patients demand "living wills" to protect elderly.' *Electronic Telegraph*, 8 December 1999.

32 'Inquiry call into "neglect" of the elderly.' *The Times*, 14 April 2000.

33   'People are just being written off by the system.' *Electronic Telegraph*, 6 December 1999.

34   *Electronic Telegraph*, 2 December 1999.

35   'Slack councils told to improve or jeopardise welfare of vulnerable.' *The Guardian*, 12 April 1999.

36   In one case, a residential home owner, faced with a long-standing allegation of mistreatment of the elderly, and who was eventually struck off the Register because of those practices, was reappointed to the local Registration and Inspection Committee ('Home owner struck off register.' *Belfast Telegraph*, 25 April 1996). For a detailed case study of the ineffectiveness of current inspection procedures with regard to private nursing homes, see the account of the death of May Hall in 'When care falls short.' *The Times*, 1 February 2000.

37   'Code to set standards for nursing home care.' *Electronic Telegraph*, 26 September 1998.

38   Jeff Smith, Counsel and Care, 'Failure of complaint system in NHS.' *Electronic Telegraph*, 27 March 1999.

39   'Elderly patients left starving to death in NHS.' *Electronic Telegraph*, 6 December 1999.

40   'In possibly thousands of cases, nursing home residents are dying from a lack of food and water and the most basic level of hygiene.' *Time Magazine*, 27 October 1997.

41   See *inter alia* the illustration of how private care homes 'manage' the inspection process in the United States, in the statement of Nursing Assistant Kathleen Duncan before the Senate Special Committee on Ageing (as cited in *Time Magazine*, *ibid.*). The hearing produced several horrific accounts of nursing home deaths through neglect and omission.

42   'In possibly thousands of cases, nursing home residents are dying from a lack of food and water and the most basic level of hygiene.' *Time Magazine*, 27 October 1997.

43   *Ibid.*

44   Evidence to the US Senate Special Committee on Ageing (as cited in *Time Magazine*, *ibid*).

45   *Ibid.*

46   The opposition of the owners' body, the National Care Homes Association, to the consultation paper on care standards, *Fit for the Future*, was not helped by one metaphor in the claim for compensation – 'If we were farmers culling sheep or cattle, there would be a compensation package.' ('Launch of consultation paper on care home standard.' *BBC Online*, 8 September 1999).

47   'Private nursing homes under threat.' *Electronic Telegraph*, 27 October 1999.

48   Charles Phillips, Myers Research Institute. Quoted in *Time Magazine*, *ibid.*

49   Diversified corporation ownership is also partly true in the UK. For example, the combine Alchemy (best known for its attempt to purchase the ailing Rover car group) was recently the subject of an inquiry by the Health and Safety Executive for allegedly 'asset-stripping' after trying to evict scores of mentally ill pensioners from its elderly care homes (*The Times*, 30 March 2000). For dramatic detail of the commercialisation of the elderly care sector in Britain (and its current crisis after over-expanding), see the report by the market analyst Laing & Buisson (cited by correspondent David Brindle) in 'Lonely old age.' *The Guardian*, 20 March 2000.

49a   *Time Magazine*, 27 October 1997.

50   Phillips, cited in *Time Magazine*, *ibid.*

51   'Patient's choking death spreads pain all round.' *Tampa Tribune*, 11 May 1998. For an even more stark case of dying by alleged neglect and abuse in a nursing home, see Eisler (1994).

CHAPTER 6

Death in Literary Discourse

At eight times seven I waxed old,
And took myself unto my rest,
Neighbours then sought my counsel bold,
And I was held in great respect;
But age did so abate my strength,
That I was forced to yield at length...
At ten times seven my glass is run,
And I poor silly man must die;
I looked up, and saw the sun
Had overcome the crystal sky.
So now I must this world forsake,
Another man my place must take.
Now you may see, as in a glass,
The whole estate of mortal men;
How they from seven to seven do pass,
Until they are three score and ten;
And when their glass is fully run,
They must leave off as they begun.

(W.M. Thackeray, 'The Life and Stages of Man'
(1811–63)[1], quoted in Ray 1946).

As in the preceding chapter, ironic humour may be the only way that commentators can deal with the commercialisation and bureaucratisation of death-hastening for the elderly.

The undertaking profession, while increasing roughly in proportion to the increase in the general population, neglected to take into account that the death rate which was 19 per thousand in 1880 would by 1960 be exactly halved. By now...funeral directors have learned that while other businessmen eagerly scan the booming population figures and project them in planning for the future, they must gloomily confine themselves to the column headed 'deaths per annum'... Mr William Krieger reports a hopeful trend 'We are coming to the end of a line, we cannot continue to expand the span of life for people indefinitely. It has to turn down. There is a slight increase in the mortality rate'. (Mitford 1978, p.52)

Early gerontological accounts of ageing have often ignored the more critical views from social history provided by literary sources. They have omitted sources that depict the lives of the common people, and which document experiences often much different from that of their betters (Blythe 1979). Not that literary and media representations are necessarily a guarantee of accuracy. Recent evidence notes that consistently fewer older people appear in the media, with a relative overrepresentation of older men (over 2:1) as compared to older women. Some 7 per cent of people on television were 60 years old compared with 21 per cent in the real world (Age Concern 1999c).

But while in the present day the elderly are notable mainly by their absence from fictional representations, historically it was their actual form of presentation that was the problem.

Evidence from literature,[2] from religious sources and from folklore suggests that ageism as an ideology has been present throughout history. Although legal statutes may have proscribed direct actions against the elderly, story-telling metaphors, allegories, and historical moralising suggest that older people, especially those now regarded as senescent, have always been represented as disposable because of their lack of utility.

A tradition-sanctified resolution endemic to those accounts is that terminating the life of elderly people should solve the perceived problems of demography and of economics. In primitive society, in medieval ballads, in folk songs and fairy stories, limiting the life of old people has been a cultural assumption. From the Greeks to Shakespeare, killing the elderly often appeared as non-problematic affairs. In more recent years, science fiction writers especially have often thought the unthinkable, confronting the dilemma of finding room for the elderly. Science fiction speculated where others would fear to tread, when faced with the demographic time bomb dilemma. From Trollope to Harrison, writers have attempted to solve in imagination that demographic crisis. In this chapter, we explore the alternative accounts of the treatment of the elderly that elucidate death-hastening experience in a variety of literary sources, past and present.

Literacy sources allow us to explore the continuing practice of elderly killing – mainly death-hastening – that more conventional sources tend to ignore. One feature of that literature is that it often does not treat the elderly as dummy figures but as agents who develop their own techniques of resistance – on some occasions single-minded elderly contrive their own voluntary termination. In particular, much has been written in literary form – especially in science fiction – of dystopian views of the demographic time bomb. More contemporary writers, novelists and especially poets have explored death-hastening experiences in care and nursing homes. They have also portrayed with considerable feeling the liminal status of those cast into the void between life and death.

Killing the elderly in literature

Nowhere has this tradition of furnishing an alternative discourse been as obvious as in the doggerel commemorating the workhouse as an institution that kills the elderly. Lord John Manners recounts of Victorian society in 'England's Trust':

> Gone are those days, and gone are the ties that then
> Bound peers and gentry to their fellow men.
> Now, in their place, behold the modern slave,
> Doomed, from the very cradle to the grave,
> To tread his lonely path of care and toil;
> Bound, in sad truth, and bowed down to the soil,
> He dies, and leaves his sons their heritage
> Work for their prime, and workhouse for their age.[3]

The workhouse gave rise to a plebeian critique, which sought to expose that institution's death-hastening role. Several contributors portrayed it as a living charnel house. In the United States, the best known is William McKendree Carleton's 'Over the Hill to the Poorhouse'.[4] Victorian England gave birth to several vivid accounts of the old person's view of the workhouse, summarised in the lines by Ebenezer Elliott.

> And Workhouse bread ne'er cross'd my teeth –
> I trust it never will.[5]

James Withers Reynolds caught its flavour in the following excerpt:

> I'll give you a sketch of our life in the union...,
> Let me see: well, the first is our grand bill of fare.
> We've skilly for breakfast; at night cheese and bread,
> And we eat it and then go to bed if you please,
> Two days in the week we have puddings for dinner,
> And two, we have broth, so like water but thinner;
> Two, meat and potatoes, of this none to spare,
> One day, bread and cheese – and this is our fare...
> I sometimes look at the bit of blue sky
> High over my head, with a tear in my eye.
> Surrounded by walls that are too high to climb,
> Confined like a felon without any crime...,
> I'll drink to your health with a tin of cold water:
> Of course we've no wine, nor porter, no beer,
> So you see we are all teetotallers here.

But the best known attack on the workhouse guardians as part of a killing machine for the elderly poor appears in George Robert Sims's 'Christmas Day in the Workhouse' (1902) in which an angry old man rejects the Christmas 'feast' – the price paid for entry was his wife's death from starvation:

> One of the old men mutters,
> And pushes his plate aside:
> 'Great God!' he cries 'but it chokes me!
> For this is the day she died'...
> Do you think I will take your bounty?
> And let you smile and think
> You're doing a noble action
> With the parish's meat and drink?
> Where's my wife, you traitors –
> The poor old wife you slew?
> Yes, by the God above us,
> My Nance was killed by you!
> Last winter my wife lay dying,
> Starved in a filthy den;
> I had never been to the parish.
> I came to the parish then.
> I swallowed my pride in coming,
> For, ere the ruin came,
> I held up my head as a trader,
> And I bore a spotless name.
> I came to the parish, craving
> Break for a starving wife,
> Bread for the woman who'd loved me
> Through fifty years of life;
> And what do you think they told me,
> Mocking my awful grief?
> That 'the House' was open to us,
> But they wouldn't give 'out' relief.
> I rushed from the room like a madman,
> And flew to the workhouse gate,
> Crying 'food for a dying woman!'
> And the answer came 'Too late'.
> They drove me away with curses;
> Then I fought with a dog in the street,
> And tore from the mongrel's clutches
> A crust that he was trying to eat.
> Back through the filthy by-lanes!

Back through the trampled slush!
Up to the crazy garret,
Wrapped in an awful hush,
My heart sank down at the threshold,
And I paused with a sudden thrill.
For there in the silv'ry moonlight
My Nance lay, cold and still. ...
She called for her absent husband, –
O God! Had I but known'! -
Had called in vain, and in anguish,
Had died in that den – alone.
Yes, there, in land of plenty
Lay a loving woman dead,
Cruelly starved and murdered
For a loaf of the parish bread.
At yonder gate last Christmas,
I craved for a human life.
You who would feast us paupers,
What of my murdered wife!

From a much earlier period, anecdotes and aphorisms depict the killing of old people and the use of their corpses for the betterment of their offspring. Often told in mock humour, they contain a kernel of folk wisdom which demonstrates their message had a legitimate source. Ashliman (1999) has collected an extraordinary series of folk stories, which illustrate how the elderly have been commonly susceptible to disposal by their sons, as their frailty is perceived.

He recounts a 'heathen' story from Steinfort in which old people were put to death, chopped into small pieces and buried in large jars in the earth. The treatment of the corpses of the elderly demonstrates the disappearance of all human affinity. Elderly corpses are dehumanised – as such they have often been a source of jest. In the medieval story *Big Peter and Little Peter* (cited by Ashliman 1999), the wealthier of the two brothers kills his poor brother's only calf. Little Peter, the poor brother, skins the animal and tries to sell the hide. By cunning, he obtains a bag of gold for his endeavours, which he persuades his brother is simply the price of the calfskin. Big Peter promptly kills his own animals but is unsuccessful in selling them on the market. He seeks to kill his brother as retaliation, but the latter manages to place his elderly mother in the way of Big Peter's axe. Thus Big Peter chopped off her head instead. Little Peter then plotted to use her corpse to obtain more gold. Taking her to the market, he poses as an apple seller and balances the severed head on her neck. A customer is insulted because she would not respond to his questions, slaps her, knocking off her head. Believing that he has killed the old woman, the customer pays Little Peter a large sum in return for not reporting him to the authorities. He returns home and shows Big Peter the money their old mother's body had brought at the market. Big Peter had an old stepmother and he killed her outright, taking the body to market hoping for a similarly high price. But instead of money, he receives only scorn and threats of arrest.

An Icelandic version[6] relates how a woman killed her old mother-in-law (who lived with her and her husband) and then set the body in a kneeling position over her husband's treasure chest. The husband thinks the 'intruder' is a burglar and stabs her. Recognising the corpse as his own mother, he enlists his wife's help to dispose of the body. The younger woman twice again sets up similar tricks. Thus, she can rid herself of her ageing mother-in-law only after she has had her 'killed' four times.

Ashliman suggests that the continuity of such stories reflects feelings of hostility towards the aged long after civilisation has developed safeguards against the literal killing of people deemed too old to be of further use. The image of the ageing parent as a troublesome burden is only thinly veiled behind the curtain of slapstick in these tales, as in a more recent story.[7] A couple takes a camping holiday in Spain with their car. Their stepmother accompanies them, but subsequently dies in her tent. Not knowing how to deal with the foreign bureaucracy, the couple roll the corpse up in a tent and tie it to the roof of their car. However, the car is stolen and the couple are forced to return home without their car – and without the stepmother they are consequently unable to prove her death to collect their inheritance.

Irrespective of the accuracy of the particular folk stories, their ubiquity suggests the prevalence of the custom of geronticide as well as the variety of defences developed by the elderly to forestall the practice.

Elderly defence against geronticide: Ashliman's collection

Folk stories – presumably the property of the older generations to pass down – commonly furnish accounts of their own value to the community. Stories include the clear moral that killing the elderly is the waste of a valuable resource. Nowhere is this value more emphasised than in the accounts of the attempt to ward off an unwilled death at the hands of their younger kin. For example, in the *Arabian Nights* three old men each tell the jinni a tale more marvellous than the one preceding it, in return for helping the merchant extend his life, the latter part of which is in thrall to the jinni.[8]

From Serbia, 'in old times, it was the habit to kill old men when they had passed fifty years'. In this story, a son felt sorry for his father and concealed him in a wine vat. The latter advised the former on how to win a bet to see the rising sun first. Consequently, the son's competitors learn that if the father had been killed, such sage advice would not have been available. Ashliman (1999) quotes a second

Serbian story. A high hill had been fortified and the leader had ordered that all the holders of the fort up to the age of 40 years were to be active in its defence, from 40 to 50 years, they were to undertake static guard duty, while those over that age were to be killed because they had no military value. This practice was continued when the occupants went on the offensive. A grandson who had secretly hidden his grandfather rather than having him slain, benefited from the latter's advice by taking a horse and its colt with him on the venture. On the trek to distant lands, the young man secretly killed the colt. When the band was defeated in the subsequent battle and the remnants found themselves lost in foreign territory, the young man could find his way home by urging his horse to seek the place where its colt had been killed. The successful return home was recognised to be a result of the elder's wise advice to his grandson; the value of such sagacity was acknowledged, and the killing of the elderly stopped.

Ashliman quotes a similar Romanian story when 'it was the custom to kill old people because they were considered useless'. In this case, the killing of the foal allowed the young man to guide his people back safely from a monster's lair. The son revealed to his fellows that his ploy drew upon his elderly father's experience and advice, and the moral is drawn: 'Our forefathers have not acted well in teaching us to kill the old men. They have gained experience and they can help our people by their advice when the strength of our arm fails.' A further Romanian story contains a similar theme – over-confident young people who believe they are cleverer than the elderly, and a king who accedes to his subjects' demands to rid themselves of those who 'had lived their lives'. The son disobeys the orders and conceals and secretly feeds his father. A drought and later a severe winter kill off cattle and crops. But the father's advice to plough the highways where grain would have fallen from passing carts saves the community, resulting in the community recognising the folly of its action towards the elderly. The geronticide order is rescinded.

In Bali, in a remote mountain village, all the old men were rounded up, sacrificed and eaten. The young men wanted to build a great house for ceremonial meetings. However, after cutting the necessary trees, none of them could tell the tops from the bottom, and the house could not be built. Then a young man spoke out and offered to solve the problem. He brought out his grandfather, whom he had hidden. The old man explained to the young men how to tell the top from the bottom and consequently demonstrated the value of the aged (Barash 1983).

Ashliman quotes a final story from Macedonia in which the old men are left to the mercy of wild beasts to save the limited food supply for the younger. In this case, the old men's advice saves the community by showing how ants have stored precious grain in an anthill. Again, the lesson was learned, the value of elderly wisdom recognised, and geronticide ceased. Ashliman demonstrates both the near-universality of the custom and of the morals drawn, with further folk stories from Germany, Greece and Japan, and from parts of Africa.

Past to future: Science fiction and geronticide

A further genre projects disposability through ageism into the future. Several generations of novelists and science fiction writers have reached not dissimilar conclusions to those of the folklore scribes about the disposal of the elderly.

In 'Parents and Children' (1888, pp.3–4) Bernard Shaw notes that if Society wishes to continue what he calls 'breeding', it must accept the inevitability of killing the elderly in order to make way for the young. Such deaths would be the only way of discouraging old people from seeking eternal life.

The grim practice is dealt with humorously in the film *Arsenic and Old Lace.* Two elderly aunts have the disagreeable habit of poisoning their gentlemen callers and burying them in the cellar. The aunts believe that they are being kind to people who are already on their way, and hold touching funeral services for all their victims.

The Victorian Anthony Trollope led the field towards a resolution with his story *The Fixed Period* (first published 1884) about a mythical British colony off the coast of New Zealand, one faced with the practicalities of supporting an elderly population. Trollope's narrator Neverbend, the First Minister, enumerates all the advantages of voluntary termination of life for citizens when they reach the age of 67 years. The assembly passes a motion intended to save the elderly from the infirmities of old age. Why should old people have to put up with declining years of sorrow and physical misery when they could end their days at an agreed date with the help of the new society's functionaries – as well as save scarce resources? Previous societies have, according to the narrator, by an ill-judged and thoughtless tenderness, failed to provide for the decent and comfortable departure of their progenitors. In the story, statistical evidence demonstrates that the sufficient sustenance of an old man is more costly than the feeding of a young one – the enfeebled old and the unprofitable young constituted a third of the colony's population. All could not be supported. Knowing their fate in advance, older people would be prepared, and would die realising that they were no longer dependent on charity, would be surrounded on their deathbeds by all available comforts, and conscious that they had benefited their country. As honoured citizens, they would save their new country sufficient to help pay off the national debt. Sanitary arrangements at the grave would abolish grief and replace it with pride. The age of departure was determined after debate to be 67 years because at that age a man's hearing would have largely disappeared, his voice would have ascended to a poor treble, or his eyesight would be dim and failing, and his limbs would have lost all the robust agility necessary for the adequate performance of productive work. Death would be peaceful – the older person's veins being opened while he was unconscious from morphine. In the event, Neverbend's leg-islation collapses under the twin impact of elderly self-interest – they disagree with the ageist depiction of themselves – and the coincident arrival of a British frigate which challenges the morbid rationality of the scheme.

Science fiction has re-worked the theme constantly. It occurs dramatically in the Victorian Walter Besant's novel *The Inner House* (1888) (referred to in Chapter 1). The book opens in 1890 with one Professor Schwarbaum revealing his discovery of the 'The Prolongation of Life Principle'. He donates the secret of the anti-ageing chemical, assuming it will be used to prolong life until a person has enjoyed everything he or she could desire, and that after two or three centuries '…contented and resigned you would sink into the tomb, not satiated with the joys of life but, but satisfied to have had your share. There would be no terror in death, because all would have felt satisfied that they had achieved all they were able.' Much further in the future, the introduction of the Great Discovery was followed by the Great Slaughter, which culled almost all the elderly so that the earth would be able to support the henceforward irreducible population (aside from accidents) in the 'better' age brackets. No one had been willing to choose death under any circumstances, and the continuance of life had been elevated into a secular religion by the College of Physicians, which controlled distribution of the chemical and was thus in a position to run the society as it saw fit. A subsequent rebellion, as a reaction to social stagnation and unchanging people, fails partly because most members of the College of Physicians are too deeply committed to their vision of the Triumph of Science to accept a renewal of the risk and anxiety of a waning elderly population.

In Kurt Vonnegut's black comedy *The Big Trip up Yonder* (1988), overpopula-tion is the result of technologies of longevity. John Macmillan Brown created emblematically-named 'Liminorians'. Medical science allows the Liminorians to live for centuries. If they chose to die, euthanasia was readily available and regarded as a 'holy duty', since death of the self meant advance for the 'higher energy' and 'truer self'. It was carried out by an electric 'petrifier' which instantly turned the moribund Liminorian into a life-like effigy constructed of *irrelium* (a much prized and versatile metal).

Frederik Pohl produced the first of many ironic fantasies of corrective mass homicide in *The Census Takers* (1956). Robert Silverberg takes the notion of insti-tutionalised population control more seriously in *Master of Life and Death* (1957). J.G. Ballard's *Billenium* (1962) furnishes a detailed account of the slow shrinkage of personal space due to overpopulation. Several science fiction contributions deal with the social problems of living in crowded conditions. John Brunner updates the Isle of Wight thesis with *Stand on Zanzibar* (1968). Brian Aldiss in *Greybeard* (1964) furnishes an ironic twist to the concern with an ageing population – humanity has become sterile due to an accident involving nuclear weapons.

Almost all the characters are old people and the novel is an account of their reactions to incipient death.

In Vonnegut's short story 'Tomorrow and tomorrow and tomorrow' (1988), the demographic problem is confronted directly. In a crowded New York apartment in the year 2158, Lou (112 years) and his wife Em (93 years) are concerned with the consequences of their grandfather's (172-years-old) longevity – due to the discovery of the anti-ageing potion, anti-gerasone. The couple and their massive extended family take turns to sleep, because of the over-crowding. 'I get so sick of seeing his wrinkled old face, watching him take the only private room and the best chair and the best food, and pick out what to watch on TV and running everyone's life by changing his will all the time.' (pp.293–4) The grandfather kept inventing excuses for not giving up the anti-gerasone. 'Sometimes I wish folks just up and died regular as clockwork. Instead of deciding themselves how long to stay around. There ought to be a law against selling the stuff to anyone over 150'. Em says she will do herself in at 150 years just by pouring the anti-gerasone down the plughole. In the event, the couple try to kill him by refilling his anti-gerasone bottle with tapwater. Unfortunately, the grand-father discovers the ruse, and the story concludes with the grandfather discov-ering an advertisement for a new 'super' anti-gerasone that will prevent wrinkles, and rejuvenate his hair.

Similar themes of the utility of elderly disposal appear in several earlier science fiction contributions. Lucien in *Dips in the Near Future* (1920) furnishes a picture of an Orwellian England beset by military conflict. Emergency legislation, the Aged Service Act, in a parallel to the military draft, provides for persons over 65 years old to be enlisted in patriotic military terms and selectively put to death to ease the food shortage. Lillian Francis Mentor draws on Rider Haggard in *The Day of Resis* (1897) to describe an African society which enjoys an annual day of cleansing. On that date, all men and women aged 65 years are ritually killed because they are a handicap to the eugenic principle on which the pure society is based. Notions of ritual cleansing to ensure the continuity of a society characterised by ideal types of male and female appear in *The Cylinder* (1918) by Victor Rousseau Emanuel. The narrator notes how that because the secret of immortality has been discovered, only elderly 'defectives' are subject to eradication.

More demographic determinism appears in *The New Gods Lead* (1932), an S. Fowler Wright short story collection. In the Great Britain of 1972, thanks to preventive medicine and improved social conditions, the age level has risen greatly. Consequently, the number of older people is disproportionately large and the younger generation find themselves dominated, exploited, and deprived of their heritage by the very old. A rebellion begins in the village of Fenny-Warford, when Michael Bede wrings the neck of his 'obnoxious old aunt' and does not cease until three-quarters of a million old men and women have been killed.

Martin Swayne's *The Blue Germ* (1918) documents a society in which chemically induced immortality results in the disappearance of enthusiasm and desire, and in a widespread slaughter of the elderly by the young, who see access to wealth and position permanently barred.

A more recent novel approach to disposing of the elderly infirm appears in J.A. Gardner's *Expendable* (first published 1954). An environmental crisis results in a decline in the earth's capacity to sustain the population. Only by searching for new worlds can life be sustained. However, that exploration will mean death for the explorers because of the extreme conditions. Therefore only the infirm and the elderly can be used for that purpose because they are expendable. The film *Soylent Green* (1972)[9] similarly postulates an environment (New York)[10] characterised by overpopulation, pollution and no resources. The government solution is to provide euthanasia centres for those over the age of 30 – age here is the determinant of death although clearly frailty is not imputed. William F. Nolan and George Clayton Johnson's *Logan's Run* (1966) determines the time for compulsory euthanasia as 21 years! Death for a flexibly determined elderly also appears in Margaret Atwood's *The Handmaid's Tale* (1987) – in which women unsuited to service the dominant males are quietly dispatched.

From the past to the present to the future, ideas about the elderly being a residual population have been common. In times of crisis – from dearth to science fiction demographic catastrophes – the old are regarded as expendable. Independently of the rise of industrialism, there is adequate evidence from literature of the way the disutility of old people has been regularly pronounced on by the working (and presumed more viable) population.

To the extent that ageism, the systematic discrimination of people on the grounds of their age, may lead to the inappropriate bracketing of all older people as 'dependent', it leads at the same time to the marginalisation of those issues concerning older people, simply because they are older. One can contemplate the segregation of an elderly person in the 'care' home in a way that one could not consider the same experience to be appropriate for a younger person. The dominant ideology historically is an image of the elderly as 'wrinklies', 'coffin-dodgers', being 'over the hill', and so on. Cultural representation in Western society has not been favourable to older people. In the present day, they may become the butt of ribald humour.

But there are other ways of dealing with overpopulation than through geronticide. Nowhere is that quandary solved more starkly than in the mechanism of Anthony Burgess's 'population police' in *The Wanting Seed* (1976). They indulge in a variety of non-geronticidal practices – mass executions of those who exceed the one child per family rule; turning spare children into cannibalistic fodder;[11] creating specially designed killing fields of mutual slaughter for soldiers; and in officially exalting the virtues of homosexuality.

Death-hastening in the care and nursing home

Several novels explore death-hastening in nursing homes. The encouragement to enter by unwilling relatives is a constant theme. Thus Sawako Ariyoshi's *The Twilight Years* (1972) documents the universal problems for the daughter-in-law carer. She tells the story of the Tachibanas, an ordinary family living in a Tokyo suburb who, after the sudden death of the husband's mother, are faced with the care of his aged father Shigezo. That task of looking after the old man falls chiefly on his daughter-in-law Akiko, who is herself a working woman. When the old man's dementia becomes too great, the rationing of nursing home facilities frustrates Akiko. There is substantial pressure on her to send him to an old people's home, where residents are rarely visited by their children. She describes how on a visit with him to the future hospice, when an elderly man dies after playing a game of GO, other residents view the incident dispassionately – 'never had a day's illness in his life'. 'They even envied the dead man' (p.122).

Doris Lessing's *The Diary of a Good Neighbour* (1983) provides an intense account of the relationship of a woman in her mid-life with an elderly female 'recluse'. When the latter is admitted to hospital, the younger woman learns how hospital staff endeavour to survive their labours in a context of an intense shortage of resources. Lon Myers' account of the ageing of a New York Yiddish community explores the life of the matriarch in the *When Life Falls, It Falls Upside Down* (1990). Death continually changes roommates. Staff are overworked. Paranoia infects the residents, who fear each other and thefts by 'illegals'.

One of the most dramatic functional accounts of a nursing home is given in Jacob van Velde's *The Big Ward* (1953). An elderly stroke victim is consigned to a public assistance building where older citizens go to die, where there is little privacy, and where the cries of patients are heard night and day. As in Myers (above), the novel vividly portrays the way the physical, emotional and financial exigencies overwhelm any sensitivity by the care and nursing staff. W. H. Auden's poem 'Old People's Home' (1932) similarly laments the death-hastening process of the elderly repository, the plight of older people destined to be abandoned and placed in institutions by families and by society.

A dismal death in the nursing home is the theme of Gwendolyn Brooks's *Death of a Grandmother* (1953). The narrator describes her grandmother as looking like a semi-corpse, ugly, repellent, and capable only of replying to questions with guttural responses. Brooks also details the de-humanising complaints of the hospital staff about the 'whines' of the elderly. The reaction of a pensioner to being encouraged to enter a so-called retirement home by his daughter is the subject of Richard Dokey's *The Autumn of Henry Simpson* (1982). 'Dokey's narrator describes a care home of the ultimate revulsion'. Nursing home death-hastening through futility and boredom is the theme of Mark Strand's poem 'Old People on the Nursing Home Porch' (1980) with the central image of elderly persons rocking quietly in the face of meaninglessness. What if they were rocking instead on the porches of their own homes, or the homes of their children? Jane Kenyon's poem 'In the Nursing Home' (1982) describes the increasingly circumscribed life of a dying resident. The final lines are a plea for God to bring an early, gentle death.

Sylvia Plath's 'Old Ladies' Home' (1955) captures the dehumanisation of the institutionalised aged, occasionally visited by children who are 'distant and cold as photos' with grandchildren 'nobody knows'. The poem is a formidable picture of the rejection of the elderly, and their waste disposal in the nursing homes. It also contains a *struldbrugg*-like caricature of the aged residents.

A similar view appears in a poem by Philip Booth, in 'Fallback' (1992) an old woman contrasts her earlier life with the present circumstances of herself and her husband as residents in the care wing of a nursing home. She is now frail and physically dependent and he suffers from dementia, as they occupy the liminal period between life and death. Philip Larkin's 'The Old Fools' (1974) laments the death-hastening experience. He complains about the conditions of existence of the institutional elderly, and includes a savage caricature of that life or death-style, with loss of memory, and drooping jaws being the defining feature of the dying elderly.

David Wagoner's *Part Song* (1979) depicts the death-hastening experience of life in a nursing home as the families of residents gather for a pathetic Thanksgiving party. The old people are immobile, detached, and waiting for death. In a short story by Gian Barriault, *The Bystander* (1982), the decrepit elderly are dumped in public institutions to rot away. The tedium of the institutional day as the inmates wait to die is vividly documented. Survival techniques under the death-hastening experience of the care home are illustrated in John Sayles's *Dillinger in Hollywood* (1980). In that short story, the inmates cultivated eccentricity as a means of maintaining notions of self within the geriatric home by the adoption of Hollywood characters. Robert E. McEnroe's *The Silver Whistle* (1984) is set in a drab, depressed, old people's home. In this case, a new inmate energises the life of the discarded to give them some purpose.

Ageism and the liminal status of the elderly

Robert Frost explores the liminal period between life and death with his poem 'An Old Man's Winter Night' (first published 1916). The old man decays in the isolated farmhouse, keeping at bay anxiety, loneliness and fear of mortality by walking noisily through the empty rooms of the house. John Ciardi's poem 'Matins' (1989) considers the death-hastening process in relation to the anonymous street people – it tells the story of a nameless old woman found frozen to death on a park bench. Even the high and mighty are transformed to irrelevant dust (in Jonathan Swift's 'On the Death of a Famous General'):

His Grace impossible! What dead!
Of old age too, and in his bed? ...
From all his ill-gotten Honours flung,
Turn'd to that dirt from whence he sprung.

In the short story by Richard Bausch *Rare and Endangered Species* (1994), the novelist analyses the unexplained suicide of an older woman. The main character, Andrea Brewer, calmly lunches with two friends, then registers at a motel and takes a lethal dose of pills. The family puzzles over the apparently inexplicable voluntary euthanasia. Yahnke and Eastman (1995) summarises the theme of Elizabeth Jolley's short story 'Mr Parker's Valentine' (1962). An old man's unwanted presence as a neighbour leads to feelings of resentment, hostility and rage that ends in 'accidental' death. New residents of an Australian house find a sitting tenant in the garden shed, a decaying old man. While the female house-holder finds some enjoyment in the old man's company, her husband increasingly sees him as an intrusion on his routine and encourages his marginalisation and death. William Carlos Williams in his poem 'The Widow's Lament' (1986) recounts an elderly widow's desire for a quiet death after the loss of her husband of 35 years. He strips away the hysterical sentimentality from the funeral rites for old people and reveals it as a bureaucratic and degrading experience.[12]

Several dramas depict the practices of death-hastening. Edward Albee in *The Sand Box* (1960) uses the metaphor of a sandbox for the nursing or care home. The son and daughter-in-law deposit the protesting mother in the sand box/nursing home, while feigning sympathy with the final disposal of the elderly. The rationale for that disposal in a death-hastening institution is explored in Edna Ferber's *Old Man Millick* (1922). The retired Millick is forced to share the small apartment of his son and daughter-in-law. He learns gradually that he has become a burden, a barrier, and an obstacle to their own life plans, tolerated as an 'old geezer'. This process of transformation from revered elder to socially disposable junk is also the subject of Allan Gurganus *A Hog Loves its Life* (1990). The grandfather mutates from the family sage to storyteller to the town oddity, 'one very old and cruelly healthy senile man', through a process of dementia.

Similarly, Olga Master's *You'll Like it Here* (first published 1982) documents the process by which an elderly woman comes to believe that a nursing home may be a desirable means of escape from the death-hastening experiences of living with her married sons. Suffering various forms of abuse and neglect at their hands, she shuttles backwards and forwards between the two domiciles. Respites are temporary while her daughters-in-law and their husbands plan to dump her in the old people's home. T.S. Winslow depicts a similar process of haphazard mistreatment and transformation in 'Grandma' (*Picture Frames* (1923)). A widowed grandmother of 73 years spends time with three different parts of her extended family.

The first well-meaningly finds a role for her by heaping her with the household chores. The second paternalistically leaves her to the instrumental care of the servants, while the third family abuses both her and one another. Each role consigns her to an inferior status ready for the liminal process.

In *The Love Story* (1947) J.F. Powers depicts an identical process through the experiences of part-time work for a retired man. The latter assumes a menial job to maintain his income and dignity. Despite his efforts to make a good impression, he is shattered and degraded when overhearing his supervisor describing him as an 'old bird' who is only fit for the 'old people's home'. Robert Vly portrays much the same sentiment in his poem 'A Visit to the Old People's Home' (1990). A son visiting his elderly mother in a nursing home becomes more concerned about his own sensitivities than conscious of the death-hastening experiences of his mother.

A kinder version of the same transformation, from well to liminal, appears in William Trevor's short story *Broken Homes* (1978). An elderly London widow is helped against her will by a teacher from a nearby school who decides that his students will decorate her kitchen free of charge, in order to encourage intergenerational understanding. The resulting carnage as the students take over the apartment results in the debilitation of the widow. Similarly misdirected good intentions are illustrated in E. Welty's short story *A Visit of Charity* (1980). A young girl visits the elder care home in order to boost her citizenship record. But instead of finding passive elders who welcome her visit, she encounters two elderly battling women who disillusion the young woman of her stereotypes of passive, caring, old folk.

This sense of the abandonment of the elderly dying and dead is more humour-lessly expressed in Thomas Hardy's (1976) 'Ah, Are You Digging on My Grave?'. A dead woman flatters herself about the reasons her grave is being visited – by her loved ones, her relatives, by her enemies and even by her dog. In each case, the answer is completely deflating – all the supposed 'visitors' are pursuing other interests without reference to her. The actual visitor is her little dog, who merely calls by to bury a bone.

Voluntary euthanasia

Several poets explore the topic of voluntary euthanasia. Thus Maya Angelou, after depicting in 'On Ageing' (1994) an old woman hanging on to life in the face of increasing senescence, develops the contrary theme in 'The Last Decision' (1994), in the experiences of an old woman, troubled by the difficult adaptation required of old age and by the tedious requirements of daily living. She yields to ageing as if it were a terminal condition, giving up reading, writing, listening, and 'living'.

In Miller Williams's 'A Day in the Death' (1992), a man lies dying in his hospital bed 'amazed how hard it is to die' and how long it takes. A nurse looks in, he tries to sleep. He wants to die but something is obstructing his terminal passage and he almost asks a counsellor for a 'push' on the way. David Ray imagines a Hemlock Society meeting where speaker after speaker emphasise that they do not want to encumber their relations as they turn into decaying vegetables. Membership of the Society is important because it may facilitate an alternative ending. A more clinical approach to the elderly choice of euthanasia appears in Francis King's 'The Tradesman' (1988). The elderly woman sorts out her affairs in order to end her life by choice by active euthanasia. After seeing two last guests she waits for the visit of a 'tradesman' and calmly arranges her self-execution with that specialist.[13]

A more cheerful outcome from a deliberate euthanasia attempt occurs for a widower who believes he has cancer in Damon Knight's 'The Resurrection Man' (1951). After the death of his wife, 80-year-old Alva Mason plots his own death in great detail to avoid wasting away – he didn't want to be trouble to anyone in his declining years. Mason digs an eight-foot deep hole with vertical sides on a mountain slope. He covers the hole with a plywood sheet for the time being, and creates a potential artificial landslide to cover it by an explosion triggered by a time-delay mechanism. Methodically he tidies up the site and leaves it until he is ready. In winter, as he feels his facilities are declining, he sets the timer and clambers into the pit with a glass jar containing a last goodbye, and falls asleep. But he wakes shortly and feels too hungry to commit suicide. Consequently, to have a meal he claws his way out of the pit, using the broken glass jar as a spade. He postpones the suicide indefinitely.

Overview

Literary sources often reveal different truths from those of more formal histories. The material noted in this chapter demonstrates several key factors regarding both geronticide and euthanasia. In accounts historical, modern, and futuristic, writers have thought the unthinkable. They have contemplated the experience of ageing – most of them negatively. Savage caricatures have been drawn of those in a liminal phase. Some of the most vivid comments have appeared over the experience of care institutions – a health warning has been issued. A few writers have conceived the mass slaughter of the elderly (and indeed of others) when powerful groups decide against them. Several have thoughtfully postulated euthanasia as a personal resolution to the end of a life. Submerged beneath more orthodox assumptions of a golden past – indeed, of a golden future – the literary contributors have hypothesised stark dystopian alternatives.

Notes

1   See also 'The Wild Old Wicked Man' by W.B. Yeats (1938).
2   For an excellent overview of literary representations of the elderly in pre-industrial society, see Fowler, D.H., Fowler, L.J. and Lamdin, L. 'Themes of old age in pre-industrial Western literature' in Stearns (1984).
3   Quoted in Quadagno 1982.
4   See Chapter 4, note 6.
5   The best source for the workhouse ballads (including Elliott, Reynolds and Sims) is in the excellent collection in the University of Oxford's Bodleian Library under 'Workhouse Literature'.
6   'The Woman that Was Killed Four Times', cited by Ashliman 1999.
7   In Briggs and Tongue's *Folktales of England* (1965).
8   Palummbo, cited in Ashliman 1999.
9   Based on Harry Harrison's book *Make Room! Make Room!* (1964).
10   New York appears frequently in the death of the unwanted. The anti-Semitic nineteenth century novelist Ignatius Donnelly had solved the overpopulation problem by providing a clinical process of voluntary euthanasia in *Caesar's Column: A Story of the Twentieth Century* (1891) 'Every day, hundreds of people, men and women, go there'.
11   As also Jonathan Swift, who proposed to solve the 'Irish question' of overpopulation, by fattening up younger members of the 'improvident' lower classes and selling them on the market as meat for the rich.
12   See also William Carlos Williams's 'The Last Words of My English Grandmother' (1986) in which the ailing grandmother protests volubly as the ambulance speeds her to final repository.
13   A similar routinisation of the last moment appears in Miroslav Holub's (1967) 'Death in the Evening' in his *Selected Poems*. Harmondsworth: Penguin.

CHAPTER 7

Death by Choice(?)

Physician-assisted Suicide and Voluntary Euthanasia

Raymond and Mary Bouldsbridge would have celebrated their diamond wedding anniversary in a fortnight. Instead, Mr Bouldsbridge will spend Thursday 22nd June alone, contemplating not only the death of his wife, but the failed mercy killing that led to his conviction for her attempted murder. The court heard that for the last six years of (her) life she had suffered from Alzheimer's Disease, gradually deteriorating to the point where doubly incontinent, and completely immobile, she required assistance from two carers three times a day, seven days a week...(fearing the withdrawal of care), distraught with anxiety and 'out of his mind', Mr Bouldsbridge decided to end his wife's suffering and his own. Attaching a hose to the exhaust of his car, he started the engine, jammed the accelerator open with a small cane, led the other end of the hose into the couple's bedroom and lay down beside his wife to die. The couple only survived because a neighbour, hearing the car engine running, followed the hosepipe and found the couple still breathing.[1]

The Voluntary Euthanasia Society called the acquittal of GP David Moor at Newcastle upon Tyne...'a huge relief to doctors and patients throughout Britain' but said guidelines were urgently needed to tell doctors how they could help dying patients without risking a similar prosecution. Had Dr Moor...been convicted of murdering 85-year-old George Liddell, a cancer sufferer, he would have faced a life sentence, which is mandatory for murder. His defence rested on the principle of 'double effect' which lays down that doctors may legally administer drugs which hasten a patient's death, as long as the intention was to ease suffering.[2]

Introduction

Geronticide means the death of the elderly person as a consequence of the actions or inactions of others – by direct coercion, or by a mix of social, psychological and economic pressures. Elderly people are subject to death-hastening pressures by others. Either they may be killed by them, directly or indirectly, quickly or slowly, or they may take their own life. The position on an elderly death continuum can, however, be distinguished if one accepts a principle of voluntariness – that sometimes older people wish to take their own lives independently of outside pressures. At one extreme is geronticide itself, a relatively clear-cut decision by others. At the other end of the continuum is voluntary euthanasia, where notionally no external factors intervene. Somewhere towards that end of the scale is physician-assisted suicide (PAS), where the individual requires assistance in that final act. However, the exact location of PAS on the determinism–voluntarism continuum is controversial – at what point does a decision by medical practitioners (as in the case of 'Do not resuscitate' orders discussed in Chapter 5) support or override any decisions or non-decisions by an elderly person? What criteria are taken into account by practitioners – the needs of the patient, of the relatives, the result of some diagnostic enquiry, or are practitioners too fallible in that decision-making process? Further – at one point does death for the older person become a function of free will rather than of external forces? When is death truly chosen by a clearly willing older person – voluntary euthanasia?

- Voluntary euthanasia is usually debated – in a myriad texts – in relation to a much wider population than the elderly, principally in the modern world in relation to the disabled, the handicapped and the terminally ill. But the evidence suggests that it is the elderly who are mainly its subject. Euthanasia, in its several varieties, cannot be discussed without reference to the tradition-sanctified ideology of ageism.

- Voluntary euthanasia and physician-assisted suicide are normally discussed in the context of the relationship between old age and some other factor – for example incurable pain or psychosocial factors such as depression.

- Attesting to the *voluntarism* of euthanasia is immensely complicated because it is difficult to decide when an individual is, or is not, acting under external pressures.

- Most of the evidence on elderly suicide suggests that it is most frequently chosen not when an individual is suffering from unmanageable pain but rather when the individual is experiencing a psychosocial problem such as a depressive illness.

- With caveats (surveys vary), older people are generally more in favour of voluntary euthanasia and physician-assisted suicide than are younger people; that is, the population most at risk may also be the population most in favour.

- However, within that elderly population stratification is evident – the groups that have the worst experience of medicine and are the most socio-economically deprived (from the elderly poor to elderly ethnic minorities) are the ones who most oppose voluntary euthanasia, believing that where it occurs through medical intervention, experience will reflect their other forms of discrimination.

- There is evidence that when voluntary euthanasia occurs by self-deprivation (i.e. when individuals starve themselves or refuse life-sustaining medication) they succumb most easily and with the least pain.

- Not every intervention by a recognised medical practitioner to assist suicide is effective – like others, medical professionals can be incompetent, lacking in appropriate knowledge, self-willed, and may be influenced by ageist ideology.[3]

A brief history of suicide and voluntary euthanasia

In most Western societies, it is a crime to assist in a suicide. Assisted suicide prohibitions are not novel. As we noted in Chapter 3, supporting euthanasia for the elderly was an approved custom in several ancient societies. In Greece and Rome, for example, voluntary euthanasia and PAS were normatively accepted ways that people of rank might dispose of themselves to avoid prolonged suffering. All the arguments used today to justify (or to condemn) the two practices were articulated before any modern biotechnology existed. The Hippocratic oath was written at a time when physicians commonly assisted suicide for ailments ranging from foot infections and gall stones to cancer and senility – the oath was a minority intrusion in the euthanasia debate within the ancient Greek medical community.

The legal prohibition of euthanasia has been a longstanding expression of the commitment to the protection and preservation of all human life. For over 700 years, Anglo-American common law tradition has punished both suicide and assisting suicide. In the thirteenth century, Henry de Bracton, one of the first legal treatise writers, observed that 'Just as a man may commit felony by slaying another so may he do so by slaying himself' – petty treason in depriving the monarch of one of his or her subjects. The material goods and household property of one who killed himself were forfeit to the king. However, 'if a man slays himself in weariness of life or because he is unwilling to endure further bodily pain…[only] his movable goods [are] confiscated'.[4] The principle that the suicide of a sane person was a punishable felony was one bedrock of English common law. In early modern society, any homicide of an adult, whether by another or by oneself, was constructed as a prima-facie felony.

Late medieval treatise writers restated Bracton; one observing that 'man slaughter' may be 'of oneself; as in the case, when people hang themselves or hurt themselves, or otherwise kill themselves of their own felony' or 'of others; as by beating, famine, or other punishment; in like cases, all are man slayers'.[5] By the mid-sixteenth century, the Court at Common Bench could observe that '[suicide] is an Offence against Nature, against God, and against the King... To destroy one's self is contrary to Nature, and a Thing most horrible'. In 1644, Sir Edward Coke published his *Third Institute*, a lodestar for later common lawyers. Coke regarded suicide as a category of murder, and agreed with Bracton that the goods and chattels, but not the lands, of a sane suicide were forfeit. William Hawkins, in his *Treatise of the Pleas of the Crown* (1716), followed Coke, observing that 'our laws have always had...an abhorrence of this crime.'

Philosophers occasionally challenged that legal proscription. During the Renaissance, English humanist Thomas More (1478–1535) defended voluntary euthanasia in his book *Utopia* (1516) (see below). More describes in sardonic terms the function of hospitals. Medical workers watch over their patients with tender care and do everything in their power to cure ills. But when a patient has a tortuous and incurable illness, the patient has the option to die, either through starvation or through opium. Similarly, in *The New Atlantis* (1626), Francis Bacon (1561–1626) wrote that physicians are 'not only to restore the health, but to mitigate pain and dolours; and not only when such mitigation may conduce to recovery, but when it may serve to make a fair and easy passage'.

Legal orthodoxy was reaffirmed in Blackstone, whose *Commentaries on the Laws of England* (1765), were the definitive summary of common law for eighteenth and nineteenth century lawyers. He referred to suicide as 'self murder' and 'the pretended heroism, but real cowardice, of the Stoic philosophers, who destroyed themselves to avoid those ills which they had not the fortitude to endure'. Blackstone emphasised that 'the law has...ranked [suicide] among the highest crimes', although, anticipating later developments, he conceded that the harsh and shameful punishments imposed for suicide 'border a little upon severity'.[7] Although common law societies gradually moved away from Blackstone's treatment of suicide, courts continued to condemn it as a grave public wrong.

Prompted in part by a half century of eugenicist concerns, in 1935 the first lobby promoting the legalisation of voluntary euthanasia (the Voluntary Euthanasia Society) was initiated by a group of London doctors. In the United States, the barrier had first been broken in 1870, when Samuel Williams proposed to the Birmingham Speculative Club that euthanasia be permitted 'in all cases of hopeless and painful illness' to bring about 'a quick and painless death'. The first society established in the United States (in 1938, originally called the Euthanasia Society) was renamed symbolically the Hemlock Society shortly after the Second World War. It now claims some 70,000 members. Its purpose is to support an individual's decision to die and to offer support when one is ready (Humphry 1998). The idea of euthanasia has gained ground in recent years, not only because of the new technologies for agonisingly prolonging life but also partly because of the discovery of new drugs, such as morphine and various anaesthetics for the relief of pain, that could also painlessly cause death.

In the United States, voluntary euthanasia and PAS have been important issues in the courts in the last decades. But as early as 1914 treatment refusal was determined as the only legally protected method of choosing death. Eleven physicians have been charged since 1935 with murder in mercy killings (eight of these since 1980). Most were acquitted, one committed suicide, and (until Dr Jack Kevorkian) none served a sentence of custody. The first of the eleven (Harold Blazer) was charged and acquitted in 1935 over the death of his daughter. She had been a victim of cerebral spinal meningitis, and he placed a handkerchief soaked with chloroform over her face until she died. He had cared for her for some 30 years (Humphry 1998). The first to be found guilty was Joseph Hassman in 1986, who had injected a lethal dose of Demerol into his mother-in-law at the request of her family. Sentenced to two years' probation, he was also fined $10,000, and ordered to perform 400 hours of community service (Humphry 1998). The most recent and controversial doctor is Kevorkian. Charged with first-degree murder in December 1990, he had connected Janet Adkins, a member of the Hemlock Society, to his suicide machine which allowed her to inject lethal drugs into her body at any time (Humphry 1998). He has been present at the deaths of more than 40 people and is currently serving a term of imprisonment as result of his crusading zeal.

The situation today

In Western societies, deeply rooted bans on assisted suicide have in recent years been re-examined and, generally, reaffirmed. Public concern is now mainly focused on how best to protect dignity and independence at the end of life, with the result that there have been limited changes in legislation and in the attitudes these laws reflect. Many Western societies, for example, now permit 'living wills', surrogate healthcare decision making, and the withdrawal or refusal of life-sustaining medical treatment. Generally, however, it remains legal only to 'pull the plug in the respirator and let a permanently comatose patient suffocate, but a crime, murder, to end that same life by a deliberate overdose of painkiller' (Stone and Winslade 1995, p.6).

Recent concern has focused on developments in the Netherlands, in Oregon State, and in the Northern Territories of Australia. In the Netherlands, assisted suicide was illegal until 1973. In that year, a physician was given a token sentence for injecting his elderly terminally ill mother with morphine with the intention to kill. This set a precedent and the Dutch courts established guidelines outlining when it was possible for a physician to assist a patient in suicide. PAS remains technically unlawful but is considered justified if the physician follows several guidelines. The patient must make a voluntary, informed and stable request. He or she has to be suffering unbreakable pain with no prospect of improvement. The physician must consult with another, and must carefully review the patient's condition. Oregon legislation has focused on PAS rather than on voluntary active euthanasia. It authorises physicians to prescribe lethal amounts of medication that patients self-administer. In 1995, the Northern Territories of Australia became the first jurisdiction explicitly to authorise voluntary active euthanasia (the legislation was overturned by the federal government in 1997). In other countries, such as Switzerland, creative interpretation of existing legislation has allowed a number of assisted deaths (Article 115 of the Swiss Penal Code prohibits assisted dying when the person assisting has 'selfish motives' – the Swiss Society for Human Dying, which has helped some 120 people die each year, has escaped prosecution by arguing that its motivations are not selfish).

In most Western countries, the patient's voluntary suicide by refusing life-sustaining food and liquids is legally recognised. Debarring legislation is only relevant where a second party is involved in the procedure.

For example in the UK, since the passage of the Suicide Act 1961, taking one's own life is not a crime, although aiding a suicide is illegal. The latter is often defined very broadly. For example, in a case involving a book of guidance published by the Voluntary Euthanasia Society, Mr Justice Woolf ruled that giving the booklet to another person could be legally construed as encouraging suicide. In view of increasing public interest in euthanasia, and in the light of the Nigel Cox and Tony Bland cases (which involved legal agreement for the termination of life support in the case of Tony Bland) the House of Lords set up a Select Committee on Medical Ethics to consider the issue in 1993. Of the interested parties, the Department of Health, the Home Office, the British Medical Association and the Royal College of Nursing all argued against any change in the law. The committee in its final report (February 1994), despite being earlier undecided on the issue, unanimously ruled that there should be no legislative change. Lord Walton, the committee chairman, reflected in a speech to the House of Lords on 9 May 1994:

> We concluded that it was virtually impossible to ensure that all acts of euthanasia were truly voluntary and that any liberalisation of the law in the United Kingdom could not be abused. We were also concerned that vulnerable people – the elderly, lonely, sick or distressed – would feel pressure, whether real or imagined, to request early death.

In Britain, doctors assisting in euthanasia may be charged with aiding, abetting, counselling or procuring suicide, an offence that carries a maximum prison sentence of 14 years.

Frequency of assisted suicide

Attempts at suicide – whether helped by others or not – are relatively frequent among the general population. Each year about 100,000 British citizens appear in hospitals as a result of deliberate self-harm, the most common form of which is poisoning with medicines or other pharmacologically active substances. As many as 95 per cent of self-poisonings are intentional drug overdoses but only around 40 per cent of patients who poison themselves express a wish to die.[6] In Britain, according to one committed source (Dr Michael Irwin of the Voluntary Euthanasia Society), up to 100,000 people a year are 'helped' to die by the double effect of pain-killing drugs every year.[7]

Approximately 6000 deaths per day in the United States are said to be in some way planned or indirectly assisted, frequently through the double effect of pain-relieving medications that may at the same time hasten death, or through the discontinuation of (or failure to start) life-prolonging treatments (Quill, Cassel and Meier 1992). Nearly 80 per cent of those deaths are 'medically managed' – that is, they are preceded by explicit decisions to stop or not to start life-sustaining treatments (Holst 1993). A survey of Washington State physicians (Back and Wallace 1996) showed that 12 per cent had received a genuine request for PAS within the year studied, and 24 per cent responded by providing a potentially lethal prescription. Another 47 per cent of physicians received requests for 'voluntary active euthanasia', and 24 per cent of those obliged with a lethal injection. The Oregon study (Ganzini *et al.* 2000) of some 1355 physicians found that 21 per cent had been asked for a lethal prescription in the past year. In Asch's (1996) study of nurses in intensive care units for adults 17 per cent said they had received requests from patients or family members to perform euthanasia or to assist in suicide.[8] In the Netherlands, between 1 per cent and 2 per cent of all deaths are believed to be from reported PAS (excluding a potentially large number of the unreported) (van der Wal *et al.* 1996).

Old age coupled with illness

Most cases of voluntary euthanasia in modern society relate not to age in itself but to elderliness coupled with some other factor, such as mental or physical debilitation or pain. Age rarely represents the only justification. Voluntary euthanasia is a much wider question than one simply involving the termination of the lives of the elderly. However, while relatively few discussions on euthanasia have focused directly on the elderly independently of other factors, ageist ideology has played its part. Several studies (for example, Carpenter 1993) have claimed that the elderly have a unique claim to an ethical unobstructed death.

The classic example of such a combination of factors occurred in the Hackethal case in Germany. In his private clinic, Dr Hackethal provided a lethal dose of cyanide to an old lady with cancerous destruction of her face. She had been a long-time patient of his and had explicitly asked to be assisted in ending her life. After her death, Hackethal publicised the case in numerous press and TV interviews. Prosecution followed. The case was dismissed as abetment of suicide, an action not punishable under German law. Hackethal was exonerated from the charge of practising illegal euthanasia. On the other hand, judgment was issued with the clear understanding that no legal facilitation of mercy killing was intended by it, and that the case did not constitute a precedent (discussed in Kottow 1988).

Easing elderly suicide

Despite the association between age and other factors, age remains the key factor. The elderly are much more prone to be exposed to the possibilities of voluntary euthanasia. For example, as we showed in Chapter 2, elderly people universally have the highest rate of suicide. They also tend to be more successful in those attempts than younger age groups, and are more likely to seek help with that termination.

Documentation of self-killing by the elderly in a variety of ghastly ways appears in the debate over the legislation on voluntary euthanasia in the Northern Territories of Australia. The Voluntary Euthanasia Society newsletter (September 1999) notes a study of the methods Australians of 75 years of age and over used to commit suicide between 1990 and 1994:

- 171 hanged themselves
- 130 used firearms
- 93 used drugs
- 78 used carbon monoxide (including car exhausts)
- 40 drowned themselves
- 34 jumped from high places
- 17 swallowed agricultural chemicals
- 15 jumped or lay in front of a moving object
- 14 used cutting or piercing instruments
- 10 burnt themselves to death
- 10 electrocuted themselves
- 2 took corrosive or caustic substances.

As the Voluntary Euthanasia Society notes, what better argument could there be that those elders wishing to die should have compassionate medical help in dying, in order to avoid extreme forms of self-violence. Elderly people often lack the technical knowledge to kill themselves quickly and comfortably. 'Botched suicides are feared because they may cause physical suffering, shame, humiliation, and a deepened sense of helplessness. Well-organised patients who carefully seek control over their dying are reluctant to embrace a casual, uncertain system to end their lives' (Block and Billings 1994, p.2040).

The Netherlands has a relatively low suicide rate, and since the acceptance of voluntary euthanasia and limited PAS that rate has decreased (Muller, Kimsma and van der Wal 1998). But many of the cases of voluntary euthanasia are likely to be elderly people who would have ended their own lives if euthanasia were not available. If any significant percentage of the euthanasia cases were to be included among the suicides, the Dutch figure would rise considerably. The decrease in the Dutch suicide rate (i.e. suicides as compared with all deaths), from a peak of 16.6 per cent in 1983 to 12.8 per cent in 1992 (in absolute numbers from 1886 to 1587), may well be due to the availability of approved euthanasia. More significant is the fact that it has taken place in the older age groups. In the 50 to 59 age group, the rate diminished from 21.5 per cent in 1984 to 14 per cent in 1992. Among those aged 60 to 69 the rate dropped from a peak of 23.2 per cent in 1982 to 14.5 per cent. Among those aged 70 and older the rate dropped from a peak of 31.3 per cent in 1983 to 19.9 per cent – a decrease of about 33 per cent in these three groups. Of the 1886 suicides in 1983, 940 were in the three older age groups. Of the 1587 suicides in 1992, 672 were in the three older age groups. The fall in suicides in the three older age groups was primarily responsible for the drop in the overall suicide rate. Comparing the five years of 1980 to 1984 with the 1988 to 1992 years provides statistically significant evidence of a drop in the older age groups that is not due to chance. These are the age groups containing the highest numbers of euthanasia cases (86 per cent of the men and 76 per cent of the women) and the greatest number of suicides. Among the older population, physical illness of all types is common, and many who have trouble coping with physical illness become suicidal. In a culture supporting of euthanasia, their distress may be accepted as a legitimate reason for supportive action in that procedure. It may be more than metaphorical to describe euthanasia as the Dutch cure for elderly suicide. It seems plausible that the remarkable decrease among the older age groups is due to the fact that older suicidal patients are now asking to receive help in dying.

the Netherlands has moved from voluntary suicide to assisted euthanasia, from euthanasia for the terminally ill to euthanasia for the chronically ill, from euthanasia for physical illness to euthanasia for psychological distress, and from voluntary euthanasia to involuntary euthanasia ('termination of the patient without explicit request'). The rationale for such extensions has been partly that it is a form of discrimination to deny the right to die with assistance to the chronically ill, who will have longer to suffer than the terminally ill, or to those who experience psychological pain not associated with physical disease. Euthanasia is preferred by patients and doctors as a safer and more certain way of assuring death, so that assisted suicide is now used relatively infrequently.

Ending patients' lives without their request has been justified by the need to make decisions for patients not competent to choose for themselves. The Dutch government's own commissioned research documented abuses of the system. In more than 1000 cases a year, doctors actively caused or hastened death without the patient's request. In more than 5000 cases, doctors made decisions that might have ended, or were intended to curtail, the lives of competent patients without discussing the decisions with them (Maas, Delden and Pijnenborg 1992).

Dworkin (1993) points out, in relation to a more limited range of elderly suicide, that current legislation produces the apparently irrational result that people can choose to die lingering deaths by refusing to eat, by refusing treatment that keeps them alive, or by being disconnected from respirators and suffocating, but they cannot choose a quick, painless death that their doctors could easily provide.

Where PAS has been approved, the vast majority using those resources has been the elderly. Thus in the first year of the Oregon legislation, of the 15 people who died as a result of physician-assisted suicide, the median age was 69 years (Snyder and Caplan 2000). In the Netherlands from 1984 to 1993, 1707 cases of euthanasia were reported. There were more male patients (57 per cent) than female (43 per cent). The average age was 62 years for men and 65 years for women (van der Wal et al. 1996). The very high suicide rate among older Americans may be due partly to concern that they may be unable to stop treatment if hospitalised. Some people now fear living more than dying, because they dread becoming prisoners of technology. There is some limited evidence from the United States – based on reported Harris opinion polls – that there has been a sub-stantial increase within the elderly population (from a minority to a majority) in favour of legitimating medical assistance in ending lives in cases of incurable terminal illness (Stone and Winslade 1995).

Voluntarism: Ageism, material and cultural pressures

When is voluntary euthanasia actually voluntary? As Battin (1994) asks, what influences shape the older person's choice? Are religious beliefs, prejudices against the handicapped and an ideology of ageism contributing to a feeling of worthlessness? Does the person fear becoming a burden? Is he or she being manipulated by family members? Or has there been frank and open communication with their intimates?

An elderly patient with a terminal illness is vulnerable. He or she may lack the knowledge and skills to alleviate their symptoms, and may well suffer from fear about the future and anxiety about the effect of the illness on others. It is very difficult to be entirely objective. Those who regularly manage terminally ill patients recognise that they often suffer from depression or a false sense of worthlessness that may affect their judgement. Decision making may equally be affected by confusion, dementia or related symptoms, which could be relieved with appropriate treatment and social support. Many elderly people already feel a burden to family and carers. They may feel great pressure to request euthanasia freely and voluntarily.

The distinction between geronticide, voluntary euthanasia and PAS suffers from vagueness and confusion over the degree of choice involved. Many cases are ambiguous. Where are the limits of voluntarism and compulsion? What constitutes independent action, one free from social pressures? Consider the following paragraph from Raphael Hytholoday in Thomas More's *Utopia*:

> ...when people are ill, they're looked after more sympathetically, and given everything in the way of medicine or special food that could possible assist their recovery. In the case of permanent invalids, the nurses try to make them feel better by sitting and talking to them, and do all they can to relieve their symptoms. But if, besides being incurable, the disease causes continuing excruciating pain, some priests and government officials visit the person and say something like this 'Let's face it, you'll never be able to live a normal life. You're just a nuisance to other people and a burden to yourself – in fact, you're really leading a posthumous existence. So why go on feeding germs? Since your life's a misery to you, why hesitate to die? You're imprisoned in a torture-chamber – why don't you break out and escape to a better world? Or say the word, and we'll arrange for your release. It's only common sense to cut your losses. It's also an act of piety to take the advice of a priest, because he speaks for God'. If the patient finds these arguments convincing, he either starves himself to death or is given a soporific and put painlessly out of his misery. But this is strictly voluntary, and if he prefers to stay alive, everyone will go on treating him as kindly as ever. (Quoted in Carey 1999, p.39)

Little has changed apart from terminology and technique. But the crux of the argument is the question of at what point is euthanasia a voluntary act and at what point is it influenced by an ideology of ageism or other external interest?

Patient choice versus medical or relational choice

The distinction between the two is rarely evident in practice. According to Eliot Freidson:

> It is my impression that clients are more often bullied than informed into consent, their resistance weakened in part by their desire for the general service if not the specific procedure, in part by the oppressive setting they find themselves in, and

in part by the calculated intimidation, restriction of information, and covert threats of rejection by the professional staff itself. (Quoted in Beauchamp and Childress 1994, p.16)

'We typically make decisions in a context of competing influences, such as personal desires, familial constraints, legal obligations, and institutional pressures' (Beauchamp and Childress 1994, p.224). Patients' choices for care in the event of terminal illness relate to an intricate set of demographic, educational and cultural factors (Garret et al. 1993, p.361). Those researchers found key variations in the degree to which elderly outpatients stated desires for life-sustaining care if they were to become terminally ill. Women wanted life-sustaining treatments less often than did men; black patients were more inclined to choose life-sustaining treatments than were white patients. Education levels and scores on a depression index also correlated with a desire for more treatment.

In the nineteenth century work of the Scots academic John Macmillan Brown (Quoted in Chapter 6), Liminorians were offered an ecological motivation for choosing death. Mortality was produced by an electric petrifier, which instantly transformed the aged Liminorians into a lifelike effigy of valuable irrelium. Humans left behind no waste product. Voluntary euthanasia materially benefited the living. Those elderly who committed suicide did so knowing that they contributed not just to the greater good in removing their encumbering selves, but also that their death furnished further benefits to the society – irrelium was their dying gift. A Durkheimian altruism prevails. Pressures from others to make that gift were hardly disinterested.

This question of differential pressures on apparently individual decision making over voluntary euthanasia was explored in a comparative study of the resort to living wills and advance directives (Hauser et al. 1997). They concluded that ethnic experience might play a crucial part in the decision-making process. Fewer members of minority groups completed advance directives, fewer desired to complete them. The researchers argued that such low use reflects differential social, welfare and medical experiences. They found the minimal use of advance directives in minority communities to be related to both a lack of trust in and satisfaction with care received and a lack of access to care. In the African-American and Hispanic groups, suspicions regarding the practice of medicine centred on specific actions that physicians might take, or might have taken, as well as a deeper lack of trust in the healthcare system. For example, several African-American participants believed that organs were removed prior to their deaths in order to be implanted into other patients.

Similarly, cultural traditions in relation to the delegation of responsibility for intimate decision making may impact on the older person's decisions to opt for continuing care or for voluntary euthanasia. For example, in Japan it may be an acceptable custom for the family to make serious medical decisions on behalf of a sick family member even without discussion with the patient or even when their decision overrides the patient's own wishes (Hoshino 1993).

Material pressures

Despite disavowals, economic decisions are still prominent in the pressures on elderly patients to end their lives.

> As one who has recently been forced to put his ageing mother into a hostel I can attest that such accommodation is expensive and scarce. There are many elderly people in the community, who would be classified by the Aged Care Assessment Teams as eligible for hostel care at 85% of the pension, but for whom no places exist. The real cost is $1,700 per month – twice the pension! (Saunders 1997, p.2)

In 1993, a Dutch pensioners' group, the Protestant Christian Elderly Society, surveyed 2066 pensioners on general healthcare issues. The survey did not address the euthanasia issue directly, yet 10 per cent of the elderly respondents clearly indicated that, because of Dutch euthanasia policy, they were afraid that their lives could be terminated without their request. According to the Elderly Society director Hans Homans: 'They are afraid that at a certain moment, on the basis of age, a treatment will be considered no longer economically viable, and an early end to their lives will be made.'[9] Cost containment is one of the main aims of Dutch healthcare policy, as it is in other jurisdictions. There is an in-built pressure to remove expensive patients.[10] General practitioners wishing to admit elderly patients to hospitals have sometimes been advised to give the patients lethal injections instead.[11]

Unlike in the Netherlands, where medical care is provided for everyone by right, in the USA many people cannot afford medical treatment. If assisted suicide were to become accepted there, death might be the only 'medical option' many could afford. Given the current push for healthcare cost containment in both Britain and the USA, medical groups and facilities may be tempted to view patients in terms of their treatment costs instead of their innate value as human beings (as noted in earlier chapters). For some, the 'bottom line' would be 'Dead patients cost less than live ones'.

An outspoken version of this creed appears in Derek Humphry's book *Freedom to Die: People, Politics and the Right-to-Die Movement* (1998). Humphry, the first chair of the Hemlock Society, argues (in a chapter called 'The unspoken argument') that assisted suicide will be legalised in Western society *chiefly* as a method of 'cost containment'. Describing pensioners as 'greedy geezers' eating up the nation's healthcare finances, Humphry proposes that Medicare and private health plans should force patients to sign 'living wills' refusing intrusive treatment as a condition for receiving coverage. Doctors and hospitals will be empowered to decline patients' and families' requests for life-sustaining care if they judge their preference for life to be 'unreasonable'. Elders should be helped to see assisted suicide as 'the morally correct thing to do' to avoid burdens on family and society. He likens this process to the old Inuit practice (see Chapter 3) of abandoning the elderly on ice floes to die once they are 'no longer productive'. Humphry praises the Oregon Health Plan, which rations care for the poor, appearing to regard life-preserving treatments as less 'cost-effective' – lethal drugs are cheap and relatively effective. Once one perceives sick and elderly people as an economic burden, those who may live a long time with continued care appear to be the greatest burden. The financial cost of maintaining the incurably ill and the senile is a growing concern, so much so that some groups have gone beyond the concept of the 'right to die' to that of the 'duty to die'. When the human machine has outlived its productive span, its maintenance is an unacceptable burden on the working strata of society, and it should be disposed of, rather than allowing it to deteriorate gradually. The political economy argument of so-called 'primitive' society comes full circle.

Recent changes in healthcare reimbursement practices – such as the development of the regional health trusts in Britain – have increased public concerns about financial incentives that may influence patient-care decisions. Reimbursement methods can create actual or perceived conflicts for those caring for terminally ill patients with expensive resource-intensive conditions. Patients and their families may fear that the quality of their care will be limited by the provider's financial considerations. Illich (1991) – after moving to rural Mexico – described as medical imperialism the situation after the building of a local hospital when peasant families were impoverished by getting dying family members the 'done thing'.

From physician-assisted suicide to voluntary euthanasia

In practice, we are discussing two different types of euthanasia with regard to the elderly. Physician-assisted suicide (PAS) occurs when a physician knowingly provides the means to commit suicide to a competent patient who voluntarily makes this request and then uses those means independently to take his or her own life. Voluntary active euthanasia (VAE) occurs when a physician intentionally provides and administers the means directly to cause death in a patient who voluntarily requests this service. In the first case, a physician (or sometimes another party, such as a close relative) provides either equipment or medication, or informs the patient of the most efficacious use of already available means, for the sole purpose of assisting the patient to end his or her own life. In the other case, at the direct request of the patient, a physician administers a medication or treatment, one intent of which is to end the patient's life. In the former case, the other party *responds* to the individual's request. In the latter, the other party *administers* as well as facilitates the final decision.

In the Netherlands, the distinction between active and passive euthanasia has been dropped in official documents. In the eyes of the law, acts of omission and commission directed at the hastening of death are identical. The definitions for euthanasia and assisted suicide in the Netherlands are by the State Commission on Euthanasia: 'Euthanasia is the intentional termination of life by somebody other than the person concerned at his or her request. Assisted suicide means intentionally helping a patient to terminate his or her life at his or her request' (Scheper and Duursma 1994, p.4). The Dutch define 'euthanasia' in a limited way: 'Euthanasia is understood [as] an action which aims at taking the life of another *at the latter's expressed request*. It concerns an action of which death is the purpose and the result' (pp.4–5). This definition applies only to *voluntary* euthanasia and excludes what the rest of the world refers to as non-voluntary or involuntary euthanasia, the killing of a patient without the patient's knowledge or consent. The Dutch call this 'life-terminating treatment'.

Differentiating the two may be illogical. As we noted earlier, in the age of advanced medical technology there is a continuum of life and death issues for the elderly. Towards the voluntary pole is the withholding or withdrawal of life support where patients shun tubes and machines, or deprive themselves of food or fluids, and allow nature to take its course. Then there is physician-assisted suicide – the patient receives medical help such as a lethal prescription but ultimately performs the actual life-taking deed, imbibing a fatal dose. Towards the geronticide pole there is active euthanasia in which a physician administers death through, for example, a lethal injection (Snyder and Caplan 1996).

Social inequality in the dying process is endemic. Treatment is not equal in that a competent person may order the removal of a life-support system, whereas one whose treatment does not include life support cannot hasten death. This unequal treatment lacks any rational basis. Further, as Capron 1992 argues: 'We have gotten to the point...when in the age of miracle cures and surgical derring-do, no illness can be said to have a natural course. There is no such thing as "natural" death' (p.142). Assistance in death may be merely the parallel of assistance in the prolongation of life by medical practitioners. The physician is caught in between – recognising the patient's right to die peacefully, naturally and with whatever dignity is possible, but foreseeing the unfortunate results that may come about when the patient exercises his legal right. About two million Americans die every year, nearly 85 per cent of them in an institution. Of those deaths, some 80 per cent involve a decision by someone to try to prolong life or to let it go. Four out of every five Americans will die a lingering, chronic illness which cannot be cured but which can be artificially prolonged.

A scenario in which natural death is accomplished by the patient's selective refusal of treatment has one major advantage over active euthanasia and assisted suicide: refusal of treatment is clearly permitted and protected by law. Unfortunately, however, most patients do not have the specialised medical knowledge to use this self-protective mechanism intelligently. Few are aware that some kinds of refusal of treatment will better serve their desires for a 'natural death' than others; few realise that refusal of treatment can be selective; they may be unable to distinguish therapeutic from palliative procedures; most do not have enough medical knowledge to foresee the consequences of refusing treatment on a selective basis. It is this that the physician must supply. Though it is crucial in making a genuinely informed decision, the patient's right to information about the risks and outcomes of alternative kinds of refusal has not yet been adequately recognised.

Medical autonomy in termination

There is some evidence that decisions made by the elderly themselves, by their kin and by medical experts – over decisions of life and death – may differ markedly. In one such study most elderly respondents (93 per cent) stated a preference for surrogate or proxy decision making by either a spouse or family member if they were unable to express decisions themselves. But only 45 per cent of the elderly respondents had actually discussed their wishes with the specified person (Gamble, McDonald and Lichstein 1991). Comparisons have been made between decisions made by elderly participants and predictions of those decisions by potential proxies, including a participant's close relatives, a nurse, a social worker and a physician in the facility. There was a low rate of agreement between decisions made by elderly participants and the decisions the potential proxies thought they would reach. The researchers particularly noted the rate of disagreement between the physicians and their elderly patients in high-risk case studies (Ouslander, Tymchuk and Rahbar 1989).

In practice, doctors actually determine euthanasia on the condition of the patient not on the basis of his or her requests. The finding that 9000 requests for euthanasia in the Netherlands led to 'only' 2300 cases of euthanasia can be interpreted in different ways. On the one hand, it shows indeed that Dutch physicians are not terminating patients' lives on demand. But it also means that the request of the patient is not, in practice, the basis on which physicians decide to perform euthanasia; rather that they base decisions on the condition of the patient. This is supported by the finding that 1000 people actually had their lives terminated without an explicit request. In many cases, it is the condition of the patient, not the request, which is the real ground for euthanasia (Jochensen 1991). Legalisation of PAS, both in the Netherlands and in other countries is usually justified in reference to the right of autonomy of patients. It may be that the judicial proceedings in The Netherlands have not so much enhanced the autonomy of patients, as the autonomy of the medical profession (Welie 1992).

Aspects of the debate
Anti-euthanasia: The 'slippery slope' thesis

There are substantial arguments that the prevailing ideology of ageism may open the door for other groups to take the same route – or have it taken for them. If voluntary euthanasia were known to be an option, people might put pressure on burdensome elderly kin as well as others to volunteer. It is hardly surprising that, according to surveys (see Quill *et al.* 1998), those who are most opposed to PAS and to voluntary euthanasia include those most likely to experience abuse and coercion – the elderly poor, and ethnic minorities.

The ethical arguments for physician-assisted suicide and euthanasia do not only apply when euthanasia is voluntary. They may also be used to justify (following the earlier eugenicist tradition) some kinds of non-voluntary euthanasia for those regarded as incompetent, as a drain on societal resources, or simply as powerless. Euthanasia might become one end of a spectrum of caring for dying patients – it will be difficult to deny euthanasia to a patient for whom it is seen as the best or most appropriate form of cure simply because that patient is now incompetent and cannot request it.

There are notorious cases of this effect. As we noted earlier, in Nazi Germany the elderly were subject to involuntary euthanasia only after it had first become legitimised amongst handicapped children and the incurably ill.

EXAMPLE OF THE 'SLIPPERY SLOPE' ARGUMENT

Letter from Dr Wurm of the Württemberg Evangelical Provincial Church to Reich Minister of Interior Dr Frick, 5 September 1940

Dear Reich Minister,

On July 19th I sent you a letter about the systematic extermination of lunatics, feeble-minded and epileptic persons. Since then this practice has reached tremendous proportions: recently the inmates of old-age homes have also been included. The basis for this practice seems to be that in an efficient nation there should be no room for weak and frail people.

Letter to Reich Minister of Justice from the Roman Catholic Bishop of Limburg, 13 August 1941

Buses arrive in Hadamar several times a week with a large number of these victims. School children in the neighbourhood know these vehicles and say: 'Here comes the murder wagon.' After the arrival of such vehicles the citizens of Hadamar then see the smoke coming from the chimney and are upset by constant thoughts about the poor victims especially when, depending on the direction of the wind, they have to put up with the revolting smell. The consequence of the principles being practised here is that children, when quarrelling with one another make remarks like: 'You are thick, you'll be put in the oven in Hadamar.' Old people are saying: 'On no account will I go into a state hospital! After the feeble-minded, the old will be next in line as useless mouths to feed.'

A former Nazi physician was asked to justify participating in the selection process for euthanasia at German concentration camps during the Second World War. After a brief pause, he responded: 'In the end, I guess the "selections" were about killing. But these people were going to die anyway. So the "selections" allowed them to die humanely. Have you ever seen someone starve to death?' (Quoted in Katz 1998).

Individual examples, however compelling, should not be allowed to outweigh the need for advocacy on behalf of the numerically greater numbers in vulnerable groups such as elderly, mentally incapacitated, and disabled people. They would inexorably be pressured, put at greater risk, and subjected to further disadvantage by any change in the present law and therefore in end-of-life care and management (Rodway 1995). It may be critical to maintain a symbolic barrier against killing.

Pro-euthanasia: The artificiality of the legal distinction

Although there are slippery slope arguments that are sound and convincing, typical formulations of the Nazi-invoking argument may be deficient in empirical evidence.

Lethal injection is merely a variant of palliative care. A well-accepted principle of medical ethics states that it is legitimate to intervene medically, even if it carries the risk of hastening death, if the intervention is designed to relieve severe suffering. It is argued that lethal injection may simply be an extreme measure of pain relief, and that the death, which accompanies the pain relief, must be accepted on the principle of double effect. Relief from suffering (rather than preserving life) should be the primary objective of healthcare providers.

Further, civilised society is obliged to acknowledge the rights of patients and to respect the decisions of those who opt for euthanasia. Since society has acknowledged a patient's right to passive euthanasia (e.g. by recognising refusal of life-sustaining treatment), active euthanasia should also be permitted. When the patient's condition has become overwhelmingly burdensome, pain management is inadequate, and only a physician can provide relief, the latter should be allowed to determine the options professionally. Almost any individual freedom involves some risk of abuse, but such abuse would be minimised by appropriate legal safeguards.

In the Netherlands, it has been claimed (Delden, Pijnenborg and Maas 1993) that the Dutch began by hastening the end of life on request and ended up with life-terminating acts that patients had not explicitly requested. We simply do not know whether unrequested life-terminating acts occurred more often in the past (although the evidence from earlier chapters suggest that that was in fact the case). To demonstrate a slippery slope one would need to show that something changed after introducing a particular practice. Delden *et al.* conclude that in the Netherlands there is no empirical data to support a slippery slope argument. For example, despite easy access, the Netherlands has one of the lowest abortion rates in the world, in part because the Dutch combine this 'tolerant' policy with comprehensive, obligatory educational and outreach programmes about birth control and family planning (Quill and Kimsma 1997).

Vagueness of professional controls

Euthanasia proposals are a primary example of the way the personal has become the public, with the abrogation of many personal rights in favour of professional practitioners. While appearing to offer more autonomy to the patient, in many cases assisted suicide gives more power to the medical practitioner. Professional practitioners can interpret vague rules with relative ease. As the Chairwoman of the British anti-euthanasia group Alert commented on the acquittal of Dr David Moor (see p.153): 'I think this is a sad day for the practice of medicine as it makes the law uncharted as to what is allowed. We cannot have a half-law when it comes to the [elderly].'[12]

A key problem in euthanasia practice in Western society is the degree of autonomy given to medical practitioners. The industrialisation process has featured the increased transfer of responsibility of decision making in intimate affairs into the hands of delegated experts. Assisted euthanasia – helping people out of this world when they decide they want to leave it – has gone on since the dawn of time. But it was seldom openly discussed. People usually died in their own homes. What happened in their last hours was known only to their closest relatives, and perhaps a doctor or a nurse. The key change has been the advance of medical technology in bringing a steadily growing majority of deaths into state and voluntary bureaucracies where life (of a sort) may be prolonged. Someone – a designated expert – has to decide what nature used to decide for us. These decisions are no longer taken privately in a small family group but in a constantly changing crowd of doctors, nurses, patients and technicians.

But independently of the problems raised more generally (in the concluding chapter) about professionalism and medicine (in relation to the actions of Dr Harold Shipman), there are two key concerns about the medicalisation of euthanasia through the PAS practice. The first of these, which we deal with below, is the extent to which procedures justified on one basis are utilised in another.

Medical decision making appears to reflect the views of the practitioners in such cases, not the views of the patients. Such rules governing decision making by medical practitioners in relation to euthanasia are permissive and flexible, rather than absolute and rigid, entailing the substitution of the prejudices and presuppositions of the professional for the intentions of the patient.

The assumption that professional rules bar medical practitioners from participating in assisting suicide by the elderly is fallacious. In many Western jurisdictions, apart from failures of detailed justification given by patients and their peers for assistance in suicide, there is considerable scepticism about the rigidity of professional codes in health care (Beauchamp and Childress 1994). It has been claimed that from the time of Hippocrates physicians have generated codes without scrutiny or acceptance by patients and the public (Beauchamp and Childress 1994). These codes have rarely appealed to more general ethical standards or to a source of moral authority beyond the traditions and judgements of physicians. In some cases, the special rules for professionals seem to conflict with, and even override, more general moral norms. The pursuit of professional norms in these circumstances may do more to protect the profession's interests than to introduce an impartial and comprehensive moral viewpoint. Other rules have traditionally been expressed in abstract formulations that dispense vague moral advice open to competing interpretations.

For example, where prohibition derives from the Hippocratic Oath, the latter is a contradictory source of advice for medical practitioners and only selectively applied. In its original form, the oath does contain an explicit injunction that the physician shall not give a lethal potion to a patient who requests it, nor make a suggestion to that effect. But it also contained explicit prohibitions against physicians accepting fees for teaching medicine, and against performing surgery. These latter prohibitions are not retained in the modern reformulation of the oath. There seems to be no *a priori* reason why the provision against giving lethal potions to patients who request it should be disallowed. What is central to the oath and cannot be deleted without altering its essential character is the requirement that the physician shall come 'for the benefit of the sick'. A physician's assistance in patient suicide may indeed be for the benefit of the patient. What the oath would continue to prohibit is physician assistance in the suicide for the physician's own gain or to serve other institutional or societal ends (Battin 1994).

There are other contradictions in the Hippocratic source. It includes, for example, a key phrase relevant to the use of opiates today: 'I will neither give a deadly drug to anybody, if asked for, nor will I make a suggestion to this effect.' But Hippocrates also wrote in his treatise *Epidemics* that 'when a doctor can do no good, he must be kept from doing harm' – in the present day, connecting an elderly individual to a life-support machine might be perceived as doing more harm than letting that person die. It may be that quality of life questions are for patients and their families to determine. The physician's realm is the efficacy of medical treatment.

Some physicians use this distinction between 'voluntary euthanasia' and 'life-terminating treatment' to avoid having a patient's death classified as 'euthanasia', thus freeing doctors from following the established euthanasia guidelines and reporting the death to local authorities. One such example was discussed during the December 1990 Institute for Bioethics conference in Maastricht, Holland. A physician from the Netherlands Cancer Institute spoke of approximately 30 cases a year where doctors ended patients' lives after the patients had intentionally been put into a coma by means of a morphine injection. These deaths were *not* considered 'euthanasia' because they were *not voluntary*, and to discuss the plan to end these patients' lives with the patients would have been 'rude' since they all knew they had incurable conditions. (Capron 1992). A more recent (1999) Dutch study suggests that doctors regularly breach the rules and that safeguards against euthanasia remain inadequate.[13]

Calls for voluntary euthanasia have not been encouraged by the failure of doctors to provide adequate symptom control, or by their insistence on providing inappropriate interventions that neither lengthen life nor improve its quality (as discussed in Chapter 5). This has understandably provoked limited distrust of doctors by patients who feel that they are being neglected or exploited. The natural reaction is to seek to make doctors more accountable. Ironically, voluntary euthanasia legislation makes doctors less accountable, and gives them more power. Patients generally decide in favour of euthanasia on the basis of information given to them by doctors: information about their diagnosis, prognosis, and treatments available and expected degree of future suffering.

Professional factors may contribute to the question of assistance in that process. Decisions to support voluntary euthanasia for the elderly may reflect differential expert knowledge. For example, decisions about cardiopulmonary resuscitation (CPR) among the extremely old and frail geriatric population, especially in nursing homes, may be viewed as imprecise because of the abysmal survival rate of CPR in this patient group. Decisions about enteral feeding, on the other hand, may be critical because more and more people are living to an age when self-feeding becomes problematic owing to advanced dementia, stroke, Parkinson's disease or other conditions (Ouslander, Tymchuk and Krynski 1993). If a doctor confidently suggests a certain course of action, it can be very difficult for a patient to resist.

Diagnoses may be mistaken. Prognoses may be fatally misjudged. New treatments, which the doctor is unaware of, may have recently been developed or may be about to be developed. The doctor may not be up to date in symptom control. Doctors are human and subject to temptation. Sometimes their own decision making may be affected, consciously or unconsciously, by fatigue, by the way they feel about the individual patient, and by the ambience of an ageist ideology. PAS gives the medical practitioner power, which can be easily abused, and a level of responsibility he or she should not be entitled to possess (see Chapter 5). The Dutch experience suggests that, where voluntary euthanasia and assisted suicide are accepted practice, a significant number of patients may make minimal input into their own life or death destiny. Allowing for hyperbole, PAS may make the doctor the most dangerous person in the state (Saunders 1997).

Pain relief? Or alleviation of psychosocial problems?

The most important finding from recent studies and one that has major implications with regard to the provision of PAS for the elderly relates to research on justifications for voluntary euthanasia. Traditionally, it has been assumed that the legitimacy of the procedure derived from a desire to ease the pain of sufferers, such as those ill from cancer. Generally, the medical profession has effected euthanasia as a means of pain relief. Conversely, older people have frequently requested it to alleviate psychosocial problems such as depressive illness. The latter population may be weighted towards the elderly but cancer is a general phenomenon and not one especially pronounced in any specific age cohort.

A research review suggests that the primary justification for PAS relates to factors endemic amongst elderly people (as noted in Chapter 2). These factors are essentially psychosocial justifications – *inter alia*, that the most isolated people, persons divorced or never married, were more likely to choose PAS. Decisions to seek that end were associated with concerns about *loss of autonomy and control* not *fear of pain* or *actual pain* (Snyder and Caplan 2000).

For example, the Remmelink Commission[14] found that, among Dutch patients, the leading reason for requests for assistance in dying was perceived loss of dignity. In only 32 per cent of the cases did pain play any role in requests for euthanasia – indeed, pain was the sole reason for requests in no reported cases. A study of patients in nursing homes in the Netherlands revealed that pain was among the reasons for requesting physician-assisted suicide or voluntary euthanasia in only 29 per cent of the cases and was the main reason in only 11 per cent (Haverkate and van der Wal 1998).

A study of 828 physicians in Washington State who admitted to having received requests for physician-assisted suicide or euthanasia revealed that severe pain played a role in only about a third of the requests (Back and Wallace 1996). Patients gave the following reasons for wanting to die: future loss of control (77 per cent); being a burden (75 per cent); being dependent on others for some or all personal care (74 per cent); loss of dignity (72 per cent); being restricted to bed more than half the time (57 per cent); experiencing severe depression or depressed mood (55 per cent); experiencing severe suffering (52 per cent); experiencing severe physical discomfort other than from pain (50 per cent); experiencing severe pain (35 per cent); and worried about medical costs (23 per cent). Pain was least often given as the reason for wanting to hasten death. Loss of control and dignity, and being restricted to bed most of the time are the reasons most often given for wanting to end one's life.

Conversely, physicians were least likely to aid those giving non-physical reasons and most likely to assist in suicide when physical pain was given as the primary reason. Physicians declined to give aid in dying to 114 of the 156 patients that requested it (73 per cent). They refused in those cases because: the symptoms were potentially treatable (23 per cent); the patient was depressed (19 per cent); the patient was expected to live longer than six months (18 per cent); and generally because the degree of suffering 'didn't justify' the requests. Critically, most of the requesting patients were men aged over 65 years who had known their physician for more than 12 months and were expected to live no more than six months. But generally in the USA many people who belong to health maintenance organisations and managed care programmes would not be familiar with the physicians who treat them. Given those circumstances, doctors would be ill-equipped to recognise if a patient's euthanasia request was the result of depression or the sometimes subtle pressures placed on the patient to 'get out of the way'.

The Dutch Penal Code Articles 293 and 294 make both euthanasia and assisted suicide illegal, even today. As the result of various court cases, doctors who directly kill patients or help patients kill themselves will not be prosecuted as long as they follow guidelines. However, a pathbreaking Dutch court decision (21 April 1993) affirmed voluntary euthanasia and PAS for psychosocial reasons. The court found that psychiatrist Dr Boudewijn Chabot was medically justified and had followed established euthanasia guidelines in helping his physically healthy but depressed patient commit suicide. Fifty-year-old Hilly Bosscher said she wanted to die after the deaths of her two children and the subsequent break-up of her marriage.[15] Euthanasia does not remain a 'right' only for the terminally ill, competent adult who requests it. As a 'right,' it inevitably is applied to those who are chronically ill, disabled, elderly, mentally ill, mentally retarded and depressed.

Amongst a different group – HIV-infected patients – requests have been found to be mainly based on depression, hopelessness and having few (and poor quality) social supports. In Emanuel's study, patients who were depressed were more likely to discuss euthanasia seriously, and to hoard drugs for suicide (Emanuel 1997). Most of the patients interested in PAS or voluntary euthanasia were not suffering severe pain. Depression, hopelessness, and psychological distress were the primary factors motivating the great majority. Emanuel (1997) comments pointedly that our usual approach to people who try to end their lives for reasons of depression and psychological distress is social support and psychiatric intervention – not giving them a syringe and life-ending drugs. There is a parallel with the 'Buddy' system amongst HIV sufferers, where one dying of that process may be 'mated' with someone who understands the problem and can sustain social support. Similarly, while clearly not all psychosocial phenomena such as depression can be alleviated by lay social support and counselling, such support can be crucial, especially amongst the elderly. It is relatively easy to provide – and indeed morally far easier than offering the alternative of death, as one might with a patient who is suffering painful and incurable physical illness.

Finally, in a comparative study of physicians in Oregon and the Netherlands (Willems *et al.* 2000), respondents in Oregon considered the fear of being a burden an acceptable justification for assistance with dying more commonly than did their Dutch counterparts. Dutch patients were slightly less likely to consider themselves as a burden (a situation presumably partly attributable to the presence of a free health service in the Netherlands).

Generally a review of all the major studies suggests that within the context of adequate palliative care, the refusal of food and fluids does not contribute to suffering among the terminally ill. Rarely does fasting cause any discomfort beyond occasional and transient hunger. Symptoms related to dehydration are few – mostly dry oral and pharyngeal mucous membranes – and are readily relieved by simple measures. Several studies show that total fasting creates hunger for less than 24 hours – unlike when small amounts are taken – and is associated with an accompanying mild euphoria. Unlike PAS, refusing food or drink is a purely personal act. While it may require information, the decision may obviate the need for physicians, nurses, or other agents of society to participate. The patient acts autonomously, independently of pressures from others.

It may be that voluntary euthanasia through not feeding or drinking may be the least painful and the least complicated way to end one's own life. That self-determination involves the medical practitioner the least. The elderly patient maximises autonomy at the cost of diminishing that of medical practitioners. In hospices, death that follows the decision to refuse food and drink is not usually considered suicide. By choosing this, the patients are conscious that their death is likely to be hastened. Hospice clinicians claim that starvation and dehydration do not contribute to suffering among the dying and might actually contribute to a comfortable passage from life. In contrast, the general public perception, and that among non-hospice medical professionals, is that starvation and dehydration are terrible ways to die.

The long-term care alternative

As in the case of Derek Humphry,[16] legalisation of euthanasia is usually championed by those who have witnessed an intimate die in unpleasant circumstances, often without the benefits of optimal palliative care. Allowing difficult cases to create a precedent for legalised killing is the wrong response. We need rather to evaluate these difficult cases so that we can do better in the future. This was clearly demonstrated in the case of Nigel Cox, the Winchester rheumatologist found guilty of attempted murder after giving a patient with rheumatoid arthritis a lethal injection of potassium chloride in August 1991.[17] Had he consulted specialists in pain management, he might have relieved his patient's symptoms without killing her. If errors of omission are acknowledged, changes can be made. The European Association for Palliative Care recently registered its strong opposition to the legalisation of euthanasia. If care is aimed at achieving *the best possible quality of life for patients and their families* by focusing on a patient's psychosocial suffering, requests for euthanasia are extremely uncommon. The answer may be not to change the law, but rather to improve standards of final care (Saunders 1997).

When patients receive comprehensive care, requests for hastened death are very rare. However, in the extraordinary circumstance when the patient's suffering cannot be ameliorated within the framework of his or her personal values, voluntary euthanasia and assisted suicide may represent appropriate extensions of palliative care (Block and Billings 1994).

Patient autonomy versus medical autonomy

The main argument in favour of euthanasia in Holland has always included the desire for more patient autonomy – that patients have the right to make their own end-of-life decisions. Yet, over the past 20 years, Dutch euthanasia practice has ultimately given doctors, not patients, more and more power. The question of whether a patient should live or die is often decided exclusively by a doctor or a team of physicians. In 1990 according to the Remmelink Report: 2300 people died as the result of doctors killing them upon request (active, voluntary euthanasia); 400 people died as a result of PAS; 1040 people (an average of three a day) died from involuntary euthanasia, meaning doctors actively killed these patients without the patients' knowledge or consent. Of these patients, 14 per cent were fully competent and had apparently never indicated that they would want their lives terminated. In 8 per cent of the cases, doctors performed involuntary euthanasia despite the fact that they believed alternative options were still possible. In addition, 8100 patients died as a result of doctors deliberately giving them overdoses of pain medication, not for the primary purpose of controlling pain, but to hasten death. In 61 per cent of these cases (4941 patients), the intentional overdose was given without the patient's consent (Remmelink Report 1991).

According to the same report, Dutch physicians intentionally ended the lives of 11,840 people by lethal overdoses or injections – a figure that accounts for 9.1 per cent of the annual overall death rate of 130,000 per year. The majority of all euthanasia deaths in the Netherlands may be involuntary deaths. The Remmelink

Report figures cited here do not include other cases, also reported in the study, in which life-sustaining treatment was withheld or withdrawn without the patient's consent and with the intention of causing the patient's death. The most frequently cited reasons given for ending the lives of patients *without* their knowledge or consent were: 'low quality of life', 'no prospect for improvement', and 'the family couldn't take it any more'. In 45 per cent of cases involving hospitalised patients who died through involuntary euthanasia, the patients' families had no knowledge that doctors deliberately terminated their intimates. Once the power to kill is bestowed on physicians, the inherent nature of the doctor/patient relationship is adversely affected. A patient can no longer be sure what role the doctor will play – healer or killer. In the words of the Dutch physician Dr Pieter Admiraal: 'The only thing passive about passive euthanasia is the physician' (Quoted in Stone and Winslade 1995).

Overview

It is not possible to do full justice to the arguments on both sides of the voluntary euthanasia debate within this limited context. The primary focus has been on geronticide rather than on situations in which self-determination may be possible in elderly deaths. However, within the wider debate about geronticide, there are three reasons for some scepticism about the development of physician-assisted suicide and legal permissiveness with regard to voluntary euthanasia.

First, both sides in the argument regularly wheel out eminent persons to support their cases – from the eighteenth century Scottish philosopher David Hume to Edmund Hillary (of Everest fame).[18] One such example is the writer Arthur Koestler, who had written extensively on the subject and took his own aged life in 1983 after the diagnosis of his Parkinson's disease and of a slow-acting leukaemia. What was remarkable about his decision, however, was not so much that Koestler should follow through his own principles, rather that it was that he assisted – some might say persuaded – his much younger wife (in perfect health) to commit suicide with him.[19] There is some suggestion that her decision was less voluntary than that of her husband. A long-term process of dying may create burdens for others; but personal decisions for suicide amongst the elderly can also have consequences for others.

Second, there is mounting evidence that while amongst older people concerns are primarily for life termination for psychosocial reasons, inadequate attention may be being given to caring processes that can potentially alleviate those phenomena. Permissive legislation allowing termination for incurable illnesses may be utilised frequently for elderly problems that appropriate resources could alleviate. Finally, as noted in the concluding chapter, legislative measures governing PAS, when they relate to professional medical decision making, are vague and permissive in the extreme. There is evident danger here that in that final act advantage may be taken against those elderly with least power, least access to economic resources, and least relevant knowledge. Ageism, in whatever form, has a continuing history in disposing of those on the socio-economic periphery.

Notes

1   'He only wanted to end his wife's pain.' *The Guardian*, 7 June 2000. See also 'Probation for mercy killing.' *The Guardian*, 30 March 1999.

2   'All I tried to do was relieve his agony, his distress and suffering.' *The Guardian*, 12 May 1999.

3   See, *inter alia*, the accounts in the *Boston Globe* (14 December 1988), the *Detroit News* (20 February 1998), the *Cincinnati Enquirer* (25 June 1998) and *Time Magazine* (27 October 1997) of elderly nursing home patients dying from medication errors.

4   Henry de Bracton (1240) *De Legibus et Consuetudinibus Angliae.*

5   A. Horne, 'The Mirror of Justices', cited in Blackstone's Commentaries (1765).

6   (1997) *Drug and Therapeutics Bulletin 35*, 6, 41–43.

7   'He only wanted to end his wife's pain.' *The Guardian*, 7 June 2000.

8   For a summary of this and related studies of medical practitioners' and the general public's changing views on voluntary euthanasia, see Stone and Winslade 1995.

9   'Elderly Dutch afraid of euthanasia policy.' *Canberra Times*, 6 November 1993.

10   'Restructuring health care.' *The Lancet*, 28 January 1989.

11   'Involuntary euthanasia in Holland.' *Wall Street Journal*, 29 September 1987.

12   'All I tried to do was ease his agony…' *The Guardian*, 12 May 1999.

13   'Euthanasia and doctor-assisted suicide around the world.' *The Guardian*, 12 May 1999.

14   In 1990 the Netherlands government installed the Commission on the Study of Medical Practice Concerning Euthanasia, the Remmelink Commission (as updated in 1996), to investigate the volume of such deaths and procedures and the safeguards.

15   'Doctor helps healthy patient die.' *New York Times*, 5 May 1993.

16   Author of *Freedom to Die: People, Politics and the Right-to-Die Movement* (1998).

17   As cited in Saunders 1997, p.5.

18   One celebrity rarely quoted in this way is Jacques Cousteau with his notorious 'to stabilise the world population we must eliminate 350,000 people per day. It is a horrible thing to say, but it's just as bad not to say it.' (*UNESCO Courier*, November 1991).

19   A rather different ending occurred with Aldous Huxley, whose wife, at his request, assisted him on the way with two injections of 100mg of LSD, and stayed alive herself.

CHAPTER 8

Dr Shipman, Social Rights, and Preventing Geronticide

No calculating utilitarian, applying Bentham's cold arithmetic of pleasure versus pain, can demand that the old be killed or starved to save money for their young. It is the old themselves who, for their own dignity and out of concern for their successors, must learn to demand less. ... Those who contribute money, both public and private, to medical research need the courage to see that they will earn gratitude by gunning for misery as well as for headline-making killers. ... There is room for plenty of theories as to what makes life worth living, but none of them can include longevity as an end in itself. ... Think of a person's life in biographical terms – in terms of achievements, experiences, responsibilities discharged and so on, not in terms of blips on a hospital scanner. It then becomes easier to see when somebody's life has been completed. When a person (or his relatives) can see that a biography is finished, it is not for the doctors to try to write a painful extra chapter. ('A time to die.' *The Economist*, 5 August 1989)

In most societies, there appears to be an elemental reverence for life which makes the deliberate killing of another person a punishable offence. Aversion to murder is probably the most universal of all attitudes. However, there have been exceptions. In Greek and Roman times, slaves and barbarians did not enjoy a full right to life. Spartan law required that impaired infants be put to death. For Plato, infanticide was one of the corner-stones of the model state. Aristotle regarded abortion as a desirable option, and the Stoic philosopher Seneca writes unapologetically of 'unnatural progeny we destroy; we drown even children who are at birth weakly and unnormal' (Quoted in Kuhse 1987).[1]

All societies kill the elderly. A few do it with immense clarity – most relatively kindly, through variations of a death-hastening process. Often, they are killed not just because they are old but because of some other converging factor. In many primitive societies, early death might be reserved mainly for elderly *females*. In the workhouse it was the aged *poor*. Under the Nazi regime, it was elderly *disabled people*. In the care and nursing home, homicidal attrition relates often to financial status, and to the routines of bureaucracy. In all societies, it has been those older people without kin support who have been the most frequent target – familial isolation is a curse in old age. The old-old, as opposed to the young-old, are most susceptible. Age of itself is rarely regarded as the justification for killing. Some other factor of social marginalisation is the precipitator. Stratification affects the elderly perhaps more seriously than it does other age groups.

Generally, with a few exceptions, the lonely survivor was the wealthy male who kept his sanity to the end, whose status was conferred by birth rather than ascribed by function, whose prospective death was not demanded by heirs desperate for their inheritance, whose abundant kin needed him more than he needed them, who possessed some knowledge or value not easily transmitted in other forms, who could if necessary buy quality care, and who lived in an relatively untasking environment. Women, although by far the majority of the elderly, seem to have survived up to that point in spite of their marginalisation and not from the good intentions of others.

Who kills the elderly?

Such a question, in one sense, is easy to answer. Society, community, tribe kills. Given pervasive anti-ageist sentiments, a notion of value based on economic con-tribution, it is the social group that kills. Grandson kills grandfather in primitive society on behalf of the larger family. Ageism and classism killed the elderly poor in the workhouse. In some societies, it was conducted with marked ritual – agency and victim were clear-cut, ceremonial meaning given to death as to birth. Others conduct the killing more grubbily – agent, intention and victim hidden behind ephemeral structures. But in the modern day, killing the elderly is an art, a craft and a profession. Functionally, it has been delegated to specialist institutions, directly to certain personnel. Differentiations in power and in expertise have located the death terminus within the medical profession

Professionalism and the case of Dr Harold Shipman

It might seem questionable to use a mass murderer of older people, such as Dr Shipman, as the model from which to derive geronticide prevention procedures. Shipman might fit into the mould noted in the political economy chapter and later reinforced by the practice of 'bed-blocking'. He is quoted as telling one Pamela Turner (whose mother he subsequently killed) 'the old are a drain on the health service' (Quoted in Whittle and Ritchie 2000, p.329). According to the toxicolo-gist Robert Forrest, he 'did it simply as a matter of convenience, getting rid of an awkward patient by killing her rather than by transferring her to another practice' (Quoted in Whittle and Ritchie 2000, p.335). Many elderly patients appear to have been lethally injected because he did not wish, for whatever reason, to carry on caring for them. Alternatively, he might have seen himself as a Raskolnikov figure (or perhaps as a Nietzschean superman entitled to ignore the rules of conventional morality). In Dostoevsky's *Crime and Punishment* (1866), Raskolnikov murders a despicable pawnbroker, an old woman no one loves and no one will mourn. Is it not just, he might have reasoned, to commit such a crime, to transgress moral law – if it will ultimately benefit humanity? But the information on Shipman's motives is anecdotal and subject to the wisdom of hindsight.

As far as we know, Shipman's crimes were exceptional. In his career, he is thought to have killed nearly two hundred people (although the precise number remains speculative).[2] His victims seem to have been entirely female (although there appears to have been an intriguing death of an elderly man who allegedly complained about his practice). The most significant thing about the victims in the Harold Shipman case is that the confirmed victims were all women, mainly past pensionable age.

Other doctors and carers have been multiple murderers. Dr Petiot lured people to his house in the 16th *arrondissement* of Paris during the Second World War with ruses of an escape route from occupied France. He then cut them up and either buried or incinerated them, keeping the money and valuables they had brought to fund their escape. He was found guilty of 26 murders, but was believed to be guilty of many more. Much earlier, the Victorian Dr Samuel Palmer of Rugely in Staffordshire poisoned 16 people, mainly to pay his gambling debts. There are more recent historical examples including the Nazi Holocaust doctors conducting extermination on a massive scale. Health provision by medical staff has not always been divorced from the mass murder of those deemed to be socially unwanted.

As far as the elderly are concerned, carer-assisted serial killing is not that unusual. Dr John Bodkin Adams was acquitted in 1957 of killing one of a long list of elderly wealthy female patients who died leaving him money and possessions.[3] Dr John Kappler committed many harmful acts against his patients and had them covered up by his colleagues and his nurse/wife (see Ablow 1994).

Mass killers of the elderly, such as the two nurses in Austria who killed 40 patients in an old people's home, have sometimes acted in the belief that they were doing their victims a favour, since they believed that their lives were no longer worth living. But Shipman does not appear to have selected those patients whose lives were especially miserable.

Shipman was both unique and representative. His practices require little reciting. Like other medical professionals, he enjoyed secret power. Death-hastening could become routine. He was an authoritative expert on life and death – his subjects the ageist-caricatured elderly. His victims trusted him. He was technically efficient at his occupation. Like other professionals, he was largely non-accountable – there were few sanctions. Disciplinary proceedings and investigative procedures were deeply flawed.

Secret power and expert authority

As experts, medical professionals enjoy secret power. Shipman could kill older people because he was a professional, with apparent access to the mysteries of life. He was a Charon figure, the boatman for the liminal between life and death, between the worlds of the living and of the dead. As a professional, he was technically efficient. 'My work was faultless. I provided the ultimate care. I prided myself on my experience in caring for people who were extremely ill. How dare they question my professionalism?'[4] He was unassailable.

The scope for life-saving treatment in modern medicine is very limited. Could it be then that in the absence of an opportunity to bring about care, Shipman resolved to bring about death? To adapt the words of Shakespeare's Richard III, since he could not prove a healer, he was determined to bring about death.

Professionalism may eschew monitoring any criminal records of doctors. There appeared to be no reason why health authorities should necessarily have such records of doctors who contract to work in their area. Similarly, while Shipman regularly over-prescribed morphine, often exceeding his budget on drugs (as scrutinised by the health authority), he also saved the authority expenditure because he relatively rarely sent patients to specialists. His few referrals made his surgery seem a cheap practice and one to be lauded in the authority records.

Such death-hastening may become routine in less extreme cases. Much of what medical practitioners and medical specialists do involves a desensitisation process. Some of their practices transgress every human instinct. They may slice living flesh. They may probe intimate parts of the anatomy accessible to no other party. They frequently inject sharp objects into their patients. These processes are often repeated. Death is part of the daily work – dealing with the dying, certifying that the individual has passed the liminal stage, and handling a corpse, are almost routine. Being a medical practitioner means a numbing experience, requiring varying degrees of detachment.

The lack of sanctions against medical professionals

Apart from over financial matters, Shipman was largely non-accountable. He enjoyed the arrogance of the professional. On the death of Ivy Lomas in his treatment room, he reputedly told a police officer that he considered her a nuisance, and that she was such a frequent attender that he had thought about putting a plaque up on the wall and reserving a chair in the waiting room for her. Doctor Palmer (see p.161) successfully poisoned people as long as he did with the same advantages as Shipman – he was their doctor, he prescribed the medicine, he signed the death certificates.

Investigatory procedures (like the inspection procedures in care homes noted in Chapter 5) are often flawed. For example, a code of conduct obliges nurses to report 'to an appropriate authority' any circumstances which could jeopardise patient care. Typically, one nurse reported a serious incident in relation to an elderly patient to the General Medical Council and to the local health authority. The complaint was rejected by the GMC because the 'information you provided did not raise sufficient concern'. 'I was expected to find witnesses and organise the witnesses before the GMC because the GMC "have no powers of investigation".' She noted routinely receiving calls from the coroner's office, trying to persuade the hospital to issue a death certificate without further ado. Suspicious deaths could be easily overlooked.[5] Extraordinarily, although 25 years earlier a pethidine addict, Shipman had escaped censure by the GMC. That professional agency, after considering psychiatrists' reports on Shipman and despite his having been found guilty of dishonestly obtaining drugs and forging prescriptions, simply sent him a warning but allowed him to continue to practise.

There are few checks on death certification by such a professional. When the GMC was informed about the police investigation of the alleged murder of Kathleen Grundy, it claimed it could have done nothing to suspend the GP because of legal restrictions. Death certificates are only used for statistical purposes by the health authority. Death rates among individual GPs are not monitored. All deaths must be notified to the Registrar of Births, Deaths and Marriages. But Shipman's local health authority had apparently no means of checking rates amongst its 230 GPs. A doctor who signs the certificate is not required to see the body. He or she must simply have 'attended' the patient in the last illness, within 14 days prior to death. The doctor is not obliged to notify the coroner of a sudden or unexpected death – that is for the Registrar to do after the families report the death. In the case of a cremation, a second GP of five years' standing is required to sign to say they are satisfied that the first doctor has given the correct cause of death. This is often a formality. The second doctor may see the body but is unlikely to examine it or look at the case notes.

After the death of a patient, a GP could retain the records of the deceased (although now they must be returned to the health authority). In the care home, even after death, the deceased may be dealt with cursorily. For example, the Director of the Registered Nursing Homes Association recently stated that she had received 12 reports of GPs refusing to visit homes – nursing home patients were being neglected in their beds, sometimes with other residents sleeping nearby, because some GPs refused to certify deaths out of hours.[6]

Ageism and blaming the elderly victim

While blaming the victim has a long and unfortunate pedigree within criminology, in one sense the victims brought death upon themselves. They attracted personal depredations and injury. Shipman singled out the most vulnerable isolated elderly women. Murder was carried out by the person most trusted – a GP who takes the Hippocratic Oath is supposed to care for them and keep them alive.

These women went trustingly like lambs to the slaughter. Within an ideology of ageism, old ladies living alone make perfect targets. There is nobody to catch the killer red-handed, nobody to raise the alarm rapidly, no reason to question the death too closely because of the victim's age. There was no mass public outcry at his court appearances – as there would have been, for example, with a suspected child abuser.

Similarly, because of the nature of the victims, it was difficult to check his practices. Most GPs, unlike Shipman, tend to avoid lists weighted towards the elderly. Shipman had a death rate of two and a half times the local average. But this was not necessarily an indication of his murderous habits, because few doctors accept lists skewed towards the elderly – for example, by including many nursing and care homes.

Professionals are frequently accountable only to their peers. They promote a notion of client–practitioner trust – rather than the blunt relationship of the cash nexus. Thus when a different patient was asked to sign a forged will on behalf of one of Shipman's victims, he said, 'If a geezer comes up to you in a pub and asks you to sign something, there is no way you'd do it without reading it all very carefully, and finding what it's all about. But if your own doctor, who you have known since you were a kid and who is extremely well-respected in the town, asks you to do him a favour and sign something, you don't think twice' (Quoted in Whittle and Ritchie 2000, p.11).

Checking Geronticide

If killing particular groups of elderly is a practice that has gone largely unchecked, ebbing and flowing in its extremities since the days of primitive society, how does one stem that tide? How does one restrain this manifest aberration from normal prohibitions on killing other humans in one's own society? Four levels of action are possible. None is new. The dilemma is the weight given to each and of putting theory into practice.

There are problems of procedure, especially with regard to the medical profession's control of dying. As in the Shipman case above, some rules need better development and more commitment to enforcement. Second, there is a question of aged. Where feasible, old people themselves are the best source of prevention – either directly or through the extensive pressure of enterprises representing the aged. Third, such geronticide disposal practices could not occur without the dominance of an ideology of ageism. While that ideology may have structural roots, its continuity through time and space requires combating at different levels. Finally, recently there have been important legal developments with regard to the rights of the elderly, especially in the field of human rights. Inevitably, the latter structures are complex, unclear in theorisation, and difficult to implement. But they offer a cornerstone of potential prevention.

Procedural Checks

As we note above, most geronticide in the present day is conducted by medical professionals – mainly sins of omission rather than sins of commission. The continuum from care assistants to medical specialists bears the brunt of obligations in relation to potential geronticide. In the case of the individual medical professional, the Shipman case teaches us that much can be done, and (sometimes) is being done, to prevent such serial murders, as well as death-hastening acts of omission, by more generic medical and care staff. One set of procedures relates to individual decision-making processes regarding voluntary euthanasia. Others relate to professional control over medical staff, especially with regard to death-hastening practices.

One key development with regard to euthanasia practices is that of the so-called 'living will'.[7] These personal imprimaturs aim to regulate the conditions of the liminal period – determine in advance the care the elderly should receive if their faculties subsequently become impaired. The Law Commission argues that any refusal of treatment in advance should not apply where life is at stake. Living wills should be allowed but they cannot require a doctor to do anything illegal, including steps to end a patient's life or providing a treatment against a patient's best interest. Second, paradoxically, more autonomy may be given to professionals. Lord Irvine's Green Paper proposes a Court of Protection with expanded powers to make decisions or to resolve disputes about personal welfare. Families would lose their traditional right to prevent doctors switching off life-support machines of comatose patients.[8]

Professionalism has often become a code for self-protection. In the light of the Shipman case, one resolution has scapegoated single-handed GPs. On the arbitrary assumption that shared practices provide for self-disciplining, the GMC has proposed that all individual-practice GPs should undergo continuing assessment and be disciplined if they do not comply with appropriate standards.[9] Each year in the UK, some £32 million is spent on fees to doctors to complete post-mortem related functions. Some of this sum would be better spent on an audit team for death certificates, recording the doctor involved and the cause and location of death. The team should undertake audits of case notes, both on the basis of suspicion and randomly.

GPs have too much freedom to remove elderly patients from their lists (which *inter alia*, acts as a sanction against possible complaints). In his annual report for 1997/98, the Health Service Ombudsman questioned the continued right of GPs to discard patients. He drew attention to guidance issued by the Royal College of General Practitioners. This recommends that, as a matter of good practice, doctors should explain to patients why they consider it necessary to remove them(!). The Ombudsman also states that the cost of treatment is not an appropriate reason to remove a patient (Age Concern 1999a).

More generally, there are problems of training and staffing in care homes. Training and pay (and by implication the treatment of the elderly as a marketable commodity) is at fault. Auxiliaries and care assistants, not nurses, conduct most work in geriatric wards and care homes. Geriatric wards in particular are depressing, often full of elderly people with different problems who are all lumped together. Routinised care processes allow little room for recognition of human individuality and needs. The recent minimum wage legislation in the UK may be one minor, but incremental step to recognising that staff in such institutions deserve better rewards, and by implication a higher level of skill, training, and qualified supervision.[10]

The Queen's Speech of November 1999 promised better protection for people in long-term care in the Care Standards Bill.[11] Regulation is currently shared by local authorities, health authorities and the Department of Health while local authority care homes may not be currently inspected. The Bill proposes to create an independent statutory watchdog to oversee all residential homes for older people,[12] to promote national standards of care for older people covering a range of matters from privacy to diet, for implementation by the year 2001. Again the problem lies in inspection practice rather than in legislative intent.[13]

Age Concern (1999a) has called for several procedural measures to eliminate discrimination against the elderly in need of health care – including investigations into no-referral from primary to secondary care and into the fear of older people who wish to make complaints. It also calls for the establishment of a National Care Commission 'to take a strategic view of long-term care and to steward the interests of older people who receive services' (Age Concern 1999a, p.7).

The elderly as active not passive: Empowerment[14] through agency

We have suggested through the episodic historical tour in this text that one of the few continuities of the social history of the elderly has been the prevalence of a culture of ageism. Whether that cultural feature remains primarily a function of demography, of political economy, of the modernisation process, of bureaucratisation or indeed, a combination of several factors, remains indeterminate. However, conclusively, it appears that the elderly, especially when conflated with one or other forms of marginal status, are readily available for death-hastening as a consequence of that ideological predisposition.

Ageism is not relevant to instantaneous resolution through procedural change. Nor is it some form of false consciousness which might be wished away and be rapidly regarded as ephemeral in the face of the onslaught of the re-education processes in postmodern societies. Ageism is an ideology, which includes amongst its other components the disregard of age in favour of youth (Bytheway 1994), and the relegation of those in need to a dummy status. Ageism means above all else the assumption that older people are incapable of rational decisions, of articulating independent modes of thought, and, in this context, resistance to death-hastening processes of de-individualisation.[15] One key aspect of that ageist ideology is the assumption that older people, especially those in care, are passive.

Most of the older academic literature (indeed, some of the literary material too) has tended to treat older people as the passive recipients of activities that are conducted against them. The image of the elderly person being often unresistingly placed in care, being woken, washed, fed, and dosed (and eventually carried out), as the conveyor belt subject of the care home's working day (and night), is common. Older people within a culture of ageism are perceived not just as the victims of such abuse, but also passive in its practice.

'Elderly people are treated and processed as commodities; their dependency is in fact socially constructed by enforced passivity. They are not considered consumers of services but rather endurers of services that stigmatise and segregate them' (Bennett and Kingston 1993, p.120). This imagery covers not only the bed-bound geriatric patient in almost post-liminal status, but is often extended to the younger elderly who have only just passed a formal age of retirement. While their spokespersons, via the several pressure groups and charities, may vocalise resistance on their part (as some do remarkable effectively), the elderly, especially the institutionalised elderly, for the most part are depicted as passive, as dummy participants in a professional game. They do not resist that contemptuous disdain.

However as we have suggested in several examples, opposition to that death-hastening process is often covert rather than direct. It appears most vividly in the Grimms' fairy tales and the folk stories recorded by Ashliman (1999) in which the elderly person frequently finds some means of demonstrating his (and occasionally) her value to the community. Typically, their intervention saves the community from impending disaster and they can no longer be ignored.

Resistance takes many forms. The problem is one of recognising it when it does not follow conventional routes. But when other avenues are closed – such as when the formal complaints procedures are perceived as inaccessible or potentially hopeless – care residents (like the elderly workhouse inmate who disrupted the Christmas dinner in George Sim's poem) have to choose from the limited available options to voice their disquiet.

In van Velde's (1953) account of a Dutch dying institution, even soiling oneself deliberately in bed – simply incontinence to the care staff – may actually be a way of resisting institutional demands. Inevitably, that final resistance is conveyed most vividly in Diamond's remarkable study (1992). For example, the nearly-blind Mrs Herman is often spoken to in baby-talk by care staff. She finally snaps and explains vociferously: 'It's not that I can't hear you, it's that I can't understand you. Most people around here talk too loud to the blind.' (p.91) Diamond notes that she would often over-pay staff for coffee even though that was against the institutional rules, as a demonstration of autonomy. Like van

Velde, Diamond notes bed-ridden residents appearing deliberately to disrupt the shift-changing timetable. Two residents, for example, would frequently demonstrate incontinence at shift changeover – chortling with laughter at the way they had disrupted the bureaucratic machine. For the staff, they were out of control, incapable, incompetent.

Recognising that opposition and its meaning,[16] in the face of being treated like a residual object, is one key to appreciating that the death-hastening process of the care home need not be a one-way dispatch. Ageism as an ideology is to be combated by recognising that resistance can take many strange forms. Some might be by the vocal research-informed demands and lobbying of the ageing enterprises. Others are, as above, the attempts by care residents located at the social residuum, constrained almost entirely by routine and by ideology, who demonstrate individuality as best they can, in resisting the ascribed liminal status.[17]

Human rights and the elderly

A final basis for combating the residual disposing of the elderly lies in that amorphous body of legislation that resides under the human rights rubric. The swathe of international rights legislation has the general advantage of furnishing a universal benchmark from which existing discrimination against the elderly can be combated and new procedures of preservation devised. Unfortunately, such legislation is often vague and contradictory in its characteristics.

Briefly, we can distinguish three separate positions with regard to human rights and the elderly – the older utilitarian view, the new equality agenda advanced by much human rights legislation, and positive discrimination proposals (often from a similar source to the second). The latter however contains its own epistemological division.

THE UTILITARIAN VIEW

This position, owing much to the older nineteenth century social philosophy of John Stuart Mill, has resonances with the political economy view documented in Chapter 2.

Callahan (1987) argued that society should develop norms excluding older people from social citizenship. Adopting a crude version of the utilitarian perspective, he argues that in a society in which health and welfare resources are finite, they should be targeted towards those for whom they will have the greatest benefits. Thus children as future citizens and younger adults as key components of the current labour force should be the primary beneficiaries. Attempts to ensure parity of citizenship for elderly people, expressed in rights to access to the full range of health and social services in contemporary society are seen as 'beyond our means'. Efforts to create participatory relationships between caring professions and service users are nonsensical, as elderly people who require care provision would receive it only on the basis of residual citizenship rights.

This view involves a notion of 'generational equity'. It proposes differential citizenship on the basis of age, relying on the concept of obligations between generations. Callahan argues, in effect, for a two-level conception of citizenship – the primary for the producers and those who have yet to contribute to society, and a second level of citizenship compensating for the lesser rights of the elderly by assuming that there exists an axiomatic caring relationship between the first and second levels. On this basis, older people will receive care without the same level of rights because of the affinity of obligations of younger people towards them. Expressive ties will compensate for the loss of formal rights.

A rather wider but similar view is taken by Alan Williams (1997), who cautions against what he calls 'the vain pursuit of immortality'. There comes a time when the inevitability of death must be accepted and 'a reasonable limit has to be set on the demands we can properly make on our fellow citizens to keep us going a bit longer' (p.820). In effect, older people must recognise when they have had a 'fair innings' and greater weight should be attached to the needs of younger people.

The utilitarian position recognises that there are other contributions to society that individuals can make apart from the simply economic ones of furnishing sustenance. Ring-fencing resources may be appropriate because the *general* contribution of the elderly to society is not as great as that of those who still have their future to live.

The generational equity debate is based upon three premises: (1) that in recent years the elderly have benefited disproportionately in terms of social spending when compared with other age groups; (2) that these gains have come at the expense of other age groups; and (3) that the elderly have had the power to make the decisions that permit this advantage to continue (Street and Quadagno 1994). It assumes that the elderly furnish a cohesive political bloc with sufficient power to determine political decisions on specific issues. Wrongly, it contends that there is a decisive age versus youth continuing contest; that elderly voting behaviour is self-interested, and that the elderly constitute a homogeneous voting bloc (*ibid.*). Such a view contains little in the way of empirical evidence.

The flaws in this rights' position need little elaboration – it is relativistic in terms of obligations; it is ageist in the treatment of the elderly as a homogeneous mass; and it is subjective in implying that the key contributions to society are made by particular types of citizen.

Its relativism is demonstrable by a simple example. In law in the elder abuse context, there has been a dilemma over the approach to the phenomenon of self-neglect. Should the individual's failure to feed, clothe, and shelter himself or herself properly be regarded as a personal or familial matter or is it a function for which the state has an obligation? (Johns and Hydle 1995) Thus in the United States self-neglect often falls outside the remit of state legislative action because of an assumption of cohesive and mutually responsible family and community ties. Individual problems which involve no apparent harm to others are largely exempt from intervention by statutory legislation. However, in Norway, for example, self-neglect may constitute an offence by the state in terms of its failure to ensure the well-being of its elderly citizens. This position makes no assumption about the nature of family and community bonds – indeed, of generational obligations.

This recognition of the differential characteristics of obligations is acknowledged in the United Nations Principles for Older Persons (1991): 'Older persons should benefit from family and community care and protection *in accordance with each society's system of cultural values*' (Clause 8) (italics added). The utilitarian position espoused by Callahan is particularistic rather than universalistic.

It is also ageist (Hugman 1998). It makes a grand assumption about the characteristics of the elderly. It makes no attempt to distinguish between them apart from on the arbitrary basis of chronological age or of retirement from waged employment. It fails to recognise that on some occasions, the older person has more in common with the young than with other elderly people. Pain (1995), for example, has argued that the older woman's experience of violent sexual assaults may place her in a category not dissimilar from younger women and one that may be quite distinct from that of elderly males.

Finally, as we have argued throughout this book, apart from the obvious divisions between the young-old and the old-old, between ethnic minority elderly and the majority community, as well as between the disabled and others, it fails to recognise the particular economic disadvantages of socio-economic class. In all societies, it is those from lower socio-economic groups who suffer the most extreme deprivation when elderly and are most liable to practices such as death-hastening. To conflate the poor elderly with the wealthy elderly on the basis of age identity is grievously to conceal their differential needs.

THE ORTHODOX HUMAN RIGHTS VIEW: EQUALITY AS A CENTRAL PRINCIPLE IN RELATION TO NEEDS

This view contains two central concepts. It assumes *equality between citizens* and it assumes *individuality*. Older people, like younger people, are individual citizens. As such they deserve the equality of treatment in terms of both rights and needs relevant to other citizens. Citizens are citizens, irrespective of socio-economic class, ethnicity, age or disability. They therefore deserve the same individual rights as other such citizens.[18]

For example, the Northern Ireland Human Rights Commission's (1998) statement of intent with regard to elderly rights:

> There is a growing realisation that people of all ages, including those beyond normal retirement age, have an equal right of access to jobs, goods, …and education…its duty under Section 75 of the Northern Ireland Act to have the need to promote equality of opportunity between persons of different ages.

Similarly Age Concern has worthily called for government legislation to make it illegal for the NHS to refuse treatment or to treat someone differently on the basis of their age (Age Concern 1999a).

Equality and citizenship are untrammelled principles. The elderly, like the young, have equality rights in the society of individual citizens. They also have – to misquote the writer Anatole France – an equal right to sleep under bridges, to beg in the streets, and to suffer death-hastening processes in care institutions! The equality and citizenship principles are inadequate because they do not recognise that many older people are manifestly already unequal as compared to other groups. Simply conferring on them equal rights – no matter how laudable as a general principle – is simply to accept their right to remain unequal.

As we have shown in this text, particular groups of the elderly are far more susceptible to being treated in a generally demeaning manner, especially with regard to their liability to fatal disposal processes, than are others, both young and old. What is required is not equal treatment but recognition of their fundamental inequality, and exposure to geronticidal practices. Positive discrimination in favour of elderly people is required, not bland euphemisms about equality of treatment independent of inequalities of conditions.

AFFIRMATIVE ACTION: POSITIVE DISCRIMINATION, LIBERAL AND NEO-MARXIST CONTRIBUTIONS

There are however other national and international standards regarding the elderly, benchmarks which recognise the inequality of condition of many elderly and which seek to remedy that inequality by positive legislative action. One body of opinion derives from a liberal democratic framework, and the other from the neo-Marxist work of Evgeny Pashukanis.

Several national statements of principle regarding the human rights of the elderly make clear the imperative for positive discrimination in favour of the elderly. They enunciate appropriate measures to ensure their needs for *extra* rights and more directive procedures to prevent them being regarded as a kind of social residuum, equal in law but not in practice.

For example, the Canadian Charter of Rights and Freedoms expressly embodies a commitment to positive discrimination on behalf of *socially unequal* groups. While this Charter is not dissimilar from (although more detailed than) the excerpt from the Northern Ireland statement of intent (Quoted above), it contains throughout a specific caveat requiring legal process to be committed to deal with social rather than legal equality. Irrespective of its concern to promote equality of treatment with regard to human rights, it contains the following provision:

> [It] does not preclude any law, program or activity that has as its object the ame-lioration of conditions of disadvantaged individuals or groups including those that are disadvantaged because of race, national or ethnic origin, colour, religion, sex, age or mental or physical disability. (Canada Act 1982, sch. B, Pt I, s.15 (2))

In other words, the Charter recognises that some individuals and groups are sig-nificantly more susceptible to social and economic disadvantage than are others.[19] Treating them simply as the equal of other, non-disadvantaged, citizens is insuffi-cient. What is required is the legal recognition of that inequality and positive dis-criminatory legal action to compensate. Citizens and social groups are not all equal, and a simple statement of human rights is insufficient. In those cases, particular elderly groups need positive discriminatory action, legislation that the notion of equal citizenship is incapable of furnishing.

Such a view (although more vaguely phrased) is embodied in the United Nations Principles for Older Persons, which, apart from recognising the need to combat the insidious ideology of ageism, also appreciates the different needs of many elderly people. The requirement to counter ageist ideologies has long been recognised.[20] The dignity of old people is inviolable. All public authorities have the duty to respect and protect it (this requires *inter alia* positive images of ageing in the media, retirement preparation, and continuing social roles after retirement (European Association for the Welfare of the Elderly 1975).

A different theoretical perspective concludes with the same thesis on the need to discriminate positively, through law (in Marxist theories of law), in the related work of two writers, Pashukanis (1978) and Balbus (1973). Their scholarship draws on an economic metaphor to demonstrate how the market economy creates 'false equivalents' which have the effect of denying individual rights and needs. Pashukanis and Balbus emphasise the distinction between the *use values* of the household and the *exchange values* of the market. In the primitive market economy, individual worth is based upon the value placed upon the materials brought for exchange on to the market. However, not merely do different individuals produce different qualities of use values (the homeworking mother produces significantly less than does the farmer who has cattle to sell on the market), but market valuation bears little relation to the actual labour required to produce the goods. Thus a baker may spend a whole day producing a hundred loaves for sale on the market. Conversely, the village axe-maker may expend a day's labour producing one implement. In the perfect economy, where there is a ready supply of both bread and axes, a hundred loaves may be valued by the axe-maker at one day's labour in exchange for a single axe. Equivalence of a day's labour is the result.

However, perfect economies rarely exist. When corn is in short supply, and there is less bread for the market, the baker may be able to demand one axe in return for 50 loaves. One day's baking comes to equal two days labour by the axe-maker. A notion of 'false equivalents' is created in which one day's endeavour is made commensurate with two days' labour.

Applied to the elderly, the metaphor becomes clear. Old people become identical to commodities in the market in which they are valued artificially (Fennell *et al.* 1988). Being defined as a senior citizen by virtue of a state pension (on reaching the legal retirement age) is a 'master status', which equates the pensioner to all other individual pensioners. A legal notion of the elderly (pension rights) creates a situation of artificial equivalents, in which differentials relating to socio-economic class (for example, access to a private pension scheme), of gender (the different demographic numbers of female elderly and their related economic security), of ethnicity, as well as of rural/urban location, are ignored under the generic notion of the pensioner. Alternative categories are disregarded with the assumption of a community of individual elders. One older person becomes equal as an object to all other older people and is deemed to have an economic, social and legal value based on that artificial status (Brogden and Nijhar 2000). They become a community of false equivalents.

The implication of this figurative approach is that older people are treated generically as artificial citizens – the only feature that makes them different from other citizens is the chronological factor of ageing. As citizens, they are then aggregated into a further artificial category of identical elderly legal citizens. But in reality as a group – as we have repeatedly argued in this book – that notional legal unity and status is fractured by many of the social schisms that affect the rest of the population. The homogenisation of the elderly conceals structural inequalities.

Remedying such inequalities, protecting the elderly from, for example, the ring-fencing of healthcare – concealed by the formal ascribed citizen status – means treating them as legal and social *unequals.*[21] Procedural positive discrimination, as in the liberal version of human rights legislation noted above, is one answer. But the critical legal approach emphasises that the social inequality of supposedly marginal groups such as the elderly be inscribed in law, thus making it mandatory, not permissive, to treat such component groups by positive discrimination. In a reverse of the utilitarian position, legal inequality is a *necessary* condition to ensure social equality. Where groups of elderly need more care or more protection – or, for that matter, more winter fuel or clothing – that should be a legislative matter enforced by criminal and civil legal sanctions. Practices such as bed blocking, ring-fencing of scarce resources to the elderly, commodifying them on the conveyor belt to the everlasting bonfire, should be combated by *enforceable* discriminatory legislation.[22]

A comparison with primitive society makes the point:

In the United States...with their monthly allocation of (food) stamps, recipients have access to any food in the supermarket. But their special claim to society's resources is limited by this meagre monthly allocation. ...

By contrast, the food taboos of many primitive societies have the effect of roping off a certain section of the supermarket for the elderly only. Moreover, they are not made to feel like second class citizens. Rather they are granted access to certain special foods as right and a privilege, and because of the unique character-istics of the age they have reached. (Barash 1983, p.191)

'There's many a slip, twixt cup and lip'

Legislation and statements of principles of positive discrimination are one thing, practice is often another.[23] Most Western countries, for example, now have legisla-tion governing the detailed rights of residents in nursing homes. They have not, however, prevented many of the death-hastening excesses illustrated in Chapter 6.

For example, the United States Congress legislation contains[24] a detailed statement of nursing home residents' rights.[25] The principles attempt to cover all aspects of residents' life in care institutions – including protection of finances, choice of physician, guarantees of privacy, equal access to care, and participation in residents' groups. Critical are such clauses as 'The facility may not use physical restraints or psychoactive drugs for discipline or when they are not required to treat medical symptoms.' As we suggested in Chapter 6 such provisions may often be more honoured in the breach than in practice.[26]

Little has been said of the importance of criminal justice intervention in nursing and care homes to enforce rights. The problems with creating such inter-ventions – from access to lack of witnesses – are well known and require little reciting (Brogden and Nijhar 2000). But there is evidence of its efficacy.[27] Menio (1996), for example, recites the several advantages of such a development: 'The images of administrators and nurses being led away in handcuffs was the scene on the evening news...' (p.161) She emphasises the importance of such cases in forcing other establishments to tend to residents' rights rather differently. Occasional emblematic prosecutions, when coupled with more proactive inspection[28] (and encouragement and employment protection for 'whistleblow-ers'[29] from concerned staff), can work wonders. Similarly, new forms of policing have been effected in other areas of business crime (Braithwaite 1989). Where the industry engages in a measure of self-regulation, its own inspectors could be held directly culpable if a higher authority finds them neglecting enforcement. Care institutions might only be annually re-registered if they demonstrated beforehand satisfaction with the rights charters. The onus must be placed much more formally on the care agencies to demonstrate their rule adherence rather than on inspectors discovering breaches.

Notes

1   For a summary of classical Greek views of the elderly and of the ageing process, see Rosenthal 1996, pp.175–80.

2   The Shipman case led to a moral panic about the relationship between GPs and elderly patients. For example, a retired GP, Dr Robert Dickson, was being investigated over the deaths of two elderly women ten years earlier. Dickson said in his defence: 'I did not intend to do her any harm. I just wanted to get her to sleep, to relieve her pain. There is not one GP I know who does not think I was unlucky. They have all used [excessive] doses.' ('New allegations over retired doctor.' *The Times*, 15 February 2000).

3   Bodkin Adams was only charged with the one offence of which he was acquitted. He had however been suspected of dispatching dozens of similar elderly ladies. When he died in 1983, he left more than £400,000, a combination of old ladies' wills and libel damages from those who had forgotten his acquittal ('Elderly Killers in the Past.' *The Guardian*, 7 February 2000).

4   'The arrogant doctor: "They will never find me guilty."' *Electronic Telegraph*, 6 February 2000.

5   Letter to *The Guardian*, 3 February 2000.

6   'GP murdered 15 women to enjoy ultimate power of life and death.' *Electronic Telegraph*, 12 October 1999.

7   'New laws required "to protect the old and infirm."' *Electronic Telegraph*, 9 December 1999. The term 'living will' (more professionally known as an advance directive) was coined by Luis Kutner in 1969 to describe a document in which a competent adult sets forth directions regarding medical treatment in the event of his or her future incapacitation. The document is a will in the sense that it spells out the person's directions. It is 'living' because it takes effect before death. See Annas (1991). There is a considerable literature on living wills – see for example Hanson and Rodgman (1996), Kuzewski (1994), Stelter, Elliott and Bruno (1992).

8   'Problems of elderly in care.' *Electronic Telegraph*, 10 December 1999. For a critique of the operation of the Court of Protection in relation to living wills see 'Revealed: cruelty of staff in NHS hospitals.' *Sunday Times*, 22 February 2000.

9   However, the problems being addressed by both government and profession are not those of 'policing' actions such as those of Shipman, but simply ones of performance and perceived problems of keeping up to date. A critical problem generally with the medical profession is that the General Medical Council has denied that a 'policing role' is one of its functions – for example, in claming that it is for an employer to ask for information when it takes on a doctor rather than for the GMC to volunteer it!

10   Although training and rewards on their own hardly affect the cases of future Dr Shipmans, the evidence of abuse in care homes frequently demonstrates that too much blame is cast on the unqualified rank-and-file of the 'industry' (Brogden and Nijhar 2000).

11   At the launch of the preceding consultation paper (7 September 1999), the Minister spoke of making 'horror stories of badly run homes a thing of the past'.

12   Note the call for this new Inspectorate in the Report of the Better Regulation Task Force, 12 May 1998. Such a development should be seen *inter alia* in conjunction with the recognition of 'grey power' by the government proposal for the development of a separate department to cater for the needs of British pensioners, 13 March 2000.

13   The response by the spokesperson for the National Care Homes Association was not positive – while emphasising the need for staff training, she also claimed: 'I have never heard that size of a bedroom harmed anyone'(!) ('Carers oppose new home regulations' *BBC News Online*, 8 September 1999). In the United States such minimal proposals were legislated for in 1987, but have not prevented many of the excesses charted in Chapter 5.

14   Generally, on the new approach to the empowerment of the elderly – and one which is illustrated by Doris Lessing's *Diary of a Good Neighbour* – see Chapter 6 and see Minkler (1996).

15   For a rosy view of a claimed decline in ageism, by the accredited inventor of the concept, see Butler (1983).

16   See the complex resistance by Mrs O'Rourke and other nursing home residents in Vesperi (1990), under the most extreme conditions.

17   There is now a considerable literature on the importance of mobilising residents to articulate their self-preservation demands and to develop respect for their personhood. Amongst others, see Williams (1989).

18   The House of Commons Health Committee described long-term care for Britain's elderly as 'mean' and 'inequitable' (10 May 1999). The problem is not inequity itself but rather inequity in the wrong direction – see Northern Ireland Human Rights Commission (1999) Belfast: Northern Ireland Office.

19   For a useful discussion of one Canadian approach to enforcing elderly rights, see the account by Chernin, Jenkinson and Lobu (1990) of the Ontario Bill of Rights for residents in nursing homes.

20   See, for example, *Charter of Human Rights for the Elderly of Europe*, s.1. Sally Greengross of Age Concern correctly makes the point that 'Charters alone will be insufficient for most people.' ('Safeguarding rights of the elderly.' *BBC News Online*, 26 May 1999).

21   One example of an oblique approach to such positive discrimination in favour of the elderly is Age Concern's call for ring-fencing of long-term care – 'Charter of Rights for Elderly?' *BBC News Online*, 26 May 1999.

22   For an excellent early discussion of the limitations and possibilities of the rights approach to combating abuse in care institutions, see Brown (1986).

23   For example, knowledge in homes for the elderly of their new obligations under the Human Rights Act 2000 appears to be minimal – 'A hard act to follow.' *The Times*, 28 March 2000.

24   2 December 1987 as part of Public Law 100–203, the Omnibus Reconciliation Act.

25   See also, for example, the Charter of Residents' Rights and Responsibilities in Australia 1991. New rules for health and care agencies – *No Secrets* – to cover the abuse of elderly people were announced by the British Social Care Minister in March 2000, after an inquiry into the 'degrading and cruel' treatment of dementia patients in Carlisle. The rules were to be implemented by October 2001 and monitored by the Social Services Inspectorate.

26   On the strategies by which nursing homes can impede the implementation of residents' rights, see the Australian study by Gibson, Turrell and Jenkins (1993).

27   For a critical appraisal of one such criminal justice intervention when a nursing home corporation's senior administrators and some of its staff were indicted for murder as a result of the deaths of residents from alleged neglect while in the care of a nursing home, see Long (1987).

28   See Glass (1988) for a detailed earlier proposal for enhancing the quality of inspections. New powers for proactive inspection – a so-called inspection 'hit-squad' (the Commission for Health Improvement) – were invoked by the Health Secretary for the first time after abuse allegations (including elderly mentally ill patients being beaten by nurses, tied to a makeshift harness and fed while on the lavatory) at a care home in Cumbria – '"Hit squad" for abuse hospital.' *The Times*, 1 April 2000.

29   On the value of whistleblowers in healthcare institutions, see Miller (1988) and the example of the student nurses who sought to draw attention to the abuse four years earlier in the cases referred to in note 29.

References

Ablow, K.R. (1994) *The Strange Case of Dr Kappler: The Doctor Who Became a Killer.* New York: Free Press.

Achenbaum, W.A. (1987) *Old Age in the New Land.* Baltimore: John Hopkins University Press.

Age Concern (1997) 'Debate of the age.' *The Millenium Papers.* London: Age Concern.

Age Concern (1999a) *Age Discrimination 1999: Turning Your Back on Us.* London: Age Concern.

Age Concern (1999b) *An Ageing Population in the Future: Statistics.* London: Age Concern.

Age Concern (1999c) 'Too old for TV?' Communications Research Group. London: Age Concern.

'A hard act to fillow.' *The Times,* 28 March 2000.

Albee, E. (1963) *The Sand Box.* New York: Signet.

Aldiss, B. (1964) *Greybeard.* London: Harcourt, Brace and World.

Alexandratos, N. (1995) *World Agriculture: Towards 2000.* New York: John Wiley.

Amoss, P.T. (1981) 'Cultural centrality and prestige for the elderly: The Coast Salash Case.' In C.L. Fry (ed) *Dimensions: Ageing, Culture and Health.* New York: Praeger.

Anderson, M. (1980) *History of the Western Family.* Cambridge: Cambridge University Press.

Angelou, M. (1994) 'On Ageing.' In M. Angelou *The Complete Collected Poems of Maya Angelou.* New York: Random House.

Annas, G. (1991) 'The health care proxy and the living will.' *New England Journal of Medicine 324,* 17, 1210–1213.

Annas, G.J. (1993) 'Physician assisted suicide – Michigan's temporary solution.' *New England Journal of Medicine 328* (21), 1573–1576 May 27.

Ariyoshi, S. (1972) *The Twilight Years.* Tokyo: Kadonsha International.

Asch, M. (1996) 'Interventional Radiology: Application Family Practice.' *Canadian Family Physician,* August 42, 1511–8, 1521–3.

Ashliman, D.L. (1999) *Folklore/and Mythology.* University of Pittsburgh: www.pitt.edu/~folktexts.html

'A time to die' *The Economist,* 5 August 1989.

Atwood, M. (1987) *The Handmaid's Tale.* London: Anchor Books.

Auden, W.H. (1932) in E. Mendelson (ed) *W.H. Auden: Collected Poems.* New York: Random House.

Auden, W.H. (1969) *Collected Shorter Poems 1927–1957.* London: Faber and Faber.

Audit Commission Report (1997) '*Improving services for older people*' London: Audit Commission.

Back, A.L. and Wallace, J.I. (1996) 'Physician-assisted suicide and euthanasia in Washington State: Patient requests and physician responses'. *Journal of the American Medical Association 275,* 12, 919–925.

Balbus, I. (1973) *Dialectics of Legal Repression.* New York: Sage.

Baldwin, S. (1995) 'Love and Money: The Financial Consequences of Caring for an Older Relative.' In I. Allen and E. Perkins (eds) *The Future of Family Care for Older People.* London: HMSO.

Ballard, J.G. (1962) *Billenium.* London: Berkley Publishers.

Barash, D. (1983) *Aging: An Exploration.* Washington: University of Washington Press.

Bardwell, F. (1976) *The Adventure of Old Age.* Boston: Houghton Press.

Barker, J.C. (1990) 'Between Humans and Ghosts: The Decrepit Elderly in a Polynesian Society.' In J. Sokolovsky (ed) *The Cultural Context of Aging: World-Wide Perspectives.* New York: Bergen and Garvey Press.

Barker P. (1983) *Union Street.* New York: Putnam.

Bates, E. (1999) 'The shame of our nursing homes.' *The Nation*, 29 March, 11–19.

Battin, M. (1992) 'Voluntary Euthanasia and the Risks of Abuse: Can We Learn Anything from the Netherlands?' *Law, Medicine, and Health Care* 20 1–2, 133–143.

Battin, M. (1994) *The Least Worse Death*. Oxford: Oxford University Press.

Bauer, M.N. (1997) 'Late adulthood: A life-span analysis of suicide notes.' *Archives of Suicide Research* 3, 91–108.

Bausch, R. (1994) 'Rare and endangered species.' In *Rare and Endangered Species: A Novella and Stories*. Boston: Houghton Mifflin.

Beauchamp T. and Childress J. (1994) *Principles of Biomedical Ethics. (4th Edition)*. Oxford: Oxford University Press.

Bennett, G. and Kingston, P. (1993) *Elder Abuse: Concepts, Theories and Interventions*. London: Chapman and Hall.

Bernabei, R. and Gambassi, G. (1998) *Journal of the American Medical Association 37*, June, 109–120.

Besant, W. (1888) *The Inner House*. London: Arrowsmith.

Bever, E. (1982) 'Old age and witchcraft in early modern Europe.' in P. Stearns (ed) *Old Age in Pre-Industrial Society*. New York: Holmes and Beier.

Biggs, H. (1996) 'Decisions and responsibilities at the end of life.' *Medical Law International 2*, 229–245.

Biggs, S., Phillipson, C. and Kingston, P. (1995) *Elder Abuse in Perspective*. Buckingham: Open University Press.

Briggs, K.M. and Tongue, R.L. (1965) *Folktales of England*. London: Routledge and Kegan Paul.

Block, S. and Billings, A. (1994) 'Patients' requests to hasten death.' *Archives of Internal Medicine 154*, 26 September, 2039–2047.

Blauner, P. (1965) 'Death and social structure.' *Psychiatry 29*, 378–394.

Blythe, R. (1979) *The View in Winter*. Harmondsworth: Allen Lane.

Booth, P. (1992) 'Fallback' in M. Kohn, C. Donley and D. Wear (eds) *Literature and Aging*. Kent, OH: Kent State University Press.

Bould, S., Sanborn, B. and Reif, L. (1990) *The Oldest Old*. Belmont, CA: Wadsworth.

Bowles, L. (1993) 'Logical conclusion.' *Nursing Times* August, 32–34

Braithwaite, J. (1989) *Crime, Shame and Reintegration*. Cambridge: Cambridge University Press.

Braverman, H. (1998) *Labour and Monopoly Capital*. Second Edition. New York: Monthly Review Press.

British Medical Association (1988) *Euthanasia*. London: BMA.

Brogden, M.E., and Nijhar, P. (2000) *Crime, Abuse and the Elderly*. Devon: Willan Publishers.

Brooks, G. (1953) 'Death of a Grandmother.' In G. Brooks *Maud Martha*. New York: Harper and Brothers.

Brown, R.N. (1986) 'Nursing home residents' rights: An overview and brief assessment.' In M.B. Kapp, J. Harvey, E. Pies, and A.E. Doudera (eds) *Legal and Ethical Aspects of Care for the Elderly*. Ann Arbor, MI: Health Administration Press.

Brunner, J. (1968) *Stand on Zanzibar*. London: Orion Millenium.

Bureau of Labor Statistics (2000) *Occupation Outlook Handbook*. US Department of Labor, Washington, July.

Burgess, A. (1976) *The Wanting Seed*. New York: Norton.

Buringh, P., Van Hearnst, S.D. and Starling, K. (1975) *Computation of the Absolute Maximum World Population*. Wageningen, the Netherlands: Centre for World Food Market Research.

Butler, E.N. (1983) 'Dispelling ageism: The cross-cutting intervention.' *Generations*, Spring/Summer 75–78.

Bytheway, B. (1994) *Ageism*. Buckingham: Open University Press.

Callahan D. (1987) *Setting Limits: Medical Care in an Ageing Society*. New York: Simon and Schuster.

Capron, A.M. (1992) 'Euthanasia in the Netherlands – American observations' *Hastings Centre Report* March/April 31.

Carers National Association (1998) *Response to the Royal Commission on Long-term Care.* London: Carers National Association.

'Care abuse worker jailed.' *BBC News Online,* 7 February 2000.

'Carers oppose new home regulations.' *BBC News Online,* 8 September 1999.

Carey, J. (1999) *The Faber Book of Utopias.* London: Faber and Faber.

Carollo, G. and De Leo, D. (1996) 'Relationship between suicide and undetermined causes of death amongst the elderly: An analysis of Italian data from 1951–1988.' *Omega 33,* 3, 215–31.

Carpenter, B. (1993) 'A Review and New Look at Ethical Suicide in Advanced Age.' *Gerontologist* 33 (3), 359–365.

'Catering for old age.' *The Times,* 15 April 2000.

Chambliss, D.F. (1996) *Beyond Caring.* Chicago: University of Chicago Press.

'Charity offers haven of care and respect for old and dying.' *Electronic Telegraph,* 10 December 1999.

'Charter of rights for elderly.' *BBC News Online,* 26 May 1999.

Chaseling, W. (1957) *Yulenger: Nomads of Arnhem Land.* London: The Epworth Press.

Chernin, S., Jenkinson, J. and Lobu, T. (1990) *Every Resident's: Bill of Rights for People Who Live in Ontario Nursing Homes.* Toronto: Community Legal Action.

Clark, C. (1967) *Population Growth and Food.* London: Macmillan.

'Code to set standards for nursing home care.' *Electronic Telegraph,* 26 September 1998.

Cohn, R.M. (1980) 'Economic development and the status of the aged.' Paper given at the Conference of the American Sociological Association, August, New York.

Cole, T. (1992) *The Journey of Life: A Cultural History of Aging in America.* Cambridge: Cambridge University Press.

'Community Care putting lives at risk.' *Electronic Telegraph,* 25 November 1998.

Cool, L. and McCabe, J. (1990) 'The "Scheming Hag" and the "Dear Old Thing": The anthropology of aging women.' In J. Sokolovsky (ed) *Growing Old in Different Societies.* Belmont, CA: Wadsworth.

Cowgill, D. (1986) *Ageing Around the World.* Belmont, CA: Wadsworth.

Cowgill, D. and Holmes, L.D. (1972) *Aging and Modernisation.* New York: Appleton-Century-Crofts.

Crewe, G. (1843) *A Case For and Against the New Poor Law.* London.

Cuttle, G. (1934) *The Legacy of the Rural Guardians.* Cambridge: W.Heffer & Sons.

Dahlin, M.R. (1994) 'Symbols of the old-age pensions movement: The poorhouse, the family, and the "childlike" elderly.' In K.W. Schaie and A.A. Achenbaum (eds) *Societal Impact of Aging.* New York: Springer.

Davis, K. and van den Oever, P. (1981) 'Age Relationships and Public Policy in Advanced Industrial Societies.' *Population and Development Review 7,* 1,1–18.

'Death rates for elderly soar in flu outbreak.' *The Sunday Times,* 9 January 2000.

De Beauvoir, S. (1973) *The Coming of Age.* Harmondsworth: Penguin Books.

De Jouvenal, M. (1966) *The Hidden Possibilities of Man.* Ashland, VA: Whittet and Shepperson.

Delden, J., Pijnenborg, L. and Maas, P. (1993) 'Dances with data.' *Bioethics 7,* 323–9.

Department of Trade and Industry (1999) *Home Accident Surveillance Systems: 21st Annual Report.* London: Stationery Office,

DETR (1997) *Road Accidents in Great Britain: The Casualty Report.* London: DETR.

Diamond, T. (1992) *Making Gray Gold.* Chicago: University of Chicago Press.

'Dobson puts accent on home care.' *Electronic Telegraph,* 22 October 1997.

'Doctors to decide right to die.' *Guardian,* 24 June 1990.

Dokey, R. (1982) 'The Autumn of Henry Simpson.' In R. Dokey *August Heat: Stories by Henry Dokey.* Chicago: Story Press.

'Dorrell proposes way of insuring home against cost of old age.' *Electronic Telegraph*, 11 March 1997.

Durkheim, E. (1964) *The Division of Labour in Society.* London: Collier Macmillan. (Original work published 1893.)

Dworkin, R. (1993) *Life's Dominion - An Argument about Abortion and Euthanasia.* London: Harper Collins.

'Dying in care.' *Detroit Free Press*, 26 February 1997.

Eastwell, H. (1976) 'Associative Illness amongst Aborigines.' *Australian and New Zealand Journal of Psychiatry 10.* 89–94.

Ebrahim, S. and Bennett, G. (1995) *The Essentials of Health Care in Old Age.* London: Arnold.

Ehrlich, P.R. and Ehrlich, A.J. (1996) *The Population Explosion.* New York: Simon and Schuster.

Eisler, P. (1994) 'Dad's last days: Tale of horror.' *USA Today*, 21 February.

'Elderly are helped to die to clear beds, claims doctor.' *The Sunday Times*, 2 April 2000.

'Elderly hip patients in danger.' *The Times*, 10 February 2000.

'Elderly patients dying because of bad management.' *Electronic Telegraph*, 18 December 1999.

'Elderly patients left "starving to death in NHS".' *Electronic Telegraph*, 6 December 1999.

Elliott, E. (1878) *Poetical Works.*

Emanuel, E. (1997) 'Whose right to die?' *Atlantic Monthly*, March.

Emanuel, V.R. (1917) *The Apostle of the Cylinder.* London: Hodder and Stoughton.

European Association for the Welfare of the Elderly (1975)

European Union (1996) *A Charter of Human Rights for the Elderly of Europe.* Brussels: European Union.

Estes, C. (1979) *The Aging Enterprises.* San Francisco: Jossey-Bass.

Evans-Pritchard, E. (1951) *Kinship and Marriage among the Nuer.* Oxford: Clarendon Press.

'Failure of complaint system in NHS.' *Electronic Telegraph*, 27 March 1999.

Food and Agriculture Organisation (1988) *World Agriculture: Towards 2000.* New York: New York University Press.

Featherstone, M. and Hepworth, M. (1989) 'Images of aging.' In J. Bond, P. Coleman and S. Peace (eds) *Aging in Society* London: Sage.

Fennell, G., Phillipson, C. and Evers, H. (1988) *The Sociology of Old Age.* Buckingham: Open University Press.

Fernquist, R.M. (1995) 'Elderly suicide in Western Europe.' *Omega 32,* 1 39–48.

Fischer, D. (1978) *Growing Old in America.* Oxford: Oxford University Press.

'France enjoys love affair with "elixir of life".' *The Times*, 14 April 2000.

Freidel, D. (1995) *Maya Cosmos.* New York: Quill.

Friedlander, H. (1995) *The Origins of Nazi Genocide.* Chapel Hill, NC: University of North Carolina Press.

Frost, R. (1916) 'An Old Man's Winter Night.' In L. and E. Mertins (eds) (1947) *The Intervals of Robert Frost.* Berkeley: University of California Press.

Gamble, E., McDonald, P. and Lichstein, P. (1991) 'Knowledge, attitudes and behavior of elderly persons regarding living will.' *Archives of Internal Medicine 151,* 277–280.

Ganzini, L., Nelson, H.D., Schmidt, T.A., Kraemer, D.F., Delorit, M.A. and Lee, M. (2000) 'Physicians Experiences with the Oregon Death with Dignity Act.' *New England Journal of Medicine 342 (8)* February 24, 557–563.

Gardner, J.A. (1997) *Expendable.* Toronto: Avon.

Garret, J., Harris, R., Norburn, J., Patrick, D. and Davis, M. (1993) 'Life-sustaining treatments during terminal illness: Who wants what?' *Journal of General Internal Medicine 8* (July), 361–368.

Garvin, R.M. and Burger, R.E. (1965) *Where They Go to Die: The Tragedy of America's Aged*. New York: Delacorte Press.

General Household Survey (1998) *Informal Carers (1995)*. London: Stationery Office.

General Household Survey (1998) *Living in Britain (1996)*. London: Stationery Office.

Gibson, D., Turrell, G. and Jenkins, A. (1993) 'Regulation and reform: Promoting residents' rights in Australian nursing homes.' *Australian and New Zealand Journal of Sociology 29*, 1, 73–90.

Gilliland, N. and Jimenez, S. (1996) 'Elder abuse in developed and developing societies.' *Journal of Developing Societies 12*, 1, 88.

Glascock, A. (1987) 'Treatment of the aged in non-industrial societies.' In P. Silverman (ed) *Elderly as Modern Pioneers*. Indiana: Indiana University Press.

Glaser, B.G. and Strauss, A.L. (1965) *Awareness of Dying*. London: Weidenfeld Nicolson.

Glass, A.P. (1988) 'Improving quality of care and life in nursing homes.' *Journal of Applied Gerontology 7*, 3, 406–419.

Glennerster, H. (1999) 'The elderly: A burden on the economy?' *CentrePiece 2* (2) pp.6–12.

Goffman, E. (1961) *Asylums*. Harmondsworth: Penguin.

Gunn, J. (1958) *The Immortals*. London: Ballantyne.

'GP's will now treat new patients from nursing homes.' *Electronic Telegraph*, 7 November 1996.

'GP murdered 15 women to enjoy ultimate power of life and death.' *Electronic Telegraph*, 12 October 1999.

Gratton, B. (1986) *The Elderly in Boston*. Philadelphia: Temple University Press.

Guemple, L. (1990) 'Growing old in Inuit society.' In J. Sokolovsky (ed) *Growing Old in Different Societies*. Belmont, CA: Wadsworth.

Guillemard, A.M. (1986) *Old Age and the Welfare State*. London: Sage.

Gurganus, A. (ed) (1990) *White People*. New York: Alfred Knopf.

Haber, C. (1983) *Beyond Sixty-Five*. Cambridge: Cambridge University Press.

Haber, C. (1994) 'Over the hill to the poorhouse: Rhetoric and reality in the institutional history of the aged.' In K.W. Schaie and A.A. Achenbaum (eds) *Societal Impact of Dying*. New York: Springer.

Hanson, L.C. and Rodgman, E. (1996) 'The use of living wills at the end of life.' *Archives of Internal Medicine*, May 13, 1018–1022.

Hardy, T. (1976) 'Ah, are you digging on my grave?' In J. Gibbon (ed) *The Complete Works of Thomas Hardy*. New York: Macmillan.

Harrison, H. (1964) *Make Room! Make Room!* New York: Bantam Books.

Hauser, J.M., Kleefeld, S.F., Brennau, T.A. and Fischbach, R.L. (1997) 'Minority populations and advance directions: Insight from a focus group methodology.' *Cambridge Quarterly of the Healthcare Ethics 6* (1), 58–71.

Haverkate, I. and van der Wal, G. (1998) 'Dutch nursing home policies and guidelines on physician-assisted death.' *Public Health 112*, 6 419–423.

Health Advisory Service 2000 (1998) 'Not because they are old': *An independent enquiry into the care of older people in acute wards in general hospitals*. London: Health Advisory Service.

Heilig, G.H. (1994) 'How many people can be fed on Earth?' In W. Lutz (ed) *The Future Population of the World*. London: Earthscan Publishers.

Help the Aged (1999) *Housing and Older People in 2025*. September, 1999. London: Help the Aged.

Hendin, H. (1996) *Seduced by Death: Doctors, Patients and the Dutch Cure*. New York: W.W. Norton.

Heumann, L.F. and Boldy, D.P. (1993) *Aging in Place with Dignity*. New York: Praeger.

'"Hit Squad" for abuse hospital.' *The Times*, 1 April 2000.

Hockey, J. (1986) *The hospice as an alternative reality on death: a sociological analysis*. Unpublished doctoral thesis, University of Durham.

Holst, L.E. (1993) 'Do we need more help in managing our dead?' *Journal of Pastoral Care 47*, 4.

Home Office (1989) *Going for People*. London: Stationery Office.

Home Office (1990) *NHS and Community Care* 1990. London: Stationery Office.

'Home owner struck off register.' *Belfast Telegraph*, 25 April 1996.

Hoshimo, K. (1993) 'Euthanasia: Current problems in Japan.' *Cambridge Quarterly of Healthcare Ethics* 2, 45-47.

'Hospital nurse accused of killing elderly patients.' *US News*, 30 December 1997.

'Hospital accused of letting patients die.' *Electronic Telegraph*, 1 December 1998.

Hugman, R. (1998) *Social Welfare and Social Value*. London: Macmillan.

Humphry, D. (1994) 'Suicide by asphyxiation after the publication on final exit.' *New England Journal of Medicine*. (letter, replies) *330*, 14, 1017.

Humphry, D. (1998) *Freedom to Die: People, Politics and the Right-to-Die Movement*. New York: St Martin's Press.

'Hundreds abused in care home.' *Electronic Telegraph*, 20 June 1996.

Hutchinson, E.P. (1967) *The Population Debate*. Boston: Houghton Mifflin.

Illich, I. (1991) *Limits to Medicine*. Harmondsworth: Penguin.

'In possibly thousands of cases nursing home residents are dying from a lack of food and water and the most basic level of hygiene.' *Time Magazine*, 27 October 1997.

'Inquiry call into "neglect" of the elderly.' *The Times*, 14 April 2000.

Institute of Actuaries (1999) *Building a Better Britain for Older People*. London: Institute of Actuaries.

Jochelson, W. (1933) *The Yakut*. New York: American Museum of Natural History.

Jochensen, H. (1991) 'Report of the Royal Dutch Society of Medicine on Life-Terminating Actions with Incompetent Patients, Part 1: Severely Handicapped New-borns." '*Issues in Law & Medicine*, 7, 3.

Johns, S. and Hydle, I. (1995) 'Norway: Weakness in welfare: International and cross-cultural perspectives.' *Journal of Elder Abuse and Neglect 6*, 3 and 4, 139–57.

Jones, H.L. (ed) (1938) *The Geography of Strabo Vol V*. London: William Heinemann and Son.

Kaberry, P. (1939) *Aboriginal Women: Sacred and Profane*. London: Routledge.

Kappeler, S. (1995) *The Will to Violence: The Politics of Personal Behaviour*. Cambridge: Polity Press.

Katz, S. (1998) 'Doctor-assisted suicide – a bad oxymoron and a bad idea.' *Connecticut Post*, 27 April.

Kearl, M. (1999) *Sociology of death and dying*. www.trinity.edu/mkearl/deathhtml

Kenyon, J. (1996) *Otherwise: New and Selected Poems*. New York: Greywolf Press.

King, F. (1988) 'The Tradesman' in R. Baird-Smith (ed) *Winter's Tales*. New Series 4. New York: Constable.

King, G. (1676–1973) *Seventeenth Century Manuscript of Gregory King, The Earliest Classics: Grant and King*. Stuttgart: Gredd International.

Knight, W.E. (1951) *The Resurrection Man*. In *Atlantic* v.233 (1974)

Kottow, M.H. (1988) 'Euthanasia after the Holocaust - is it possible?' *Bioethics* 2 (1), 58–69.

Kuhse, H. (1987) *The Sanctity of Doctrine in Medicine*. Oxford: Clarendon.

Kuzewski, M. (1994) 'Whose will is it anyway? A discussion of advance directives.' *Bioethics 8*, 1, 27–48.

Landa, L.A. (1960) *Gulliver's Travels and Other Works*. New York: Houghton Mifflin.

Langton. J. (1999) 'America's aged lifers turn jails into geriatric homes.' *Prison Connections, 17*, 37–40.

Laczko, F. (1990) *The Growth of Retirement Since 1951*. Guildford: Pre-Retirement Association.

Larkin, P. (1974) 'The Old Fools.' In P. Larkin *High Windows*. London: Faber and Faber.

Laslett, P. (1985) *The World We Have Lost*. New York: Macmillan.

Laslett, P. (1987) 'The Emergence of the Third Age.' *Aging and Society*. London: Methuen.

'Launch of consultation paper on care home standard.' *BBC Online*, 8 September 1999.

Lerner, D. (1964) *The Passing of Traditional Society.* London: Collier Macmillan.

Lessing, D. (1983) *The Diary of a Good Neighbour.* New York: A.A. Knopf.

Levi-Strauss, C. (1936) *The Savage Mind.* Chicago: University of Chicago Press.

Logue, B.J. (1990) 'Modernization and the status of the frail elderly: Perspectives on continuity and change.' *Journal of Cross-Cultural Gerontology 5,* 345–374.

'Lonely Old Age.' *The Guardian,* 17 February 1998.

Long, S. (1987) *Death without Dignity.* Austin, TX: Texas Monthly Press.

Longmate, N. (1974) *The Workhouse.* London: Temple Smith.

'Long Term Care Needs of the Elderly'. *Electronic Telegraph,* 11 March 1997.

Lucien (1920) *Dips in the Near Future.* London: Headly Brothers.

McDowell, E.E. (1997) 'Death's challenges from the perspective of three generations of the elderly.' *Journal of Long-Term Health Care 16* 3, 4–14.

McEnroe, R.E. (1958) *The Silver Whistle.* London: Alcan.

McFarland, A. (1970) *Witchcraft in Tudor and Stuart England.* London: Routledge.

Maas, P., Delden, J. and Pijnenborg, L. (1992) 'Euthanasia and other medical decisions concerning the end of life.' *Health Policy* (special issue) 22 (1+2) Amsterdam: Elsevier.

Mahajan, A. (1992) 'Social dependency and Abuse of the Elderly' in P. Krishnan and K. Mahadevan (eds) *The Elderly Population in the Developed and Developing World.* New Delhi: Vedams Book International.

Malthus, T. (1798) *Essay on the Priciple of Population as it Affects the Future Improvement of Society.* London: Joseph Johnson Bookseller.

Master, O. (1991) *The Rose Fancier.* New York: W.W. Norton and Co.

Matcha, D.A. and Hutchinson, J. (1997) 'Location and timing of death among the elderly.' *OMEGA 34,* 4, 393–403.

Maxwell, E., Silverman, P. and Maxwell, R. (1982) 'The motive for geronticide.' *Studies in Third World Societies 22,* 67–84.

Maxwell, R.J. (1979) 'Doomed status: Observations on the segregation of impaired old people.' *Psychiatric Quarterly 51,* 1, 3–14.

Maxwell, R.J., Silverman, R. and Maxwell, E.K. (1990) 'The motive for geronticide.' In J. Sokolovsky (ed) *The Cultural Content of Ageing.* New York: Bergin and Garvey.

Medical Research Council (1994) *The Health of Britain's Older People.* London: MRC.

Menio, D.A. (1996) 'Advocating for the rights of vulnerable nursing home residents: creative strategies.' *Journal of Elder Abuse and Neglect 8,* 3, 59–72.

Mentor, L.F. (1897) *The Day of Resis.* New York: G.W. Dillinghen.

Miller, B. (1988) 'The right to health care free from abuse.' *The Health Service Journal 17.*

Minkler, M. and Estes, C. (1984) *Critical Perspectives on Aging.* New York: Baynod.

Minkler, M. (1996) 'Critical perspectives on ageing: New challenges for gerontology.' *Ageing and Society,* 467–489.

Minois, G. (1989) *History of Old Age.* Oxford: Blackwell.

Minturn, L. and Stasak, J. (1982) 'Infanticide and Terminal Abortion Procedure.' *Behavior Science Research 17,* 70–90.

Mitford, J. (1978) *The American Way of Death.* London: Quartet.

Mullan, P. (1999) *The Imaginary Time Bomb.* London: I.B. Tauris.

Muller, M.T., Kimsma, G. K. and van der Wal, G. (1998) 'Euthanasia and assisted suicide: Facts, figures and fancies with special regard to old age.' *Drugs and Ageing.* September 13 (3), 185–91.

Murphy, J. (1931) 'Dependency in old age.' *Annals of the American Academy of Political and Social Science 154,* 38–41.

Myers, L. (1990) *When Life Falls, It Falls Upside Down.* New York: Grove Werdenfeld.

'New laws required "to protect the old and infirm."' *Electronic Telegraph,* 9 December 1999.

Newby, H. (1977) *The Deferential Worker.* Harmondsworth: Penguin.

'NHS complaints at record high.' *The Guardian,* 17 January 1999.

Nolan, W.F. and Johnson, G.C. (1966) *Logan's Run.* New York: Dial Press.

Northern Ireland Human Rights Commission (1999) *Draft Strategic Plan.* Belfast: Northern Ireland Office.

'Nursing home manager "drugged" resident.' *Electronic Telegraph,* 11 July 1997.

'Nursing home manager abused patients.' *Sunday Life,* 23 May 1999.

'Nursing home strains graveyard.' *Electronic Telegraph,* 19 December 1995.

Office of Population Census and Surveys (1994) *General Household Survey: People Aged 65 and Over.* Department of Helth. London: HMSO.

'Older males more likely to kill themselves.' *Toronto Star,* 20 August 1998.

'Old people are made to pay for care that should be free.' *Electronic Telegraph,* 2 December 1999.

Oldfather, C.H. (ed) (1838) *Dioderus of Sicily Vol II.* London: William Heinemann and Son.

Ouslander, J., Tymchuk, A. and Krynski, M. (1993) 'Decisions about enteral tube feeding among the elderly.' *Journal of the American Geriatrics Society 41,* 70–77.

Ouslander, J., Tymchuk, A. and Rahbar, B. (1989) 'Health care decisions among elderly long-term residents.' *Archives of Internal Medicine 149* 1367–1372.

Pain, R. (1995) 'Elderly women and fear of violent crime.' *British Journal of Criminology, 35,* 4, 584–598.

Palmore, E. and Manton, K. (1974) 'Modernization and status of the aged: International comparisons.' *Journal of Gerontology, 29* 205–210.

'Paramedic tells of hospital leaving patients to die.' *The Sunday Times,* 16 April 2000.

Pashukanis, E. (1978) *Law and Marxism: A General Theory.* London: Ink Links.

'Patient's choking death spreads pain all round.' *Tampa Tribune,* 11 May 1998.

'Patients demand "living wills" to protect elderly.' *Electronic Telegraph,* 8 December 1999.

Pearson, F.A. and Harper, F.A. (1945) *The World's Hunger.* New York: Cornell University Press.

Pearson, J.L., Conwill, Y., Lindesay, J., Takahashi, Y. and Crane, E.D. (1997) 'Elderly suicide – a multi-national view.' *Ageing and Mental Health* (32) 107–111.

Pelling, M. and Smith, R.M. (eds) (1991) *Life, Death and the Elderly.* London: Routledge.

Pepe, M.C., Applebaum, R., Straker, J.K., and Mehidizadeh, S. (1997) 'Evaluating the effectiveness of nursing home pre-admission review.' *Journal of Long Term Health Care 16,* 3.

Petronio, S. and Kovachls, S. (1997) 'Managing privacy boundaries: Health providers' perceptions of residents' care in Scottish nursing homes.' *Journal of Applied Communication Research 25,* 115–131.

Phillipson, C. (1982) *Capitalism and the Construction of Old Age.* London: Macmillan.

Piore, M.J. (1984) *The Second Industrial Divide.* New York: Basic Books.

Plath, D. (1984) *Work and Life Cause in Japan.* New York: New York State University.

Pohl, F. (1956) 'The Census Taker.' in *Magazine of Fantasy and Science Fiction,* February 1956.

Posner, R.A. (1995) *Aging and Old Age.* Chicago: Chicago University Press.

Post, S.G. (1990) 'Infanticide and geronticide.' *Aging and Society 10, 3,* 317–330.

Post, S.G. (1991) 'Euthanasia, senecide, and the aging society.' *Journal of Religious Gerontology 8,* 1, 57–65.

'Private nursing homes under threat.' *Electronic Telegraph,* 27 October 1999.

'Problems of elderly in care.' *Electronic Telegraph,* 10 December 1999.

Quadagno, J. (1982) *Aging in Industrial Society: Work, Family, and Social Policy in 19th Century England.* London: Academic Press.

Quill, T., Cassel, C. and Meier, D. (1992) 'Care of the hopelessly ill.' *New England Journal of Medicine 327,* 19 1380–1384.

Quill, T. and Kimsma, G. (1997) 'End of Life Care in the Netherlands and the United States.' *Cambridge Quarterly of Healthcare Ethics 6*, 2 189–204.

Quill, T. E., Meier, D.E., Black, S.D. and Billings, J.A. (1998) 'The debate over physician- assisted suicide; empirical data and convergent views.' *Annals of Internal Medicine* 1 April 128, 552–8.

Ray, D. (1995) 'Hemlock society' in *Kangaroo Paws*. Kirksville, MO: Thomas Jefferson University Press.

Ray, G.N. (ed) (1946) *The Letters and Private Papers of W.M. Thackeray*. Cambridge, MA: Harvard University Press.

'RCN report rationing by steath.' *Electronic Telegraph*, 2 December 1999.

Reid, J. (1985) '"Going Up" or "Going Down": The status of old people in an Australian aboriginal society.' *Aging and Society, 5* 69–95.

Remmelink Report (1991) *Commsion on the Study of Medical Practice Concerning Euthanasia: Medical Decisions Concerning the End of Life*. The Hague: Sdll.

'Revealed: Cruelty of staff in NHS hospitals.' *The Sunday Times*, 22 February 2000.

Reynolds, J.W. (1846) 'Written from the Newmarket Union.'

Rich, B.A. (1996) 'Elements compromising the autonomy of the elderly.' In L.B. Cebnik and F.H. Marsh (eds) *Advances in Bioethics: Violence, Neglect and the Elderly*. Greenwich: JAI Press.

Rodway, A. (1995 June) 'Pro-euthanasia lobby represents the minority view in Britain.' *British Medical Journal*, p.310.

Rosenthal, J.T. (1996) *Old Age in Medieval England*. Philadelphia: University of Pennsylvania Press.

Royal College of Nursing (1974) *An Inspector Calls? The Regualtion of Private Nursing Homes and Hospitals*. London: RCN.

Royal College of Physicians (1999) *Report*, November 1999.

'Rover "saviours" face nursing home inquiry.' *The Times*, 30 March 2000.

Royal Commission on the Poor (1834) *Commission for Inquiring into the Poor Laws: Reports of Assistant Commissioners, XXXVII*. London: HMSO.

Royal Commission on the Aged Poor (1895) *Minutes of Evidence XIX*. London: HMSO.

Royal Commission on Long-Term Care (1999) *With Respect to Old Age: Long Term Care – Rights and Responsibilities*. London: The Stationery Office.

Saunders, P. (1997) 'Euthanasia: the road to mass killings.' *The New Australian 20,* January, 6–12.

Sayles, J. (1980) 'Dillinger in Hollywood.' *Triquaterly*, Spring 1980.

Scheper, T. and Duursma, S. (1994) 'Euthanasia: The Dutch experience.' *Age and Aging 23*, 3–8.

Scott, D. and Wishy, B. (eds) (1975) *America's Families: A Documentary History*. New York: Harper and Rowe.

Seale, C.F. (1989) 'What Happens in Hospices? A Review of the Research Evidence.' *Social Science Medicine 28*, 6, 551–559.

Shaw, B. (1888) 'Parents and Children: Misalliance.' in D.H. Laurence and D.J. Leary (eds) (1995) *B. Shaw: The Complete Works Vol. III*. Harmondsworth: Allen Lane.

'She only went in for a sore knee.' *Electronic Telegraph*, 6 December 1999.

'Shortages in the NHS: Denying eldery patients dialysis.' *Electronic Telegraph*, 10 March 2000.

Silverberg, R. (1957) *Master of Life and Death*. New York: Avon Publishers.

Silverman, P. and Maxwell, R.J. (1984) 'Cross-cultural variation in the status of old people.' In Stearns (ed) *Old Age in Pre-Industrial Society*. New York: Holmes and Meier.

Simmons, L.W. (1945) *The Role of the Aged in Primitive Society*. New Haven, CT: Yale University Press.

Smith, A. (1880) *An Inquiry into the Nature and Causes of the Wealth of Nations*. Second edition. Oxfold Claredon Press.

Smith, D.S. (1973) 'Parental power and marriage patterns.' *Journal of Marriage and the Family. 35*, 419–428.

'Slack councils told to improve or jeopardise welfare of vulnerable.' *The Guardian*, 12 April 1999.

Smyth, N. (1888) *The Place of Dying in Evolution.* London: T. Fisher Unwin.

Snyder, L. and Caplan A.L. (1996) 'Die-hard: End of life care in America.' *Pennsylvania Medicine 99*, 10-11, July.

Snyder, L. and Caplan, A.L. (2000) 'Suicide: Finding common ground.' *Annals of Internal Medicine 6*, 132, 21 March.

Social Trends (1999) *National Population Projections.* ONS. London: Stationery Office.

Spenneman, D.H.R. (1998) *Essays on the Marshallese Past.* Albury, NSW.

Spitzer, S. (1975) 'Towards a Marxian theory of deviance.' *Social Problems, 22* 638–651.

Stack, A. (1980) 'The effects of age composition on suicide in traditional and industrial societies.' *Journal of Social Psychology 111*, 143–4.

Stannard, D.E. (1978) 'Growing up and growing old.' In S.F. Spicker, K.M. Woodward and D. Van Tassel (eds) *Aging and the Elderly.* Atlantic Highlands, NJ: Humanities Press.

Stearns, P.N. (1978) *Old Age in European Society: The Case of France.* New York: Holmes and Meier.

Stearns, P. (1984) 'Old age family conflict: The perspective of the past.' In R. Wolff and K. Pillemer (eds) *Helping Elderly Victims.* New York: Columbia University Press.

Steinmetz, S. (1988) *Duty Bound: Family Care and Elder Abuse.* Newbury Park: Sage.

Stelter, K., Elliott, B. and Bruno, C. (1992) 'Living will completion in older adults.' *Archives of Internal Medicine 152*, 954–9, May.

Stone, T.H. and Winslade, W.J. (1995) 'Physician-assisted suicide and euthanasia in the United States.' *Journal of Legal Medicine 15*, 2, 481-508.

Strand, M. (1980) 'Old people on the nursing home porch.' In M. Strand *Selected Poems.* New York: Atheneum.

Street, D. and Quadagno, J. (1994) 'The state, the elderly, and the intergenerational contract: Toward a new political economy of aging.' In K.W. Schaie and A.A. Achenbaum (eds) *Societal Impact of aging.* New York: Springer.

Sudnow, D. (1967) *Passing On.* Englewood Cliffs, NJ: Prentice-Hall.

'Survey reveals opposition to entering care homes.' *Electronic Telegraph*, 14 December 1997.

Swayne, M. (1918) *The Blue Germ.* London: Hodder and Stoughton.

Swift, J. (1996) In *Jonathan Swift: The Selected Poems.* (edited by A. Norman Jeffaries) London: Trafalgar Square.

'The arrogant doctor: "They will never find me guilty."' *Electronic Telegraph, 6 February 2000.*

'The Future of the NHS.' *The Guardian,* 4 April 2000.

Thomas, K. (1976) 'Age and authority in early modern England.' *Proceedings of the British Academy, 62*, 205–208.

Tonnies, F. (1955) *Community and Association.* London: Routledge and Kegan Paul.

Tout, K. (1989) *Ageing in Developing Countries.* London: Oxford University Press.

Townsend, P (1963) *The Family Life of Old People.* Harmondsworth: Penguin.

Trollope, A. (1993) *The Fixed Period.* Oxford: Oxford University Press.

Turner, V. (1957) *Schism and Continuity in African Society.* Manchester: Manchester University Press.

United Kingdom Central Council (1994) *Professional Conduct: Occasional Report on Standards of Nursing in Nursing Homes.* London: UKCC.

United Nations (February 1998) *Fourth Review and Appraisal of the Implementation of the International Plan of Action of Ageing: Work Population Projections to 2150.* New York: UN Population Division.

US Department of Commerce, Economics and Statisitcs (1999) Administration Bureau Report of Cencus.

US Department of Commerce, Economics and Statisitcs, Age and Statistics Branch (2000) *Current Population Reports*, Series pp.23–190, Washington: US Census Bureau.

van der Wal, G., van der Maas, J., Bosma, J.M., Onwuteaka-Philipsen, B.D., Willems, D.L., Haverkate, I. and Kostense, P.J. (1996) 'Evaluation of the notification procedure for physician-assisted death in the Netherlands.' *New England Journal of Medicine 335*, 135–40.

van Velde, J. (1953) *The Big Ward.* Amsterdam: W. Querido.

Vesperi, M. (1990) 'The reluctant consumer: Nursing home residents in the post-Bergman era.' In J. Sokolovsky (ed) *Growing Old in Different Societies.* Belmont, CA: Wadsworth.

Victor, C. (1987) *Old Age in Modern Society.* London: Croom Helm.

Vonnegut, K. (1965) 'Fortitude.' In K. Vonnegut *Wampeters, Foma and Granfallons.* New York: Delacorte Press.

Vonnegut, K. (1988) 'Tomorrow and tomorrow and tomorrow.' In K. Vonnegut *Welcome to the Monkey House.* New York: Dell.

Wagoner, D. (1979) 'Part song.' In D. Wagoner *In Broken Country.* Boston: Little, Brown and Co.

Walker, A. (1980) 'The social creation of dependency in old age.' *Journal of Social Policy 9*, 45–75.

Walker, A. and Maltby, T. (1997) *Ageing Europe.* Buckingham: Open University Press.

Weber, M. (1964) *The Theory of Economic and Social Organisation.* New York: Free Press.

Weissert, C.S. (1998) 'Governing health: The politics of health policy.' *Journal of Health Politics, Policy, and Law 23*, 6.

Welie, J.V.M. (1992) 'The medical exception: Physicians, euthanasia and the Dutch criminal law.' *Journal of Medicine and Philosophy August 17*, 4, 419–37.

Wells, H.G. (1895) *The Time Machine.* London: Heinemann.

Wells, H.G. (1901) *Anticipation of the Reaction of Mechanical and Scientific Progress Upon Human Life and Thought.* London: Chapman and Hall.

Welty, E. (1980) 'A Visit of Charity.' in *Eudora Welty's Newsletter*, Summer 1980, IV, 2.

Weisman (1982) *Essays upon Heredity and Kindred Biological Problems.* Oxford: Clarendon Press (Originally published in 1899).

'When care falls short.' *The Times*, 1 February 2000.

White, R. (1983) *The Roots of Dependency.* London: University of Nebraska Press.

Whittle, B. and Ritchie, J. (2000) *Prescription for Murder.* London: Warner.

Willems, D.L., Daniels, E.R., van der Wal, G., van der Maas, P.J. and Emanuel, E.J. (2000) 'Attitudes and practices concerning the end of life.' *Archives of Internal Medicine.*

Williams, A. (1997) 'Rationing health care by age: The case for.' *British Medical Journal 314*, 15 March.

Williams, C. (1986) 'The last words of my English grandmother.' In A.W. Litz and C. MacGowan (eds) *The collected Poems of William Carlos Williams Vol. 1.* New York: New Directions.

Williams, C. (1986) 'The widow's lament.' In A.W. Litz and C. MacGowan (eds) *The collected Poems of William Carlos Williams Vol. 1.* New York: New Directions.

Williams, C. (1989) 'The experience of long-term care in the future.' *Journal of Gerontological Social Work 14*, 3/4, 820–825.

Winslow, T.S. (1923) *Picture Frames.* New York: Knopf.

Wright, S.F. (1932) *The New Gods Lead.* London: Jarrold.

Yeats, W.B. (1938) 'The Wild Old Wicked Man.' In R.J. Finnegan (ed) *W.B. Yeats: The Poems.* New York: Macmillan.

Yahnke, R.E. and Eastman, R.M. (1995) *Literature and Gerontology.* Westport, CT: Greenwood Press.

Yoke, C.B. and Hassler, D.M. (1985) (eds) *Phoenix from the Ashes.* New York: Greenwood Press.

Zelhovitz, B. (1990) 'Transforming the middle-way: A Political Economy of aging policy in Sweden.' In J. Sokolovsky (ed) *The Cultural Context of Aging.* New York: Bergen and Garvey Press.

Subject Index

aborigines 52, 59, 60, 61, 74, 75–6
abuse, care homes 119–21, 129
accountability, of medical professionals 184, 185–6
Action on Elder Abuse 121
After Many a Summer 112
Age Concern 31, 32, 34, 41, 43, 49, 53n5, 139, 188, 189
ageing
    cultural definitions 74
    and decline 17–21
    as disease 15, 21
    fear of 18
    literary descriptions 17–21
    as problem 11, 13, 52
    and senescence 24
    social prejudices about 33
    see also elderly; population, ageing
ageism, ideology of
    blaming the victim 186–7
    combating 187
    death-hastening 87–90, 123
    empowerment 189–91
    euthanasia 156, 181
    human rights 193, 195
    literary sources 139, 145, 148, 150–2
    modernisation 79–80
'Ah, Are You Digging on My Grave?' 152
Alert 173
Aleuts 70
Alice's Adventures in Wonderland 18
All Moonshine 27
almshouses 94
Also Sprach Zarathustra 25
Alzheimer's disease 44, 51
Amassalik Inuit 65
American Sociological Association 28
'An Old Man's Winter Night' 150
Arsenic and Old Lace 145
As You Like It 19
Asmat 76
attrition, death by 12, 78–106
Audit Commission 46
auto-euthanasia 123
Autumn of Henry Simpson, The 149

Back to Methuselah 13
bed blocking 43, 46

Big Peter and Little Peter 142–3
Big Trip to Yonder, The 146
Big Ward, The 149
Billenium 146
Blue Germ, The 148
Bororo 63
British Geriatric Society 46, 129
British Medical Association 126, 160
Broken Homes 152
Bureau of Labor Statistics 39
bureaucratisation
    care institutions 108–35
    death 109–13
    geronticide 21–2
Bushmen 65
Bystander, The 150

Canadian Charter of Rights 194–5
cancer
    cost implications of curing 29
    men and women 34
    screening 44
    treatment 44, 45
capitalism 58
cardiopulmonary resuscitation (CPR) 175
care homes
    abuse 119–21, 129
    authority structure 117–18
    bureaucratisation 108–35
    businesses 131–4
    demand for 37–8
    direct death-hastening 126–7
    dying in 113–15
    ethnography of death-hastening 124–6
    failings 130–1
    inspections 129–31, 197
    institutional features 115–19
    literary sources 149–50
    making death 'ordinary' 121–4
    organisational goals 119
    private sector 132–4
    profiteering 134–5
    regulation 128–9, 189
Care Standards Bill 189
carers 39
    gender 40
Carers National Association 40
Caring For People (White Paper 1989) 135n3
Census Takers, The 146
ceremonial killing, of elderly 12, 61–2, 65, 78

Author Index